International Narcotics Control

First published in 1934, *International Narcotics Control* is concerned with dangerous drugs solely as a subject of international administration. The ultimate questions that this study seeks to answer bear upon the form and function of the international organisms which have been set up to deal with drug traffic. What relation shall the function of a body bear to the method of its appointment, to its composition, and to source of its responsibility? What type of organism will secure the best response from national administrations? What should be the method of contact between national and international bodies? The answers to questions such as these can be found in this study.

Divided into two parts, the book discusses important themes like the establishment and the work of the Opium Advisory Committee, the origin and functioning of the Permanent Central Opium Board; and the control of raw opium production in India, former Yugoslavia, Turkey, and Persia. This is an important historical reference work for scholars and students of criminology.

International Narcotics Control

L. E. S. Eisenlohr

Routledge
Taylor & Francis Group

First published in 1934
by George Allen & Unwin Ltd.

This edition first published in 2024 by Routledge
4 Park Square, Milton Park, Abingdon, Oxon, OX14 4RN

and by Routledge
605 Third Avenue, New York, NY 10017

Routledge is an imprint of the Taylor & Francis Group, an informa business

© L. E. S. Eisenlohr, 1934

Publisher's Note
The publisher has gone to great lengths to ensure the quality of this reprint but points out that some imperfections in the original copies may be apparent.

Disclaimer
The publisher has made every effort to trace copyright holders and welcomes correspondence from those they have been unable to contact.

A Library of Congress record exists under LCCN: 35005576

ISBN: 978-1-032-90263-0 (hbk)
ISBN: 978-1-003-54680-1 (ebk)
ISBN: 978-1-032-90265-4 (pbk)

Book DOI 10.4324/9781003546801

INTERNATIONAL
NARCOTICS CONTROL

by

L. E. S. EISENLOHR

LONDON

GEORGE ALLEN & UNWIN LTD

MUSEUM STREET

FIRST PUBLISHED IN 1934

PRINTED IN GREAT BRITAIN BY
UNWIN BROTHERS LTD., WOKING

TO

My Father

BERTHOLD A. EISENLOHR

PREFACE

THIS book is concerned with dangerous drugs solely as a subject of international administration. Possibly it will interest the student of this general field as well as the student more particularly interested in narcotics as a social danger. For the development of principles and methods of international administrative organization has gone farther in the field of narcotics control than probably in any other. For the pioneer in international planning in many other spheres there may be much useful precedent in the experiments which have been made in drug control.

The ultimate questions that this study seeks to answer bear upon the form and function of the international organisms which have been set up to deal with the drug traffic. What relation shall the function of a body bear to the method of its appointment, to its composition, and to the source of its responsibility? What type of organism will secure the best response from national administrations? What should be the method of contact between national and international bodies? The answers to questions such as these can be found only be examining the work that has been done. And here a second series of questions has to be borne in mind: What important proposals have been made? from what sources have they come? how have they been received and what type of opposition has been raised against them? with what success have they been applied? These questions are fundamentally important wherever international control or supervision is developing.

Strictly speaking, only the manufactured drugs—morphine, heroin, cocaine, and their derivatives—should be included in a study of the international control of narcotics. The raw materials from which they are made—opium and the coca leaf—are controlled, so far, only domestically. Nevertheless, I believe it is essential to include them here, first because their supervision

7

is in some measure implied in the three existing international conventions, second, because the League Opium organization is actually studying the possibilities of direct international supervision over the production of raw materials, and third, because some of the important opium-producing countries have developed important systems of control which will form the groundwork for any future system of international supervision.

The debt that any student owes his teachers is always too great to be fully expressed. I shall say only that I owe much of this debt to Professor Henry Russell Spencer of Ohio State University; to Professor McIlwain and Dr. Friedrich of Harvard University; and to Professor William E. Rappard of the Graduate Institute of International Studies at Geneva. In the immediate preparation of this book, whose controversial subject-matter makes me hasten to acknowledge my sole responsibility for every expression of opinion and interpretation of fact therein, I have had the inestimable advantage of advice and criticism from Professor Pitman B. Potter, Professor Hans Wehberg, and again of Professor William Rappard. Mr. L. A. Lyall and Mr. Herbert May of the Central Opium Board, and Mr. A. E. Blanco of the Anti-Opium Information Bureau: Geneva, gave me generously of their time and interest in reading the finished manuscript and discussing it with me. In Mr. Duncan Hall, Chief of the League Opium Section, I have had the particular benefit of a critic whose views are not always mine. To Sir Malcolm Delevingne, Sir John Campbell, Dr. Schultz, Mr. A. C. Chatterjee, and Mr. T. P. Sinha I am deeply indebted for the time they have given me in discussing particular phases of the opium problem. Finally, I owe my friends Violet, Richard, and David Greaves a debt of patience and encouragement which I shall not attempt to measure.

L. E. S. EISENLOHR

GENEVA
July 1934

CONTENTS

9

CONTENTS

Part Two

*THE CONTROL OF
RAW OPIUM PRODUCTION*

INTRODUCTION

THE habit of indulging in some kind of narcotic is very ancient. Certainly the earliest literature of man makes reference to it, and the earliest trade records indicate that opium was a well-known commodity in the commerce that flourished between India and China long before the Crusades.[1] The Arab traders are the first who are known to have been familiar with the drug called opium, and to have introduced it into China, probably about the sixth century. It was for long not thought of as a vicious article as its use was moderate and its medicinal value recognized. The habit of smoking opium mixed with tobacco was introduced by the Dutch in the middle of the seventeenth century, when its use began to develop rapidly.

In other parts of the world different plants with a narcotic content were discovered and used. The Indians of South America found a shrub known as the coca plant, whose leaves were chewed for the stimulating effect they produced. The same shrub was also introduced into the East Indies in the nineteenth century. Hemp grew in India and Africa, and was consumed throughout the East variously as hashish, ganja, and bhang.

Opium, however, until modern chemistry discovered the alkaloids obtainable from it and from the coca leaf, was the chief narcotic of addiction. It was the lucrative article of commerce, the cause of wars, the subject of imperial edicts, parliamentary debates, royal investigations, and international conferences. Its history is, in fact, almost as colourful as the dreams it has created in the mind of man. The Chinese emperors, when they conquered Amoy and Formosa in 1683, first came into contact with the problem of opium smoking which, until well into the eighteenth century, was serious only in the district around Amoy. It was not, however, until the European trader

[1] *Report of the International Opium Commission*, Shanghai, 2, p. 44.

13

developed the opium traffic that it became a menace to Oriental civilization. Portuguese traders early in the eighteenth century were the first to import foreign opium into China, and from some two hundred chests in 1729 imports increased gradually to about one thousand chests in 1769.[1] Chinese merchants also brought it from India in the days of the East India Company, but after the British succeeded in breaking through the isolation of the Chinese Empire and securing the open door in trade, an increase of staggering proportions took place in the export of opium from India to China. What had been a minor article of domestic commerce in 1700 had by 1796 become a grave menace to the welfare of the Chinese people. In 1729 the Emperor Yung Cheng issued the first edict against smoking, but the proclamation availed nothing against the steady tide of foreign opium. It cannot be doubted that Chinese merchants entered into the trade themselves and shared in the great profits which it brought in, but European enterprise was a far more important factor in the growth of the trade.

The edict against smoking was renewed in 1796, but the evil had become so great that in 1800 an edict was finally issued prohibiting as well both the importation of opium from abroad and its cultivation at home. With that prohibitory edict international troubles began. Illegal as it was, the Indian opium trade made incredible advances in the next thirty years. The average annual import between 1821 and 1828 was 9,708 chests;[2] between 1828 and 1835, 18,712 chests; and between 1835 and 1839, 30,000 chests. The determination of the Government to stamp out the evil seemed only to increase the zeal of the smugglers and the daring of the many Chinese officials who connived at the illicit traffic.

Against this influx of opium the Chinese Government was helpless, having to combat not only the resourcefulness of

[1] See Morse, *International Relations of the Chinese Empire*, vol. i, chap. viii. [2] A chest contains 140 lb.

its enemies at home and abroad, but also the growth of addiction in China with its accompanying demand for the drug. On the whole, however, the opinion of the Chinese people seems to have been opposed to the trade, and the Emperor had therefore some domestic support for the edicts against it which he caused to be proclaimed. Their chief result, however, was only to turn the trade into illicit channels.

Whatever may have been the true causes of the so-called Opium War between Great Britain and China, and there is great division of opinion on the subject, there can be little doubt that its immediate cause was an incident growing out of this illicit traffic in opium which succeeded the proclamation of the imperial edict prohibiting the trade: Commissioner Lin, an honest imperial official, had twenty thousand chests of opium, which were being illicitly imported into the country, destroyed.

The act of Commissioner Lin may serve to explain the outbreak of hostilities between the two countries. Whatever may have been the part of the Government of Great Britain in the beginning, the terms of the treaty which ended the war opened the channels of trade to all commerce, from which opium was not excluded, and stipulated that the indemnity which was demanded of the Chinese Government be paid to the opium merchants who had suffered loss through the action of Commissioner Lin. The declaration frequently made that Great Britain made war on China in order to force the opium trade upon her must be regarded in the light of these facts.

After these incidents China suffered in silence. The opium habit spread, and the Government, forced by the course of events to permit the continued import of the drug, found no prohibitive measures within China itself of any avail. Furthermore, the growing of opium was taken up by the Chinese. In the last half of the nineteenth century opium exports from India to China averaged 3,500 tons every year, the highest amount being nearly 5,000 tons in 1879–80.[1] What the figure for Chinese production during this period was is not ascertainable.

Meanwhile, the opium situation in India was as alarming as in China itself. Indeed, although the consumption of the drug was not great, as in China, the problem was actually much more serious in character, for the production and trade in this commodity was so great that it would have been entirely impossible to balance the Indian budget without the revenue from the opium monopoly. This actual incorporation of the production of opium into the economic life of India was to cause the Government of India in the twentieth century a multitude of problems.

Until the beginning of the twentieth century the only measures taken to combat the spread of drug addiction and cut down the consumption of opium were those taken by the Chinese Government, but as it was not able to prohibit the import of Indian opium these measures had little effect. In England in the last decade of the nineteenth century an energetic and idealistic group, headed by Joseph Alexander, exerted its influence in Parliament to secure a change in the policy of the Government of India with regard to its Chinese opium trade. Already at this time it was realized how closely opium was bound up with the financial life of India, and the reform group had the foresight to see that any diminution of the Chinese opium trade would need to be preceded by a complete reorganization of Indian finances. It proposed, therefore, that a Royal Commission be appointed to study the problem from this angle, but the motion was opposed by Gladstone and Lord Kimberley, Secretary of State for India, with the result that the Royal Commission, which was subsequently appointed in 1893, had for its mandate "a general inquiry into the production and consumption of opium in India." Obviously the matter of the trade

[1] Chinese Maritime Customs statistics, reported to the Hague Opium Conference, 1912.

with China was not to be touched. As regards India itself, the report of the Commission in no way changed the policy there, but on the contrary sanctioned conditions as it found them, and thus secured the maintenance of the old policy for another two decades.[1]

However, the effect of the continued agitation of the reform group was so strong that in spite of this serious setback it was possible to pass only eleven years later, in 1906, the following resolution in Parliament: "That this House re-affirms its conviction that the Indo-Chinese Opium Trade is morally indefensible, and requests His Majesty's Government to take such steps as may be necessary for bringing it to a speedy close."[2] The Chinese Government, in September of the same year, decreed the abolition of poppy production and opium smoking, and two months later opened negotiations with the British Government which resulted in the 1908 Agreement, whereby opium exports from India to China were to be reduced *pari passu* with the reduction in Chinese poppy cultivation. The state of Chinese public opinion was such that it was not difficult for the Chinese Government to carry out its part of the bargain. Upon the most authentic information available—and there is little doubt as to its reliability—both the production and the consumption of opium in China had practically ceased by 1913, four years after the agreement was reached. Simultaneously the Indian Government ended the exportation of opium to China before half the term of years in which the Agreement was to be fulfilled had run its course, and so a contentious subject in the history of Anglo-Chinese relations was at length terminated.

[1] For a full account of the anti-opium movement in Parliament, see H. G. Alexander's life of his father, *Joseph Gundry Alexander*, Swarthmore Press, 1921.
[2] The reform group was materially aided by the change in Government which took place at this moment, for the General Election of 1906 brought in a large radical majority, only too ready to find, in the policy of the preceding Government, material for censure.

In order to make possible the execution of the treaty with China it was necessary to do what the Government of India had refused to do ten years previously, namely, to study the reorganization of revenue and the modification of the opium monopoly. From this point of view the agreement had perhaps greater significance to the opium fight than it had in its more direct and obvious effect upon the Chinese situation. For although it had been well comprehended in some quarters for a long while that the opium question presented certain very important economic aspects, yet this was the first time this most important fact was brought home to the administration. The experimentation which the Government of India has since carried out on the basis of this principle has the most valuable implications for the opium situation at the present moment, in particular for those countries which now find themselves in the same position with regard to their opium production as India in 1911. Though the general economic situation in these countries is far from being identical with that of India, and although this important factor must be taken into consideration, still the lessons learned by the Indian administration in the twenty years past can be applied in the work which these countries have now to undertake. It is perhaps not generally realized by those who are working for the reduction of opium cultivation that there is as a result of the Indian experiment a great deal of material available which will simplify the efforts of other countries in the same field.[1]

Almost simultaneously with this important development in regard to the Chinese opium trade there grew up a movement of the same kind in the United States. It was sponsored mainly by Bishop Brent, a missionary, and Dr. Hamilton Wright, a physician, both having first-hand acquaintance with the opium situation in the Orient. The acquisition of the Philippines at the close of the Spanish-American War had, furthermore,

[1] See below, chapter on India.

created a special interest in the subject in America, which prompted President Theodore Roosevelt in 1909 to invite the Governments of the opium-smoking colonies and territories to meet in Shanghai and discuss the problem. The parleys resulted in the adoption of a series of resolutions recognizing and defining the narcotic danger and urging action against it.

It was, in fact, at the Shanghai Conference that the first general recognition was given to the existence of the problem of addiction to manufactured drugs. Heretofore opium, and three or four other natural products, had been considered alone as agents of addiction. Although no specific measures were framed to check the drug danger, it is worth while to note this earliest recognition of a menace to public welfare which has since taken on such vast proportions. The Fifth Resolution framed by the Shanghai Conference declares:

That the International Opium Commission finds that the unrestricted manufacture, sale, and use of morphine cause a grave danger, and that the morphine habit shows signs of spreading: the International Opium Commission therefore desires to urge strongly on all Governments that it is highly important that drastic measures should be taken by each Government in its own territories and possessions to control the manufacture, sale, and distribution of this drug, and also such other derivatives of opium as may appear on scientific inquiry to be liable to similar abuse and productive of like ill effects.

It is interesting to note that it was considered sufficient at this time for "each Government in its own territories and possessions to control the manufacture, sale, and distribution of this drug"; in other words, that the dimensions of the problem did not as yet demand international action. It is also interesting to see that morphine was apparently the only narcotic whose abuse was causing concern. To the harassed anti-narcotic reformer and administrative official of to-day the pristine simplicity of the problem in 1909, as opposed to the infinite complexity to which neglect has permitted it to grow to-day, is a subject upon which he does not like to dwell.

The Conference was chiefly important because it symbolized the awakening of a world-wide determination to rid the world of the opium evil and of the realization that addiction to manufactured drugs was also beginning to menace the welfare of humanity. The importance of the Shanghai Conference was, however, gravely modified by the fact that the representatives who were sent to it were not empowered to draw up a convention. It would have been impossible to summon the Conference with this end in view, for there was no apparent willingness on the parts of the Governments to commit themselves definitely to any agreement at this time. But the Shanghai discussions showed that a considerable basis of agreement existed, and the United States Government at once urged the calling of a conference.

Two years later the Hague Opium Conference met.[1] By this time it was possible to draw up a convention which called for the control of the production of raw opium and the gradual suppression of opium smoking in those territories and colonies in which it existed. To what limits and by what means the production of opium was to be reduced was not specified in the Convention, neither was a definite programme for the suppression of opium smoking laid down. Among the proposals submitted by the United States as a basis for discussion at the Conference was one which envisaged the restriction or control of poppy cultivation in those countries where it was as yet unknown, in order that the measures of reduction being undertaken in India and China, and under consideration likewise in Persia,[2]

[1] The Conference was proposed by the Government of the United States, and convoked by the Government of the Netherlands.

[2] As a result of the Shanghai Conference, Persia passed a law providing for a seven-year programme of reduction of opium consumption. But this was not to affect production.

might not be nullified by the development of the industry in other countries. The Russian Government, however, opposed the proposition on the grounds that it would be detrimental to the development of a yet almost untried field of Russian agriculture.[1] This valuable measure was thus defeated.

The most important contribution to the agenda of the Conference was made by the British Government, which recommended that the problem of the manufactured drugs, as well as that of opium, be included in the discussions. The principle of limiting the manufacture, use of, and trade in drugs to medical and scientific purposes was accepted, but the means of determining these needs and of effecting the desired limitation were not established. That the problem was international in scope and would have to be dealt with as such was a fact which had become apparent since the meeting of the Shanghai Conference three years earlier. A suggestion contained in the American draft plan called for the appointment of an international commission to supervise the carrying out of the Convention, but the suggestion was tabled, being opposed by the Chinese, the French, and the British, who nevertheless, with all the other Governments represented, declared themselves in favour of limiting the production of drugs,[2] and advocated the free communication of all relevant information between the various national administrations for their mutual benefit.

Unfortunately, the conservatism of the Conference was seconded by delay on the part of the High Contracting Parties in ratifying the instrument which they had drawn up. The result was that when the World War broke out in 1914 the legislation called for in the Convention had not yet been passed in the great majority of the countries, and the measures which ought to have been ready to control the production of drugs during the war and, much more, at its close, were lacking at a time

[1] Conference Internationale de l'Opium, 1912. *Actes et Documents,* tome 1, p. 4.   [2] Ibid., tome ii, pp. 1–2.

when the need for them was most acute.[1] Obviously, after 1914 the Governments had little time to devote to the drug problem, but if the Hague Convention had been vigorously applied the problem would never have reached the proportions to which it has grown to-day. The provision of some machinery of international supervision, and the prompt ratification of the Convention, would have done much to prevent this development.

In short, the Shanghai Conference and the Hague Convention were fatally conservative and fatally weak. If the reduction of opium cultivation and the limitation of drug manufacture had been undertaken in 1909 and 1912 in a vigorous, systematic, and scientific manner, the enormous growth of the manufactured drugs industry during the war would have been checked and controlled at its close, and the tremendous wave of narcotic addiction which since the war has been the chief preoccupation of the narcotics fight need not have occurred. But what is easy to perceive now was less easy to forecast at that time. Only a pessimistic seer would have foretold the extent to which this menace was to spread and in how brief a space of time. Still, the fact remains that the most critical moment in the history of the narcotics fight was passed unheeded, and the opportunity of preventing the unchecked spread of drug addiction was lost when at Shanghai and The Hague the represented Powers failed to pursue a strong and determined policy against the production of opium and to carry out promptly and vigorously the measures agreed upon at the Conference. And though ignorance may plead innocence as regards the subsequent and unforeseen development in narcotic drug addiction, this fearful scourge would have been avoided had the Governments but met squarely the task for which they were assembled. It is not to be inferred that the Governments were responsible for the tide of addiction

[1] By 1919 only seven States had declared their intention of putting the Convention into operation, namely, Belgium, China, Honduras, Luxemburg, Netherlands, Norway, and the United States.

that swept the world, and has continued to sweep it since 1914. That was the almost inevitable outcome of the war. The war-time need for opiates naturally necessitated the development of the manufactured drugs industry. But that this development should not have been curbed and checked, brought under control and within the bounds of medical necessity, and that at once at the very beginning of the danger, and before it had grown to proportions which made it almost impossible to cope with, this was undoubtedly the fault of the Governments. And much more was it their fault that the age-old problem of opium cultivation had never been met, and that therefore an unlimited and unchecked supply of opium and the coca leaf continued to provide the drug industry with its raw materials.

The events of the war years put the whole opium question in the background, and the Hague Convention, insufficient as it was, lay dormant. Meanwhile, the increase in the extent of addiction to manufactured drugs had become so great that some sort of organized international action was imperative. The Netherlands Government, which had been acting as repository for ratifications of the Hague Convention, therefore proposed to the Peace Conference that the League of Nations take over this task.[1] It was decided at the Conference that the ratification of the Peace Treaty should imply ratification of the Opium Convention of 1912 as well. In addition, the Peace Conference provided in Article 23, paragraph *c*, of the Covenant that the members of the League would "entrust the League with the general supervision over agreements with regard to the traffic in opium and other dangerous drugs." The First Assembly, after some discussion of the method by which this duty could best be executed, agreed to appoint a permanent organ, the Advisory Committee on the Traffic in Opium and Other Dangerous Drugs, which should be composed of the repre-sentatives of the principal drug manufacturing and opium-grow-

[1] See Chapter I.

ing countries. It was promptly set up and held the first of its meetings in 1921. Thus the first piece of machinery of dimensions suitable to deal with the problem was constructed. It had three important qualities: permanence, internationalism, and generous terms of reference which permitted it to carry out a wide programme of activity. Unfortunately, these virtues were not unmixed. Conservative interpretation of its competence limited the activity of the Committee to urging upon Governments the execution of the Hague Convention, to which end various administrative measures were devised. Furthermore, mere internationalism proved to be insufficient, for it could and did exclude from the membership of the Committee States which, as non-producers and consumers of opiates, would have tempered the Committee's conservative attitude and furnished a needed element of impartiality. Finally, the need for keeping an international organ free from the national interests of its component members became apparent, and was not met by the Advisory Committee whose members were intended to and did represent their respective national points of view.

But by the time the Committee was organized and had begun to function, the problem of manufactured drugs had completely eclipsed the problem of opium smoking, and with it even the meagre provisions of the Hague Convention for the reduction of the production of opium were put aside, for the manufactured drugs problem was in so advanced a stage that it could only be met by direct attack at the traffic and regulation of the manufacture of these substances. Thus the more fundamental but less urgent question of limiting the supply of the raw materials, opium and coca leaves, was left to future consideration. Only in 1931 was the question again seriously raised of attempting to meet the opium problem as such,[1] virtually all of the League's anti-narcotic activity having meanwhile been directed against the traffic in dangerous drugs. The wisdom of this procedure,

[1] See below, pp. 145, 210.

though it was dictated by circumstances rather than by foresight, has become none the less apparent.

From the beginning two means for achieving the object of the Hague Convention with respect to the manufactured drugs were considered. But in the opinion of the Advisory Committee the one, direct limitation of manufacture, was unnecessarily drastic, and it was therefore the second, regulation and control of the traffic, which was adopted. This decision proved to be the choice of a by-path which narrowly escaped leading to the morasses of defeat. Many of the schemes which the Committee worked out and submitted to the States for adoption were excellent, it is true, but they were after all only schemes of control. The best of sieves will not hold water. The insufficiency of any method of attacking the problem, short of cutting down directly the actual output of the drug factories, was recognized in the Committee itself, but only by a minority which was easily overruled. However, on one occasion at least the view of the majority was expressed in terms that gave the best of the argument to the other faction. This was when, in respect of one of the most excellent measures of control devised by the Committee, the import and export certificate system, the objection was raised that tightening the control over the legal trade in drugs would only divert the flow of the illicit traffic to other channels. To this the chairman of the Committee replied that it was an objection which could be applied to all the restrictive measures passed by the Committee, for any restriction could only have the effect of enhancing the returns of the illicit traffic. This was an accurate reflection, and ought to have convinced the Committee that its most useful action was to limit at once the output of substances which, when control was attempted, were simply turned into other channels of distribution. With production thus reduced it would, of course, still have been necessary to police the channels of trade. But this task would have been both easier and productive of better results than any attempt to control an unregulated and unknown volume of manufactured drugs.

The first serious consideration to be given to the view that direct limitation of production ought to be undertaken came in 1923, when the United States asked to be allowed to bring definite proposals to that effect before the Committee. These proposals raised a storm of discussion, but the decision was finally reached that the time was ripe for calling another conference, which in addition to studying the American proposals should elaborate measures for giving greater effect to the Hague Convention.

The First and Second Geneva Opium Conferences were consequently called, by virtue of a resolution of the Fourth Assembly, and held in 1924-25 under the auspices of the League of Nations. It was soon seen, however, that the basis on which the Conference had been authorized to proceed could not survive the antagonism which it met on all sides. The Governments were no more ready to pledge themselves to so ambitious a plan as that implied in the American Proposals and the Assembly resolution than they had been in 1912. In the middle of the Conference the plan had to be abandoned and its supporters to content themselves with the rule of the majority, whose opinion continued to be that the effective control of the trade would eliminate the illicit traffic, and hence, automatically, limit the production of narcotic drugs to the amounts needed for medical and scientific purposes.

To many the work of the Conference was a keen disappointment, but its achievements ought not to be overlooked even if it failed to accomplish the main purpose for which it was called. Of the most signal importance was the establishment of an independent, international board, whose function was to watch the trade in drugs and, on the basis of regular quarterly reports received from all the Governments, to point out any excess or irregularity in the trade. It was to be composed of specialists in the problem who were to meet not as representatives of their respective Governments, but as a technical body, reporting to the Council of the League of Nations, and ultimately responsible to the signatories of the Geneva Convention. Thus two of the principal deficiencies of the Advisory Committee were met in the establishment of the Permanent Central Opium Board.[1] The work and development of this Board is taken up in a later chapter. It is sufficient to say here that its organization turned out to be the most significant contribution of the Geneva Conference to the anti-narcotic cause, and one which has largely redeemed its failure in other respects.

The contest on the issue of control versus direct limitation had been close. Indeed it had also been so bitter that one important delegation had left the Conference partly on that account.[2] The fact that this fundamental disagreement remained was one of the reasons why the defeated principle of the direct limitation of drug manufacture was soon revived. Another was

---

[1] Shortly after the Board began to function, the Assembly of the League, at its 10th Session, agreed that the composition of the Advisory Committee should be altered to permit the representation on it of some of the drug-consuming countries, and asked the Committee itself to study the question. The result of its deliberations on the subject was the addition of seven new States to membership on the Committee. In this manner the third defect in the system was remedied. The present composition of the Advisory Committee is as follows, the final column being those States added by reason of this resolution:

Bolivia	Japan	Austria
China	Netherlands	Belgium
France	Portugal	Egypt
Germany	Siam	Mexico
Great Britain	Switzerland	Poland
India	U.S.A.	Spain
Italy	Yugoslavia	Uruguay

[2] The United States. The Chinese delegation subsequently also left, because of the decision reached in the First Conference regarding smoking opium, a decision to which both the Chinese and Americans were strongly opposed.

the discovery of several sources of the illicit traffic in European factories, and the fact that statistics showed an increase in the reported world manufacture in the years following the Geneva Conferences.[1] This fact is not to be blamed on the ineffectiveness of the Geneva Convention, for that instrument was not ratified by a sufficient number of States to bring it into effect until 1928. But it served to intensify the impatience of those who believed that the end of the evil could only be attained by a system of direct limitation of drug manufacture. This opinion was held not only by many of the Governments—chiefly by those which were the victims of the drug traffic—but also by small but informed and active private groups which by their influence upon public opinion, in so far as it is interested in the drug problem, are a contributing factor in the determination of official attitudes. Finally, the opposition of one or two important manufacturing groups which had opposed direct limitation since it was first proposed, gave way under repeated attacks and the very real fear that exposure of their illegal activities would follow further resistance. The result was that the Tenth Assembly of the League of Nations, in 1929, passed a resolution ". . . recalling the proposals made in connection with the Geneva Conference of 1924–25 for direct limitation by agreement between Governments of the manufacturing countries of the amounts of such drugs manufactured . . ." and requesting "the Advisory Committee to prepare plans for such limitation, regard being had to world requirements for medical and scientific purposes. . . ."[2]

The Advisory Committee accordingly set to work to consider by what means the mandate given it by the Assembly was to be fulfilled. Meanwhile, a most important set of inquiries was undertaken by the opium section of the League Secretariat to ascertain the exact extent of the drug trade, to separate if

[1] Consult League Document O.C. 1072, Part II (1930).
[2] 10 A.P., p. 498.

28

possible the licit from the illicit trade, to locate the sources of the latter as well as the victims of it, to establish an estimate of the legitimate needs of the world in drugs, the total amount manufactured, the manufacturing countries, and any other particulars that would be of use to the Conference which was to consider the direct limitation of the manufacture of drugs to their medical and scientific needs. This statistical work of the opium section cannot be overrated. The only valid criticism that has been made of it is that it was too comprehensive, too detailed, and too thorough, and hence of little use to anyone who had not the time to give to a complete study of the material it contained. This is a criticism which borders closely on the laudatory. The energetic attitude of the opium section was symptomatic of a renewed life in the anti-drug movement all along the line. Lethargy and indifference gave way to activity, and even opposition was broken down when those Governments which had most opposed the limitation of drug manufacture by direct means were persuaded or obliged to accept the principle. Obliged is not perhaps too strong a word, for it was scarcely possible for a Government to be represented on the Advisory Committee of the League and remain actively opposed to an idea which, by majority vote of the Assembly, it was the Committee's duty to study and to develop. This was the position in which several of the Governments on the Committee found themselves.[1] But the thesis of the direct and quantitative limitation of the manufacture of drugs had won the day, and it had become impossible to oppose it any longer without an unwelcome loss of influence and prestige.

It is not to be wondered at nor unduly criticized that the

[1] During its 13th Session the Opium Advisory Committee put itself publicly on record as having always been opposed to limitation, by leaving unchallenged a statement to this effect made by the President on February 14th. See Communique II of the Anti-Opium Information Bureau: Geneva.

Governments of the drug manufacturing countries should have opposed a system of direct limitation of the manufacture of drugs, considering the difficulties in which such a scheme would inevitably involve them with the industry. Especially is this true considering that the effects of the Geneva Convention, in which many of the Governments had the utmost faith, had scarcely had time to manifest themselves. Furthermore, carrying out its provisions did not present the administrative difficulties which the proposed plan involved. For the first of these three reasons, at least, it can also be understood why the Governments of the manufacturing countries, having once adopted the principle of limiting the production of drugs, should seek to carry it out by the method which should elicit the minimum of opposition from the industry. These considerations account for the fact that the Advisory Committee, on which the drug producing countries had a majority representation,[1] drew up a plan which, while assuring the limitation of the manufacture of drugs, at the same time assured that the industry should become the virtual monopoly of the existing manufacturers, by making the admission of new participants difficult. From the administrative point of view the plan was blameless, but it proved impossible of realization for two reasons to which the Advisory Committee had failed to attach sufficient importance.

The first was that the manufacturers could not agree among themselves upon a just allotment or quota distribution of the drugs which they were to produce annually among them. Originally these quotas were to have been allotted on the basis of the present manufacture of each country for legitimate pur-

[1]
China	India*	Portugal
France*	Italy*	Siam
Germany*	Japan*	Switzerland*
Great Britain*	Netherlands*	Yugoslavia

Composition of the Advisory Committee at this time. The manufacturing countries are marked *. India and Italy, however, manufacture very small quantities. Yugoslavia began to manufacture in 1933.

poses, but although it was well known which of them were responsible for at least a part of the illicit traffic, no authority existed to establish this fact and to make the adjustment on the proper basis. The Advisory Committee therefore decided to let the manufacturers adjust the matter among themselves,[1] but they also found it utterly impossible to do this by negotiation. After a few sessions of the Limitation Conference it became clear that any agreement on quotas was out of the question, and the idea was abandoned in favour of an alternative scheme.

Intimations that general opposition to the quota system existed among the non-manufacturing countries were frequent while preparations for the Conference were under way, and it is likely that the quota system would have broken down even if the manufacturing countries had been able to agree on the quota allotments, for the temper and strength of the consuming countries was unmistakable. Their attitude, not only in demanding limitation, but also in demanding a scheme which should safeguard their special interests, had been developing ever since the Geneva Conference six years earlier. The Press and private societies and individuals who interested themselves in the question and who formed public opinion were generally supporting the position of the consuming countries. And, finally, the validity of the arguments put forward by the consuming countries gave them, it must be admitted, a definite moral advantage over the manufacturing countries, who could never, in public conference, have put through a scheme which threatened, if it did not actually propose, to give them a monopoly of the drug industry, and the control of the supply and price of products vital to the medical profession.

The Conference for the Limitation of the Manufacture of Narcotic Drugs was held in Geneva from May 27 until July 13, 1931. Its long duration is partly explained by the conflict of opinion which has just been described, and to which so much

[1] *Minutes of the Opium Advisory Committee*, 12th Session, p. 106.

attention has been given here because it illustrates the type of difficulty which has presented itself time and again in the anti-narcotic movement.

A brief description of the situation in the narcotics industry and of the manner in which it is now, under the Convention just drawn up, proposed to control the production of drugs, is necessary to complete the history of this work and to define the basis from which it is to continue.

If the world production of narcotics is to be limited to the needs of the medical profession and of science, it is obviously essential that these needs be known. As yet, however, it has not been found possible to do more than estimate them, since no attempt to ascertain them with any exactitude has yet been made in most countries.[1] A few countries demand accounts of their pharmacies as to the amounts of drugs dispensed; others follow the control of narcotics only as far as the wholesaler. In others there is no way of arriving at the figure of consumption except the unsatisfactory one of adding together the amounts imported and manufactured and subtracting from this sum the amounts exported and kept in stock. Various attempts have been made locally to ascertain the quantities of drugs used by physicians and in hospitals, and although these have produced some valuable results they have in general remained too localized to be useful in establishing accurate figures for national and world needs in opiates. The best available information as to the world's annual legitimate consumption of drugs was that furnished to the Limitation Conference by the Secretariat of the League of Nations, giving the following figures:[2]

Morphine	..	..	..	9·0 tons	
Heroin	..	..	..	2·0 tons	Total: 16·5 tons
Cocaine	..	..	..	5·5 tons	

[1] Germany, Great Britain, and the United States can give quite accurate figures of legitimate requirements.

[2] See League Document L.F.S. 73 (i).

INTRODUCTION

It is interesting to compare with these figures those for the actual quantities of the substances reported as manufactured in the years 1929, 1930, 1931, 1932.[1] These were:

	1929	1930	1931	1932
	Tons	Tons	Tons	Tons
Morphine	13·0	9·2	8·3	7·0
Heroin	3·6	3·9	1·2	1·2
Cocaine	5·6	4·7	4·0	3·9
Morphine used in the manufacture of drugs not covered by the Convention ..	38·0	21·0	18·0	16·4

Germany is the greatest single manufacturer of narcotic drugs producing more than one-third of the total world manufacture. Switzerland and Great Britain came next in order in 1925, but their manufacture has since then steadily declined, while that of France and the United States has as steadily increased. These are the five principal drug manufacturers. There is in addition Japan producing approximately 3 per cent of the total world manufacture of morphine and its products, and responsible for over one-third of the total world cocaine manufacture. Russia also produces, but consumes her own manufactured drugs, and the Netherlands, Italy, and India each manufacture only small amounts. Turkey is the last to be mentioned, having only in the past two years developed a considerable drug industry which gave other drug manufacturers no little concern, especially as Turkey had refused to adhere to any of the Conventions. Although the Turkish Government has now established control over its drug industry, pirate factories turned out, on the

[1] Permanent Central Opium Board. Report to the Council on the Work of the 11th, 12th, and 13th Sessions (Document A. 35. 1932, XI) for 1929–31. For 1932, see Report of the Board to the Council on the Work of the 14th, 15th, and 16th Sessions (Document C. 495. M. 250. 1933, XI).

Government's own admission, some ten tons of drugs in 1930 alone. The great danger from Turkey has been that it produces the opium used for morphine manufacture, and is therefore beyond the reach of any international supervision exercised by means of keeping watch over imports of raw materials.

No one of the manufacturing countries can be charged singly with the responsibility for the illicit traffic in drugs, nor can any of them entirely escape blame. The most that can be said is that recent discoveries of illicit trade channels have led to the implication of this or that industry, but it must be remembered that only a small part of the contraband trade is ever uncovered. The source of the other nine-tenths remains at most a subject of conjecture. A study on the channels of the illicit traffic recently made by the League Opium Section[1] reveals that the actual manufacture of drugs for illicit purposes is only one of the sources of the illicit trade, and that the latter is also largely supplied out of licit quantities of drugs which pass into the illicit traffic at various subsequent points where control is either weak or entirely lacking. Much of the blame may thus fall on a country which does not have any drug industry, but which imports the drugs and permits their re-export or other distribution without sufficient regulation. It is easier to point out the consumer than the supplier of contraband drugs. Egypt is the most glaring example of a country which seems to have become the definite objective of the smuggler. In the past ten years, according to the report of Russell Pasha, Director of the Central Narcotics Intelligence Bureau in Cairo, a half-million out of a population of 14,000,000 has become addicted to drugs.[2] A similar cry comes from China, which points an accusing finger at Europe, and from India, where it is claimed that addiction to cocaine, of Japanese origin, is spreading rapidly. The United

[1] See League Document C. 587. M. 228. 1930, XI. Analysis of the International Trade in Morphine, Diacetylmorphine, and Cocaine for the years 1925–29. *Provisional.*

[2] *Minutes of the Advisory Committee,* 13th Session, p. 72.

States seems to be the principal victim of narcotic addiction among the manufacturing countries. The cases of smuggling of manufactured drugs which have been uncovered have been principally on the East coast, while large quantities of opium come in from Oriental ports.[1]

The elusive character of the drug traffic, the devious channels through which it can be effected, the tremendous profits involved, the assured and inevitably increasing demand for the drugs, and the ease with which they can be handled undetected, make the problem of control extremely complicated. It was the hope of the Conference which met in Geneva in the summer of 1931 to avoid these difficulties entirely by rendering impossible the manufacture of more drugs than are strictly necessary for the satisfaction of medical and scientific needs. It remains to be seen with what success the Limitation Convention will meet. In April 1933 it had received a sufficient number of ratifications to make it effective. Its provisions are of such a nature that the effective limitation of the manufacture of narcotics is finally in sight. The manufacture of heroin for export has been prohibited, except under exceptional circumstances, and some of the contracting parties have in addition agreed that its use is not essential to medicine and shall therefore be abandoned in favour of less harmful substances.[2] Any possible leakage through the manufacture of codeine has been stopped by submitting it also to regulation, though of a less stringent type than that provided for morphine and cocaine.

The Convention has also gone a step farther in the development of international control machinery in that it contemplates the establishment of an organ with yet more direct powers than those of the Central Board. This is the Supervisory Body, provided for by virtue of Article 5, paragraph 6, of the Convention.

[1] *Minutes of the Advisory Committee*, 13th Session, p. 229.

[2] The countries which have abandoned the use of heroin are Austria, and Poland, and the United States, which has prohibited opium imports for heroin manufacture.

It is composed of one member appointed by each of the following organs: the Advisory Committee, the Permanent Central Board, the International Health Office at Paris, and the Health Committee of the League of Nations. The new organ is thus assured of high technical qualifications and of a membership independent of national interests. The function of the Supervisory Body is to receive annually from each of the Governments estimates of its requirements of narcotic drugs for the coming year, to demand explanations of them if they seem excessive, and to furnish estimates for any country which does not supply them. The Convention also secures wider powers to the Permanent Central Board, which is now enabled to establish its decisions on the basis of the estimates which are transmitted to it by the Supervisory Body. The Board has in addition been empowered to draw up, at the close of each year, a comprehensive report on the international trade in drugs and each country's part in it. The powers of the Supervisory Body and the Central Board thus complement each other: the first sees that each year the legitimate amount of drugs to be manufactured is established, and the second that the production and trade for that year remain within the bounds thus drawn. Ultimate responsibility is still in the hands of the individual Governments, for even the Board's authority to recommend is strictly limited, and its most powerful weapon is the publicity it can give to any irregular situation. Because of this, Article 15 of the Limitation Convention is of the greatest importance, for it requires of the signatories the creation of a special administration to apply the provisions of the Convention. This Article ought also to hasten the application of recommendations made by the Advisory Committee.

The importance of the Convention lies chiefly in the fact that it enables the Governments to keep better informed as to the course and volume of the drug trade and thus to regulate their individual parts in it in such a manner that the international production of drugs may remain within definite and legitimate limits. The significance of this step toward international centralization and control is very great, and will be more fully dealt with later.[1]

Of equal importance, though bearing on a different phase of the narcotics control problem, are certain provisions in the Convention which aim at establishing strict domestic control over the quantities of raw opium and coca leaves imported into the manufacturing countries for the purpose of producing drugs. These provisions do no more than carry a step farther the principle already recognized in limiting the manufacture of drugs to medical and scientific needs, namely, that the only effective attack on the drug menace has to be made at the very roots of production. Effective though the provisions for limiting manufacture may be, it must be remembered that behind this industry there is the opium grower, and sometimes a revenue-collecting Government, interests which, in certain parts of the world, have to be reckoned with. Obviously, if the quantity of drugs henceforth manufactured is to be greatly reduced the production of raw opium will have either to undergo a corresponding reduction or find some other outlet. As to the latter, there are only two which it is possible to envisage. Either there will be an increase in the quantities of opium exported to those territories where opium smoking has not yet been eliminated, thus rendering that problem more difficult, or, what is certainly more dangerous and perhaps more likely because it is more profitable, the establishment of drug factories in countries not party to the Limitation Convention, or in remote territories where control is not practicable. This has happened already in Turkey and Bulgaria, where suppressive measures have been taken since, but the clandestine activity was only shifted to Manchuria where the problem of control is for the moment hopelessly difficult.

For a time it seemed that a second door would be closed to the producers of opium. The sequel to the movement against

[1] See pp. 198 et seq.

opium smoking, which was begun at Shanghai and The Hague in 1909 and 1912, was enacted in 1931 at Bangkok. At the invitation of the Siamese Government and under the auspices of the League of Nations the Governments of those territories where opium smoking is still permitted met to discuss ways of arriving at an eventual complete elimination of the custom. But this renewed attempt to deal with the problem proved as abortive as the First Geneva Opium Conference of 1924–25.[1] The burden of the agreement reached was that the reduction of smoking with a view to its complete prohibition within the space of a few years could not be attempted until opium was brought under strict control, both as to production and export.

Definite action may nevertheless have to be taken by the Colonial Governments sooner than they expected, for the League Assembly, which has shown itself fully aware of the development of the narcotics problem, in 1931 passed the following resolution, presented by the delegate of Panama:

> . . . that the Secretary-General ask the Advisory Committee on the Traffic in Opium and Other Dangerous Drugs and the competent organs of the Secretariat of the League of Nations to undertake as soon as possible the compilation of all documentary material likely to serve as the basis of the work of a conference on the limitation of opium production, and for this purpose to send a questionnaire to all Governments Members or Non-members of the League of Nations.

The year 1931 was the most fruitful for the anti-narcotic movement since the League entered upon this field of activity. The Conference for the Limitation of the Manufacture of Drugs, and the proposal to hold another conference to secure the reduction of poppy cultivation, crystallize not only one, but ten years' achievements. It must be remembered, however, that

---

[1] Held simultaneously with the Second Geneva Opium Conference which discussed the control of drug manufacture. It was attended by representatives of the Governments in whose territories smoking is permitted.

these accomplishments, important as they are, are in substance but the adoption of certain principles, the agreement on a line of action. They do not represent an object attained; rather they point the road to a goal. That is much, but the road is still to be travelled.

Two primary tendencies stand out in the development of the control over the traffic in narcotics as it is presented in the previous pages. The first is the tendency to centralize control in an international organism. The second is the tendency to strike directly at production, leaving as secondary the consideration of the control of the traffic.

These two tendencies are apparent throughout, not only since the League of Nations adopted the management of the problem, but since the Chinese undertook to pull up the poppies in 1907, and the Hague Conference studied the proposal to set up an international commission. At the present moment the first of these two tendencies is being furthered in the Supervisory Body, which must, however, in the future be still further developed, for the existing international organization is not endowed with sufficient power to make it fully effective, while national administrations still maintain enough absolute discretion to prevent perfectly co-ordinated action. The second tendency, meanwhile, has just received the most complete recognition with regard to the manufactured drugs, and is about to be extended to the production of opium.

The following pages will deal with the questions raised in considering further the development of these two tendencies. Part One will discuss more fully the internationalization of control, in the attempt to destroy some of the misconceptions which have hindered its more rapid development in the past, and to point out the reasons for and the possibility of the continuation of this evolution which has so much significance for the success of the drug fight. Part Two, in dealing with the limitation of opium production, involves problems which are chiefly, and for the moment, of an economic nature.

Perhaps the conclusions which resolve themselves from this study may prove of some value in hastening the destruction of a grave social menace.

Part One

THE ORGANIZATION OF INTERNATIONAL CONTROL

CHAPTER I

THE ESTABLISHMENT OF THE OPIUM ADVISORY
COMMITTEE

1. *Introductory*

THE first organized international action against the narcotic traffic
was begun on December 15, 1920, when the Advisory Committee
on the Traffic in Opium and Other Dangerous Drugs was set up
by resolution of the First Assembly of the League of Nations.

The act of the Assembly marked the realization of a concept
which had its origin in 1912. The idea of a permanent international organization to supervise the trade in opium and drugs
was contained in one of the points submitted to the Hague
Opium Conference by the Government of the United States. It
was too widely opposed at that time to be given concrete form,
although the Conference recognized the need for some sort of
responsible supervision when it asked the Netherlands Government to undertake to secure the ratification of the Hague Convention, and to see that it was faithfully executed by its signatories.

The passage of ten years saw many political changes. Not the
least of these was the development of opinion with regard to
internationalizing control in a number of fields heretofore considered the exclusive domain of national sovereignty. The work
of the Peace Conference was a continuous revelation of the
extent to which this realization had permeated the minds of the
peoples, and the drafting of the Covenant of the League of
Nations was at once the embodiment of this idea, and the
highest achievement of the Conference. Although public attention has been attracted chiefly to the work of the League in
settling disputes and preventing the outbreak of war, its more
important function has been what has aptly been called "the

organization of peace." The ambitious framers of the Covenant laid the foundations of an institution whose activity was to reach into the farthest corners of the world and into many fields of human enterprise. Besides the task of preventing war and its immediate corollary, the securing of disarmament, the League embarked upon the difficult and diverse paths of economic organization, financial regulation, the equitable government of the mandated territories, the regularization of international communications and transit facilities, the world organization of health and sanitation, co-operation in intellectual and educational fields, and finally upon such social problems as the protection of children, the fight against the white slave traffic, and against the illicit trade in opium and other dangerous drugs. These were the lines upon which the organization of peace was undertaken. Although international co-operation in most of these fields had not been unknown before the war, never before had so far-reaching and thoroughgoing a programme of institutionalization been drafted.[1]

2. The Origins of the Committee

In the light of these developments it was natural that the control of the drug traffic should have been undertaken by the League. Although this task has been referred to as the unwelcome foundling on the doorstep, it was fully in line with the rest of the humanitarian work which the League undertook. Moreover, it was in line with the development of drug control itself, for the Hague Convention was in need of some competent hand which should secure its ratification and watch over its application, a task which the League was better able to perform than the Netherlands Government.

There had been great difficulty in securing the ratification of the Hague Convention. Although a Second Opium Conference

[1] See H. R. G. Greaves, *The League Committees and World Order*, Oxford University Press, 1931.

44

was held at The Hague in July 1913 for the purpose of securing further ratification of the Convention, and again, in June 1914, a Third Conference for the purpose of putting the Convention into effect as between the Powers which had ratified, the results were very discouraging. Only thirteen States had signed and ratified before the outbreak of the war,[1] and only four were added to this number before the signing of the Peace Treaties.[2] Of these only seven had signified their readiness to put the Convention into effect by the close of the war.[3] Credit is due to the Government of the Netherlands for urging the Peace Conference to provide in the terms of the Treaty that the signatories thereof should, automatically, become adherents to the Hague Opium Convention.[4] A like provision was made in the Peace Treaties with the rest of the Central Powers.[5] Equal credit is due to the Government of Great Britain for urging in the League of Nations Commission at the Peace Conference that the international control of the opium trade be undertaken by the League. Mr. David Hunter Miller, in *The Drafting of the Covenant*, said: "There are, as a matter of fact, a number of matters, such as, for instance, the international control of opium, morphia, and other dangerous drugs which the competent British officials are particularly anxious to bring within the scope of the League. . . ."[6] The British proposal later became incorporated in the Covenant as Article 23 (c), and establishes the League's function in the following terms:

Subject to and in accordance with the provisions of the international conventions existing or hereinafter to be agreed upon, the Members of the League: . . .

---

[1] Belgium, China, Denmark, Great Britain, Guatemala, Honduras, Italy, Netherlands, Portugal, Siam, Sweden, United States, Venezuela.

[2] Brazil, Ecuador, Nicaragua, Norway.

[3] See p. 22, f.n. 1, above.   [4] Article 295, Treaty of Versailles.

[5] Treaty of St. Germain, Article 247; of Trianon, 230; of Neuilly, 174. See Liais, *La Question des Stupéfiants Manufacturés et l'Œuvre de la Société des Nations.*   [6] Part I, p. 219.

Will entrust the League with the general supervision over the execution of agreements with regard to . . . the traffic in opium and other dangerous drugs.

The signing of the Peace Treaties made the Hague Convention law in twenty-seven additional States, bringing the total number of adherents to forty.[1] Of these all but eight had become members of the League of Nations by the time the First Assembly was convened.[2] Although unfortunately among these eight were included two of the most important drug manufacturing countries, the United States and Germany, whose collaboration could with difficulty be dispensed with, the First Assembly nevertheless united the great majority of States which had an interest in the work, and it was therefore excellently constituted for constructing the machinery which should consummate this particular task of the League.

The Second Committee of the First Assembly was charged with the study of the application of Article 23 of the Covenant. As the basis of his report to the Committee on the question of the opium traffic, Sir William Meyer, representative of the Government of India, and *rapporteur*, used a memorandum communicated to the Secretary-General by the Netherlands Government. The substance of the memorandum was that the Netherlands Government considered that the League ought now to succeed it in supervising the execution of the Hague Convention, and suggested that a committee composed of those States which were directly concerned with the subject should consider the means whereby the League could best carry out this function. The Second Committee of the Assembly happened to be thus qualified; though, if one were to judge by the amount of discussion which the question raised, very little interest in the subject could be attributed to the Committee. Beside the excellent

[1] Spain ratified the Hague Convention January 25, 1919.
[2] Austria, Bulgaria, Ecuador, Germany, Honduras, Hungary, Spain, United States.

report of Sir William Meyer, in which the situation with regard to opium and drugs was reviewed, the Hague Convention sketched, and two alternative proposals made for the organization of the League's opium work, only one notable contribution to the solution of the problem was offered. This was the resolution put forward by Mr. Barnes, of the British delegation. Sir William Meyer had concluded his report with the suggestion that the obligation of the League under Article 23 (c) might be executed in either of two ways: (1) it might simply be left to the Council of the League, which would be assisted by the Secretariat and would report annually to the Assembly, or (2) it might be desirable to appoint a special committee composed of the members of the League most interested in the opium problem, which committee should assist the Council and the Secretariat. Mr. Barnes proposed that the second of the two plans be adopted, and in this view the representatives of China, Portugal, the Netherlands, and Siam concurred. It is important to note the terms of Mr. Barnes's resolution, which, with only slight amendment, was adopted by the Second Committee and, later, by the Assembly in plenary session.[1]

[1] The relevant passages of the Assembly resolution are the following (see 1 A.P., p. 538):

"That having regard to the duty placed on the League by Article 23 of the Covenant to supervise the execution of arrangements with regard to the traffic in opium and other dangerous drugs, the Assembly concurs with the Netherlands Government in its view that it will be preferable for the League to undertake the duties placed upon the Netherlands Government by the Opium Convention with regard to the collection of data and dealing with disputes;

That for this purpose and for the purpose of enabling the League to exercise its general supervision over the execution of arrangements with regard to this traffic, the Secretariat of the League is entrusted with the duty of collecting information as to the arrangements made in the various countries for carrying out the Opium Convention, the production, distribution, and consumption of the drugs, and other necessary data;

That in order to secure the fullest possible co-operation between the various countries in regard to the matter, and to assist and advise the Council in dealing with any questions that may arise, an Advisory Com-

The resolution states that the League of Nations will take over the task which the Hague Convention had imposed upon the Netherlands Government. This task was threefold, consisting, first, in securing the ratification of the Convention; second, in collecting information regarding the methods adopted by the various Governments for executing the Convention; and, third, in settling questions arising out of its application. The first of these tasks was practically accomplished with the signing of the Peace Treaties. The second, Mr. Barnes suggested, should be assumed by the Secretariat of the League, and the third by the committee which Sir William Meyer proposed setting up. Mr Barnes, furthermore, approved the lines upon which Sir William Meyer had proposed that this committee should be organized, adding the important condition that the Council be empowered to name as assessors the representatives of any countries especially concerned with the drug traffic.

It seems from this review of the course of events leading up to the establishment of the Opium Advisory Committee that considerable ambiguity as to its duties and competence was permitted to exist. The Committee from the first suffered from this lack of definition, and its work was considerably retarded by the fact that it was possible to defend a very con-

---

mittee be appointed by the Council, which shall include representatives of the countries chiefly concerned, in particular Holland, Great Britain, France, India, Japan, China, Siam, Portugal, and shall, subject to the general directions of the Council, meet at such times as shall be found desirable; . . .

That the Council be authorized, if and when they think it necessary, to add as assessors to the Committee not more than three persons not representatives of Governments, having special knowledge of the question; and that the travelling expenses and allowances of such Members shall be paid out of the funds of the League;

That the Advisory Committee shall, three months before the beginning of every Session of the Assembly, present to the Council for submission to the Assembly a report on all matters regarding the execution of agreements with regard to the traffic in opium and other dangerous drugs; . . ."

servative policy simply by referring back to the early discussions of its functions. The British view at the Peace Conference, as stated by Mr. David Hunter Miller, contains no hint of limiting the League's work to supervising the execution of the Hague Convention. Article 23 (c) itself was included in the Covenant as a British amendment, and in view of its origin it may fairly be given a liberal interpretation. A different note, however, was struck in the First Assembly, due perhaps to the fact that the memorandum of the Netherlands Government had directed attention more especially to the Hague Opium Convention. The resolution of Mr. Barnes can hardly be construed otherwise than as proposing that the League should succeed to the task of the Netherlands Government, an unfortunately narrow representation of the case.

The Council of the League at its 12th Session considered the report of the Assembly on the opium question, and in view of the resolution adopted by it, the Advisory Committee on the Traffic in Opium and Other Dangerous Drugs was formally constituted.[1] Its members were to be eight in number, one appointed by each of the Governments named in the Assembly resolution, i.e. China, France, Great Britain, Holland, India, Japan, Portugal, and Siam. The idea of special assessors which Mr. Barnes had put forward in the Second Committee was developed by the Council in such a way as to answer a different need than the Assembly had foreseen. Instead of representing Governments with a special interest in the drug traffic, the three assessors were selected as individuals with a special and technical knowledge of the question, and an active interest in the work which the League had undertaken. Thus Sir John Jordan, who played an important part in the negotiation of the Indo-Chinese opium agreement of 1907, was thoroughly acquainted with the Chinese opium situation and a strong defender of the Chinese position. M. Henri Brenier was equally

[1] 12 C. 6.

familiar with the opium problem, having for long been in the service of his Government in French Indo-China. Thirdly, Mrs. Hamilton Wright, the widow of Dr. Hamilton Wright, had collaborated with her husband in his anti-opium work in China, and was well qualified to carry on the policy which he had defended at the Hague Conference.

It is interesting to note that at the time the Advisory Committee was set up, no thought seems to have been given to the inclusion of States with a direct interest in the manufactured drugs. Only incidentally, in the membership of France and Great Britain, was this interest represented, and even these two States were primarily concerned with the opium problem in their colonies and possessions. This fact had a noticeable effect upon the work of the Committee, as the following pages will show. The idea of the Assembly was to have the Advisory Committee composed of representatives of Governments having to cope with the opium-smoking problem. It was thought that these representatives would be able to formulate realistic and practicable measures which their Governments would be inclined to adopt, and that the exchange of criticisms and experiences would further a general solution of problems common to them all. If it had not been for the fact that opium smoking provided important revenues for the Governments of the colonies, this view would have been more plausible. But members representing Governments in whose territories opium smoking was still permitted and still financially important would necessarily place considerable emphasis upon these aspects of the problem. Such a result was unavoidable, the more so because the general acceptance of the thesis that opium smoking was detrimental to society was still hedged round by qualifications frankly dictated by fiscal and other considerations.

Nevertheless, the Advisory Committee was organized along the lines which have just been indicated, although already at this time a section of opinion was beginning to advocate that advisory bodies be constituted at least in part of persons entirely independent of any special interest in avoiding the unequivocal solution of the problem to be dealt with. This principle was in part applied when the Mandates Commission was organized, and again when the Permanent Armaments Commission was seen to be unsuitable and was supplemented by the Temporary Mixed Commission on Armaments. Even regarding the organization of the Opium Advisory Committee the Assembly has not maintained its original views unaltered. Although the adoption of a resolution in 1929 to add seven non-manufacturing countries to the Committee did not mean a complete repudiation of the principle upon which it had been constituted, it was an admission that these principles had not shown themselves to be entirely satisfactory. Some element of opinion had from the first been in favour of a committee representing non-producing interests in some proportion. Something of this was clear when the appointment of assessors went unopposed. As a result of the proposal of Uruguay the Fifth Assembly added a Bolivian member to the Advisory Committee to represent the consuming countries of Latin America.[1] In the Sixth Assembly the Irish Free State delegate was supported by Japan and Sweden in proposing a change in the composition of the Advisory Committee in favour of the consuming countries.[2] In the Seventh Assembly the Italian delegate proposed that the Committee be composed equally of producing and consuming countries.[3] Finally, in 1928 Italy was given a seat on the Committee to represent the point of view of the consuming countries. The next year the Venezuelan delegate once more raised the subject, and as a direct result of this the Tenth Assembly resolved that there should be more effective representation on the Committee of the non-producing countries.[4] To the seven new members appointed at that time two more representatives of

[1] 5 A.C. v., p. 16. [2] 6 A.C. v., p. 37.
[3] 7 A.C. v., p.17. [4] 10 A.C. v., p. 56.

non-manufacturing countries have been added since.[1] But at the time the Advisory Committee was set up the general view taken was that repeated conference between representatives of the countries directly concerned, familiarity with each other's problems, and the resulting publicity, would achieve the ends which the Committee was intended to serve.

3. The Representation "of the Countries Chiefly Concerned"

The Secretary-General of the League of Nations, presiding at the first meeting of the Opium Advisory Committee, expressed the hope that its members, while representing their Governments, would also bear in mind the international aspect of their work.[2] This was pure optimism. Several important discussions which took place in the earliest sessions of the Advisory Committee indicated at once the tenor of mind of its members, and may be well worth examining here for the picture they present of the forces and motives at work beneath the activities of the Committee.

In the 1st Session of the Advisory Committee, Sir Malcolm Delevingne, delegate of Great Britain, proposed that the Secretariat, through the International Health Organization, undertake an investigation into the medical and scientific requirements of opium and drugs all over the world. It was obviously essential to the work of the Committee that it have at least an approximate idea of the amount of narcotics needed for medical and scientific purposes if it was to attempt to limit their production to this quantity. But the delegate of India at once raised strong objections. Mr. (now Sir) John Campbell claimed that it was distinctly

---

[1] Canada and Sweden. Persia and Turkey were added at the same time, in 1934.

[2] *Minutes of the Advisory Committee*, 1st Session, p. 3.

beyond the competence of the Committee to authorize an investigation into the needs of raw and prepared opium with a view to their subsequent limitation. The Hague Convention imposed provisions for limitation of production upon the manufactured drugs alone, and it was therefore outside the competence of the Committee to consider measures which aimed at extending that principle to raw and prepared opium as well. The Chinese delegate, Mr. Tang Tsai-Fou, advocated a more liberal interpretation of the Committee's competence, claiming that it was qualified to take any steps in advance which might serve the anti-narcotic fight. His contention was, however, overruled, and Mr. Campbell secured the passage of a resolution which confined the proposed investigation to the manufactured drugs.[1]

China, nevertheless, had her innings in the Council, where the Chinese delegate, Mr. Wellington Koo, as *rapporteur* on the opium question, did not hesitate to suggest that the Advisory Committee's recommendation fell short of the highest possible achievement, and that, in view of the general interest in opium production and the growing opinion that abuse must be stopped by striking at production itself, the proposed investigation ought by all means to be extended to opium as well.[2] As the Government of India was not represented on the Council the amended recommendation was passed without opposition.

The Government of India, however, was not content to let this decision go unchallenged. When the report of the Opium Advisory Committee came before the Assembly, Mr. Sastri, the delegate of the Government of India, was ready with a fresh argument. Mr. Sastri explained that there were non-medical and non-scientific uses of opium in India which were nevertheless legitimate, that a large portion of the population consumed opium regularly as a kind of general preventative and cure-all, and that to deprive the people of this simple remedy for their

[1] *Minutes of the Advisory Committee*, 1st Session, p. 17.
[2] 13 C. 276.

ills was unthinkable.[1] It would be impossible to conduct an investigation into the needs of opium in India unless this important consideration were kept in mind.

A simple observation upon Indian opium production at that time, which, however, Mr. Sastri did not make, might not be inappropriate here. Revenue from the sale of opium by the Opium Monopoly of the Government of India amounted to 4 per cent of the total revenue. Of this 4 per cent, three-fifths were derived from the sale of opium at home and the other two-fifths from the sale of opium abroad. The latter item was in process of diminution because of the recent abolition of the auction system of sale for export. This fact gave to the domestic sale of opium a correspondingly increased importance.

Whatever connection this fact may or may not have had with the attitude of the Government of India toward investigation, it is impossible to doubt that they were anxious not to interfere with the domestic use of the drug. The argument of Mr. Sastri prevailed in the Assembly, and in order to meet the demands of the Government of India a resolution was passed whereby the Advisory Committee was authorized to conduct an investigation into the "legitimate," instead of into the "medical and scientific," requirements of opium and drugs.[2]

It is a question whether the resolution of the Assembly was an improvement on the original Committee proposal. The Committee, it is true, had confined the investigation to the manufactured drugs, but the Assembly, while extending it to cover raw and prepared opium as well, recognized as legitimate a very

[1] The Indian fashion of taking opium is by eating instead of smoking. Small pills of opium are chewed or dissolved in water and the solution drunk. Although the contention is that it is not a drug of addiction when taken in this manner, it would appear that the consumer receives the full morphine content of the opium, whereas, in smoking, the largest part remains in the ashes. While opium smoking is not permitted in India, the habit of eating it, and its sale for this purpose, is considered legitimate.

[2] 2 A.C. ii., p. 490.

questionable use of opium. Medical opinion has increasingly condemned it, and the Government of India itself is beginning to recognize that its position cannot much longer be maintained.[1]

The incident demonstrated the ease with which a strong national interest could overrule an international project. Unquestionably, the Indian attitude gave a severe setback to opium control. Other opium-producing and consuming countries have naturally been able to resist investigation and refuse to take measures for suppression simply by pointing to India.

Perhaps the most glaring example of the part which politics could play in the Advisory Committee was given at the 2nd Session of the Committee when the situation with regard to opium in China was under discussion. China, motivated by the same type of interest that had dictated the attitude of India in the previous Session, protested against submitting its opium problem to foreign investigation. It had been suggested in the 1st Session of the Committee that the consular representatives of the European Powers in China be authorized by the Chinese Government to make representation to the provincial governors in an effort to get them to enforce the Chinese laws against the production of opium. In the Council, however, where the Chinese delegate had the advantage over his colleague on the Advisory Committee because of the absence of British Indian opposition, Mr. Koo had succeeded in deferring the recommendation for consular representation until the Chinese Government should have made a thorough investigation into the production of opium. But at the 2nd Session of the Advisory Committee the report of the Chinese delegate on the results of the investigation met with the severest condemnation. Not only the delegate of India, but also the two League assessors, M. Brenier and Sir John Jordan, the defender of China, accused the Chinese Government of failing to meet its obligations under the treaty

[1] See chapter on India for fuller discussion.

of 1911 with India,[1] and declared that the report presented to the Committee was entirely invalid. The Committee thereupon refused to accept it, and in its report to the Council recommended again that foreign consular representation be made in China. The Chinese member on the Committee, while not denying that conditions in China were not what they ought to be, nevertheless maintained that his Government would refuse to tolerate any foreign action in China, unless such action came directly from the League, and unless it was applied equally to all other countries. In establishing these two conditions the Chinese delegate very adroitly placed himself in a strong position. Conditions in the Native States in India were not better than in China, nor was the Indian Government any more able than the Chinese to secure law and order in these regions. If consular representation was to be applied in China it must also be applied in India, and in any other country where for one reason or another it appeared impossible to enforce laws against opium and drugs.[2] None of the States represented on the Advisory Committee could have escaped this description. The fact placed the Committee in an embarrassing position, for the idea of League investigation, and much more of consular representation, lost its charm when applied to themselves. The Chinese proposal, therefore, that a new investigation be conducted in China, this time by a more reliable agency, was agreed to, as more desirable than a general, world-wide League investigation. The one advance which was realized as a result of this clash of interests was the passing of a motion that the Council might at its discretion invite parties to the Hague Convention to appoint committees of investigation upon which the League should also have its representation. This was intended as a compromise, for

[1] See chapter on India and the Introduction.
[2] Although the Government of India disclaims responsibility for what goes on in the Native States, it provides the only point of contact, politically, between those States and League, or any particular Government.

it granted the justice of the Chinese position by admitting the right of the League to investigate conditions in any country, and at the same time, by intimation, prevented an immediate general investigation by giving discretionary power in the matter to the Council. It was doubtless expected that this discretion would be exercised, at least for the moment, only with regard to China. That, in any case, was the result feared by the Chinese. It so happened, however, that in the Council China was again able to carry her point, and consequently a second all-Chinese committee of investigation was authorized.[1] The consequences of this play of interests are obvious.

In significant contrast to the treatment received by the Chinese at the hands of the Committee is the manner in which it dealt in its next session with the question of the Hong-Kong opium supply. The British opium monopoly of Hong-Kong was reported to have put in a greatly increased demand for opium in that particular year.[2] In spite of Sir John Jordan's request that the asked-for increase be refused because the colony was already receiving enough opium to satisfy the needs of the Chinese population there, the British delegate gained his point by maintaining that the increased orders were only intended for the Government reserve stocks, which were depleted. The Chinese delegate was only able to point out that the Hong-Kong monopoly was making the task of his own Government more difficult, and Sir John Jordan to declare that it was clear that the monopoly existed solely for the purpose of revenue and that no increase should be allowed pending the receipt of further information, when the chairman raised the question whether the discussion was in conformity with the rules of procedure. A negative vote of five to two abruptly ended the debate.[3] No reference to the

[1] For the full account of these discussions, see *Minutes of the Advisory Committee*, 2nd Session, pp. 13–18, and 18 C. 543.

[2] Hong-Hong receives its opium supply from British India.

[3] *Minutes of the Advisory Committee*, 3rd Session, pp. 15–16.

discussion was made in the Committee's report to the Council. In view of the lengthy examination of the Chinese situation at the previous meeting, and the caustic criticism of that Government made by the Advisory Committee in its report to the Council, it is impossible not to remark the difference in the attitude toward an influential European Power, the rapidity with which criticism of its policy was silenced, and the valid interest of another Power disregarded. In view of the Chinese difficulties then under consideration a proposal by the Committee to investigate the Hong-Kong matter would have been no more than appropriate.[1]

The contagious quality of these expressions of national interest is well demonstrated by the action of that body with regard to certain proposals for calling a new international conference which a special American delegation brought before the Committee. The Americans felt that the purpose of the Hague Convention was not being achieved by the Committee, and that the measures of the Convention itself were not equal to meeting the problem. The Convention aimed at the limitation of the production of opium and drugs, but the means which it provided for realizing this aim had not proved adequate. Mr. Stephen G. Porter, representing the United States, therefore declared that the control of the production of raw opium must be effected to the end that there would be no surplus of this raw material available for non-medical and non-scientific purposes. And in order that his position on this point might be clear he added that if the Hague Convention was to be carried out according to its true spirit "it must be recognized that the use of opium for other than medical and scientific purposes is an abuse and not legitimate."[2] The delegate of India promptly recalled the objections to this formula which he and his colleague in the Fifth Committee of the Assembly had raised on a previous

[1] *Minutes of the Advisory Committee*, 3rd Session, pp. 15–16.
[2] *Minutes of the Advisory Committee*, 5th Session, p. 15.

occasion,[1] but whereas he was alone in upholding his view before, seven other Governments now found it possible to take a similar stand by invoking Article 6 of the Hague Convention. Article 6 is vague enough to be interpreted to suit almost any interest: "The Contracting Powers shall take measures for the gradual and effective suppression of the manufacture of, internal trade in, and use of, prepared opium, with due regard to the varying circumstances of each country concerned, unless regulations on the subject are already in existence." The delegates of France, Germany, Great Britain, Japan, the Netherlands, Portugal, and Siam accordingly accepted the American proposals with the reservation that the use of opium and the trade in it are legitimate as long as they are in accordance with the provisions of Article 6 of the Hague Convention. These seven (out of ten) members of the Advisory Committee, in accepting a proposal for the improvement of the Hague Convention, were, in fact, by their reservation, refusing to go farther than its weakest provision, a sorry index of the progressive attitude of the Committee.

These were some of the early indications that the effect of bringing together countries with conflicting interests was not to produce a constructive plan, but to make the vulnerable spot in each a weapon of defence in the hands of the others. If the Assembly, when it set up the Advisory Committee, believed that an interplay of interests would achieve the solution of the Committee's problems, it was soon apparent that the theory was fallacious. It produced conflict rather than co-operation, and it fettered the talents of the members of the Committee, as individuals, for constructive work by demanding of them, as delegates, the constant defence of a national position at variance with the general interest. The mere inequality of nations, in their dealings with each other even as members of an international body, militated against the emergence of fair or constructive

[1] See above, p. 53.

results from this method of pitting one against the other. After nine years this defect was remedied to some extent when the seven non-manufacturing countries were added to the Committee by the Assembly. But the handicap under which the Committee laboured in the meantime must be kept in mind while considering its work, with which the next chapter deals.

CHAPTER II

THE WORK OF THE OPIUM ADVISORY COMMITTEE

1. *Introductory*

THE work of the Committee must be carefully examined and its results weighed if one is to arrive at a just evaluation of its usefulness. But this in itself is not sufficient. It is even more necessary, in order to establish a valid criticism of the Committee, to trace its acts to their origins, to discover what influences were responsible for their success or failure, and thus to search out those elements in the composition of the Committee which have been productive of useful work and those which have retarded or impeded its progress. Only in this manner will it be possible to consider the means whereby a more efficient organization may be effected, or whether such a step seems advisable.

It has already been seen that the representation of national interests had its results in the early work of the Advisory Committee, and that even outside the Committee the attitude of Governments caused serious setbacks in its progress. These factors had the unfortunate effect of setting narrow bounds to the field of activity upon which the Committee entered, and of weakening the authority of its recommendations. It was also seen that the political interests represented in the Advisory Committee were reinforced rather than checked in the Council and the Assembly, so that the system as it worked out in actual practice was far from being what the originators of the Committee idea had had in mind. Fencing rather than co-operation resulted in the Committee itself, and in the executive organs of the League upon which the Committee depended for the enforcement of its recommendations, there was not only a lack of forceful action, but even a lack of interest, except from those members whose voices merely prolonged the debates of the Committee. Added to these constitutional drawbacks was the lack of response and co-operation of the Government administrations.[1] It is well to keep in mind these circumstances which, without being the fault of the Committee, yet hindered its progress to a great extent and were important in determining the course of its activity. Constituted on other lines, the Committee might have pursued another line of action, one determined by a single, progressive, and co-ordinated interest, rather than by the clash and compromise resulting from several conflicting interests. It must be remembered that there was a definite contradiction between the task of the Committee and the manner in which it was organized to deal with that task. It had a definite problem to solve, yet its position was such that it had of necessity to place greater weight upon the difficulties than upon the possibilities of solution, to pursue progress in form and to evade it in substance.

2. *Investigations and Inquiries*

It was obviously necessary to establish a broad foundation of facts, to gather statistics and information on any number of subjects, before constructive measures could be undertaken. The first acts of the Committee, therefore, were to set on foot various inquiries into the several aspects of the problem. The first of these has already been touched upon, namely, the inquiry into the "legitimate" needs of opium and drugs. The sixty-three members of the League or signatories of the Hague Convention were approached with the request that they investigate their needs in these drugs and report the result of their research to the Secretariat. Four out of the sixty-three furnished the desired information within the appointed time, seven others saying

---

[1] See the following section.

they were unable to give the information asked for. The four to have replied were Belgium, Canada, Luxemburg, and Siam, all of whom, with the sole exception of Luxemburg, gave inadequate information.[1] Lest it be thought that this was an extreme instance of negligence on the part of the Governments, it may be well to cite one or two other cases.

A second important investigation to be undertaken was the inquiry into the traffic in cocaine. Governments were requested to furnish information on the manufacture, distribution, and medical needs of cocaine. The astounding result of this demand was that actually not one of the important cocaine manufacturing countries replied, these being France, Germany, Japan, the Netherlands, Switzerland, and the United States. Although twelve States replied, none of them was important as a producer of cocaine.[2]

A third inquiry to be attempted was an examination into the conditions relating to free ports and zones. It had been seen at once that these districts, where customs regulations did not exist and control was difficult, furnished admirable breeding-places for the illicit traffic. The Governments were therefore requested to inform the Secretariat of the measures of control which they had undertaken in the free ports or zones existing in their territories. Seven States replied, four of which had no free ports or zones, and two of which could give no information. Only one, Germany, was able to state definitely that she was about to place customs officials in Hamburg and Stettin to control the imports and exports of drugs.

As the Committee based its work on the Hague Convention, and as the Assembly had, by its resolution of December 15, 1920, given to the Secretariat the special function of "collecting the information as to the arrangements made in the various countries for carrying out the Opium Convention with regard

[1] *Minutes of the Opium Advisory Committee,* 2nd Session, p. 72.
[2] Ibid., 4th Session, p. 66.

to the collection of data,"[1] one of the first recommendations made by the Committee at its 1st Session was that the Secretariat send out to all the Governments a questionnaire designed to discover how much legislation had actually been passed in conformity with the Hague Convention. The questionnaire was duly circulated, and very satisfactory reports were returned by most of the States. In this instance, however, the Committee ignored the opportunities for comparison and co-ordination of the various legislative measures reported on, which this fund of information made possible. Mr. John Campbell proposed that the Secretariat establish from the information at hand in the answers to the questionnaire, what the positions of the various countries were with regard to the importation of raw opium, but nothing came of this proposal. On the other hand, Sir Malcolm Delevingne, also in the 1st Session, suggested that the Secretariat be kept progressively informed of the state of affairs existing in the several countries, by requesting an annual report from every Government, which should indicate what progress had been made in the application of the Hague Convention, and give statistics of the trade in, and production of, drugs and opium. These annual reports have not received the attention from the Governments which their fundamental importance merits. Obviously the information contained in them must furnish the basis of any constructive recommendations which the Advisory Committee might make for the Governments. Out of 63 Governments, 28 sent in annual reports for 1922, the first year for which the system was to function. Among these were Great Britain, France, Italy, Japan, and the United States. Unfortunately only five, Canada, France, Great Britain, New Zealand, and Poland, submitted fully satisfactory reports in the form requested by the Secretariat. For 1923, 29 reports were received, and again 28 in the following year. However, after the Geneva Conferences, and due, no doubt, to the special stipulations con-

[1] 1 A.C. ii., p. 162.

tained in the Geneva Convention, more attention was given to the matter of annual reports. For 1927, 38 reports were submitted to the Secretariat, and 45 for 1928. This figure represents approximately three-fourths of the States from which reports should be received, not, perhaps, a poor result to have obtained. But only too often the reports were incomplete, or too general to be useful for compiling a complete and coherent record of developments. From one region in particular there has been an exceptionally bad record. The 20 Latin-American States have together, in the seven years from 1922 until 1928, submitted only 25 reports, whereas during this period 140 reports should have been received from them. Between 1925 and 1928 no report was received from China; while Persia, one of the largest producers of opium in the world, sent in its first report in 1928. Before the Geneva Conference no reports had been received from Germany, Latvia, Luxemburg, Mexico, Monaco, Panama, Portugal, Yugoslavia, or Switzerland; 18 States have never submitted a report, though fortunately none of these can be considered important from the point of view of the drug traffic.[1]

A much stricter control, based on more accurate and detailed information than had previously been received, was envisaged by the Advisory Committee in 1930, when at its 13th Session it drew up a revised form for the annual reports. This was particularly important because certain provisions of the Geneva Convention called for accurate statistics of the import, export, and manufacture of drugs, and because it was necessary to have precise information on the development of the various lines of activity recommended by the Committee to the Governments, such as the import certificate system, internal administration, and measures taken against the illicit traffic. In view of the fact that, in the words of the Committee's report to the Council after its 13th Session, the annual reports "form the most important

[1] *Minutes Advisory Committee*, 13th Session, Appendix 4, p. 397.

source of information available to it regarding the general state of the traffic,"[1] it seems that this increased severity with regard to the annual reports might with profit have been adopted very much earlier. Complaints from the Secretariat, repeated in the reports of the Committee to the Council, appear regularly, and it is evident that the insufficiency of information at the disposal of the Committee could only have hampered its work in the most serious way.

The attempt of the Advisory Committee to reach an estimate of the world's annual requirements in drugs by asking the various Governments to submit the required information, did not meet with success, as has already been shown. Inasmuch as it was essential to establish the medical and scientific needs of the world in order to achieve the aims of the Hague Convention, the Committee made a further effort in this direction by requesting the Secretariat to make an investigation into these needs in the various countries, and on the basis of information thus obtained, establish the world average.[2]

When the Advisory Committee met again in 1922, Dr. Norman White, of the Health Committee, reported that although investigations had been carried on in Denmark, Sweden, and Switzerland, the Health Committee was of the opinion that the figures for no one country could be applied to another because of the variety of conditions existing in the respective States.[3] Subsequently, at the request of the Health Committee, two members of the Opium Committee, Mr. John Campbell and Dr. Anselmino, were appointed to sit on a joint subcommittee intended to extend both the time and the scope of the investigation. This subcommittee, which was composed of Dr. Carrière, Director of the Federal Public Health Service at Berne, Mr. A. E. Blanco, member of the Opium Section, the Polish Minister of Health, and the two above-mentioned members of the

[1] *Minutes Advisory Committee*, 13th Session, Annex 6, p. 382.
[2] Ibid., 1st Session, p. 17. [3] Ibid., 2nd Session, p. 5.

Advisory Committee, presented a report at the 4th Session of the Advisory Committee.[1] The report stated that the abuse of drugs resulted chiefly from the careless use of them in the practice of medicine, and suggested that in order to arrive at the figure of consumption in every country the formula, "Production plus Import minus Export equals Consumption," should be applied. The strictly medical needs should then be ascertained by questioning doctors, hospitals, and dispensaries, by checking up the amounts imported under the certificate system, or by multiplying the average amount of drugs needed for a patient by the number of patients treated in a year. The amount of the illicit traffic could then be deduced. Unfortunately these methods were not at the time practicable in most of the countries, for control was not strict enough to make the figures available. Germany and the United States were cited in the report of the subcommittee as having an accurate system of supervision which other countries would find it profitable to adopt. However, even in these countries it has not been possible to reach an accurate legitimate consumption figure, although attempts have for some years been made to do so. The figure upon which the world's annual needs of drugs is based was calculated by the Health Section of the League after a long investigation which was terminated in 1929.[2] This figure is not without value as an approximate indication of the amounts of drugs annually consumed, but, due to the impossibility of employing the same methods of investigation in every country, it is far from satisfactory. A part of the figures are based on the quantities of drugs dispensed by the registered pharmacists, or by physicians and hospitals. This method gives a figure which may safely be said to represent legitimate consumption. Other countries sent in figures based on commercial statistics, while still others simply took the quantity sold by the wholesale dealers to retailers. These two methods tend to

[1] C. 23, p. 352.   [2] See Document O.C. 1112.

produce a figure which includes all or at least a part of the illicit as well as the legitimate consumption. An average world consumption figure based upon such divergent calculations fails to indicate either the legitimate needs in drugs or their total consumption. Although the Health Committee's work was extraordinarily exhaustive, it was, because of the impossibility of securing comparable figures, of no great value in determining legitimate world needs. This fundamental information, upon which any effective limitation must necessarily be based, has not yet been obtained.

These attempts of the Advisory Committee to establish a solid groundwork of facts upon which to base its work did not, as the above account shows, result in an enviable measure of success. The annual progress reports of the Secretariat, which give a résumé of the work of each succeeding year, indicate that there was a great deal of dissatisfaction with the results, and that this was blamed almost entirely on the laxity of national administrations which consistently failed to comply adequately with requests for information. That the Committee's work must have been seriously hampered by these dilatory actions is evident. The Committee itself felt the limitations which this unfortunate circumstance imposed upon it, and expressed its dissatisfaction in its report to the Council on the work of the 12th Session, saying that it had been

... seriously hampered in the preparation of the annual statistics by the fact that a number of important Governments have failed to send in their reports until many months after the date laid down by the Council, and the Committee hopes that the Council will impress, in the strongest possible manner, on the States members of the League, that the annual reports should be dispatched not later than July 1st in the case of European countries, or October 1st in the case of Eastern countries.[1]

[1] *Minutes Advisory Committee*, 12th Session, Annex 2, p. 200.

3. *National Administrative Systems*

Probably the most important single explanation of this lack of co-operation on the part of the individual Governments lies in the fact that most of the Governments had no administrative departments for dealing uniquely with drug questions. Generally the functions which the Governments were called upon to exercise in this field were a part of the activity of the Ministry of Health or of the Interior, administrative divisions which also had a variety of other tasks to perform. The effective control of the production and trade in drugs necessitates the services of more than one administrative department as well as definite location of responsibility in one particular branch. From the time a consignment of opium is imported, manufactured into morphine or heroin, exported, or distributed among the pharmacies and dispensaries of a country, the customs agents, sometimes the revenue officials, the health officers and medical inspectors, and not infrequently the police and the judiciary are called in to lend their respective services to its control. This necessary diversity of function has to be reconciled with the equally essential centralization of responsibility.

There must be some definite organ to formulate policy and co-ordinate the work of different departments which normally do not act together in as close relations as this type of problem demands. This twofold need was not met by the drug manufacturing countries in 1920, and only by those opium-growing and consuming countries which had instituted monopolies, namely, India and Siam, Macao, the Straits Settlements, Hong-Kong, and other colonial possessions. Directly or indirectly, by creating the necessity for a responsible organ to act on its recommendations, or simply by its emphasis on the general importance of the problem, the Advisory Committee has been the cause of an increasing attention to the perfection of administrative machinery. Although the response to this need was at first slow, it has gained momentum in the last years, especially since the ratification of the Geneva Convention.

Great Britain was the first State to organize narcotics administration on a basis suitable to national and international needs. The administration of the Dangerous Drugs Act of 1920, which was passed in conformity with the obligations assumed under the Hague Convention, was put into the hands of a special division of the Home Office. The Home Office works in formal and informal consultation with the Ministry of Health, but as the problem is considered to be mainly one of police control the responsibility remains with the Home Office. The necessary medical inspection is made by the Regional Medical Officers of the Ministry of Health, and the Customs Officers and Postal Officials co-operate in regulating the licit trade and in the prevention of smuggling.[1] Thus by employing the field forces of the other administrative divisions, while maintaining responsibility in the Home Office, efficiency, co-ordination, as well as definite central authority are assured. The Home Office maintains direct contact with the Advisory Committee of the League by sending Sir Malcolm Delevingne, the Under-Secretary in charge of the Division, to sit as British delegate. Great benefit has resulted from this fact, not only to the Home Office, which is thus in a position to make its principles and policies felt and understood on the Committee, but to the Committee as well, which has its recommendations thus communicated directly to the department responsible for executing them, and which receives the benefit of the expert administrative ability of its British member.

As the Home Office is directly occupied chiefly with domestic problems, it works in close consultation with the Foreign Office and the Colonial and Dominions Offices in matters that relate to other countries and to the Empire. In order that co-ordination may also be maintained in this branch, a special

[1] League Document O.C. 776.

standing committee representing the three departments is appointed.[1]

It is the opinion of the Home Office that the system which it has adopted embodies the essential factors of efficient administration. Its virtues are briefly summed up, in a statement sent to the League Secretariat, in the following words:

Unification of control is regarded as being of the greatest importance for efficient administration and direction of policy. All the information both on the national and international sides is thus concentrated in a single Department, and the delays and semi-paralysis which often follow on a divided authority are avoided.[2]

Experience has proved the correctness of this view.

When it was suggested in the 3rd Session of the Committee that the exchange of information regarding cases of illicit traffic and seizures of drugs be communicated directly between the competent central bureaux, it was discovered after investigation that such central bureaux did not exist. Great Britain could point to the Dangerous Drugs Division of the Home Office, but the rest of the Governments indicated only that their departments of public health were generally responsible for the work connected with the control of narcotics. In 1926, after the Advisory Committee had spent five years in urging on the Governments the acceptance of the system of import authorizations, and in stressing the desirability of establishing in each country a central narcotics bureau, it was found that only two countries, Guatemala and the United States, had established such bureaux. In Australia and New Zealand the Customs Department was empowered to issue import authorizations, in India, Panama, and Siam the Department of Finance and Revenue, and in twenty-five other States the ministries of the interior or the departments of public health were more or less vaguely designated.[3]

---

[1] League Document O.C. 776.   [2] Ibid.
[3] *Minutes Advisory Committee*, 8th Session, p. 103.

As indicated above, a pronounced change has come over administrative methods in the past two years. Unfortunately, it has been less widespread than could well be desired, but those countries which have undertaken a reform in this branch of their administrations have effected thorough changes. What has been a convention in Great Britain for a decade has been elaborated and institutionalized in Portugal by the Portuguese Decree of 1928, in a Permanent Commission on the Traffic in Opium and Other Drugs. This Commission is composed of the head of the Portuguese Legation at the League, a Portuguese member of the International Health Organization, the Lisbon Police Director, the Director of the Institute of Legal Medicine, a representative of the Superior Council of Hygiene, of the Health Service of the Ministry for the Colonies, and of the Customs Department, an inspector of the pharmaceutical service, and an administrative officer of the Ministry for the Colonies. It will be seen at a glance that there are united in this Commission not only all of the interested administrative units, but also a liaison officer to establish and maintain constant co-operation with the Advisory Committee of the League. The head of the Portuguese Legation at the League, M. de Vasconcellos, is also the Portuguese member of the Advisory Committee. There is not a special central narcotics bureau, but the Commission's work is to co-ordinate the services of the State, to propose measures to the Government in conformity with international conventions, to establish co-operation with other Governments, and to elaborate the annual report of the Government for the League. The Portuguese have stressed a phase of the narcotics problem which has only recently begun to receive the attention which is due it. It has formed a Criminal Subcommittee in the Commission, whose special function it is to take care of criminal cases arising out of the application of the narcotic laws, and to co-operate with similar institutions in other countries.[1]

[1] Communication from the Portuguese Legation at the League to the Secretariat, January 5, 1931.

As yet these "similar institutions" are rare, although since the resolution passed by the Advisory Committee in 1930 regarding the unification of police control a number of Governments have reported that the process of centralizing police control in their territories is under study.[1] Great Britain, Germany, Austria, the United States, the Netherlands, and Egypt are definitely in a position to offer direct international police co-operation.

In Japan an Imperial Decree came into effect on April 31, 1931, which is a variated form of the Portuguese plan. It lays more stress on the direct co-operation of the administrative departments concerned than on ministerial counsel, although this has also been provided for in an Interministerial Opium Council which investigates and deliberates under the direction of the Minister for Home Affairs. But in addition to this organ there is a body of executive officers appointed by the Cabinet on the recommendation of the Minister for Home Affairs from among the high officials of the departments concerned. This group of executive officers is specifically entrusted with carrying out the plans of the Council.[2] The Treaty Division of the Department of Foreign Affairs maintains contact with the League and with other Governments.[3] This lack of direct relationship between the national administrative machine in Japan and the League opium organization is a serious defect in an otherwise carefully laid plan. The Advisory Committee has not enjoyed the fullest measure of Japanese co-operation in the past precisely on this account. Responsibility and continuity of action have been difficult to get from Japan for the reason that every year or two a new delegate or a substitute delegate, generally only vaguely informed as to the exact position and intentions of his Government, has been sent to sit on the Advisory Committee. The reform in internal administration might profitably have included provisions for closer co-operation with the League

[1] *Minutes Advisory Committee*, 14th Session, p. 204.

[2] Japanese Imperial Decree, No. 38, issued March 31, 1931. See archives of the League Secretariat.

[3] League Document O.C. 1379.

organization, although it is not impossible that in actual practice the plan will work out on these desired lines.

Reports from the Governments received by the Secretariat in 1931 show one development of particular interest in the drug administrations, namely, a growing readiness to co-operate on an international scale and through the League. Six Governments have placed the responsibility for the exchange of information on illicit traffic and seizures with the League division of their departments of foreign affairs.[1] Germany, Great Britain, the Netherlands, and Egypt, by sending as their representatives on the Advisory Committee the officials in charge of drug administration, have also emphasized the international character of the drug problem and the value of collaboration between national experts, which the Advisory Committee permits.

In all, seventeen Governments have undertaken reforms in their drug administration divisions since the activity of the Advisory Committee began. In many of the countries opium and drugs do not present a serious problem, and therefore a drastic reform was not necessary. New Zealand, however, presents an example of the danger there is in allowing laxness in narcotics administration simply because no problem is known to exist. Such countries offer favourable conditions to smuggling bands and may easily become centres of illicit traffic. New Zealand, until 1929, was unaffected by the trade in drugs, but in that year the customs uncovered the traces of a ring of smugglers who were taking advantage of the laxness of the drug laws to make New Zealand the base of their activity. A glance at the system in use in New Zealand will reveal its defects, which are unfortunately shared by most of the countries which have no present drug problem. By virtue of the Dangerous Drugs Act of 1927 the Governor-General makes the regulations which he considers necessary, and judges which drugs are to be considered dangerous and to fall under the terms of the law. The Comptroller of Customs

[1] Finland, France, Italy, Holland, Persia, Portugal.

is authorized to issue import and export certificates, the Minister of Health or any Justice may order the search of premises, the Director-General of Health grants licences for the sale and distribution of drugs, and any customs, health, or police officer may arrest a suspect. This complete separation of the various functions which must be performed and the lack of any attempt to correlate them, the reference to the Governor-General of so specialized and technical a task as the formulation of narcotics regulations, and the absence of any provision for securing co-operation with other countries or with the League of Nations, sum up the deficiencies of the system. They were inherent in nearly all of the administrations when the Advisory Committee began to function. The improvement which has gradually come about since may be cited as one of the most significant achievements of the Committee.[1]

It is evident that a large part of the lack of success which met the recommendations of the Committee, and which still meets them, though in diminishing measure, must be attributed to the fact that the Governments were not prepared technically to carry them out. In criticizing the achievements of the Committee this fact must not be overlooked, for the Committee had not only to devise schemes for controlling the illicit traffic, but also to seek and urge the development of the machinery necessary for carrying them out. This is necessarily a work of persuasion. Of itself the Committee can do nothing in an administrative way. It has the power alone of advising a course of action or a method of administration. The effectiveness of such recommendations depends upon the attitude of national administrations.

4. Regulating the Illicit Traffic

The type of the Advisory Committee's work has been almost entirely regulatory. The Committee has not considered itself

[1] The Permanent Central Board claims a measure of the credit for this development. See Chapter IV.

competent to undertake any action not based on the letter of the Hague or the Geneva Convention. In declining to depart from the letter of these two instruments it has confined itself to the elaboration of schemes for controlling the traffic and the trade in drugs, hoping thereby to effect indirectly the limitation of their cultivation and manufacture. Discussions of principle and of fundamental changes in policy have been raised from time to time, but the Committee has decided against making any recommendations on new lines, either on the ground of incompetency or because of opposition to the suggested programme itself.

(a) *The Import Certificate System.*—In the 1st Session of the Opium Advisory Committee two proposals for the control of the drug traffic were put forward by Sir Malcolm Delevingne, the British member, both intended to reinforce the provisions of the Hague Convention for keeping the trade in drugs within legitimate bounds.[1] The first suggestion was that the Opium Section of the League Secretariat collect and circulate to all the Governments information on the laws and regulations in force regarding the imports and exports of drugs. With this information on hand every exporter could be held responsible for conforming with the law of the particular country with which he happened to be dealing. The alternative suggestion was that the Governments adopt a system of import certificates to be procured by the prospective importer of drugs from his Government, and presented to the Government of the exporting country before any export was permitted.

The import certificate system as thus proposed was an improvement on the provisions of the Hague Convention for controlling the trade, as set down in Article 13. This provided that import and export should be effected only by holders of Government certificates, but omitted to limit the subsequent activities of these licensees, or to establish any control over the

[1] Hague Opium Convention, Article 10.

individual consignments of drugs as they entered or left the country. Nevertheless, Sir Malcolm's scheme still left room for improvement. The importation of drugs was not directly controlled or limited by it, and no check was provided over the issuing of certificates by importing Governments. Yet it was well known that few Governments were in a position to know their exact requirements in drugs, or, therefore, to be able to limit its imports to "legitimate" amounts. In partial rectification of these omissions the Committee adopted a resolution at its 2nd Session, presented by Prince Charoon, Siamese member, providing that the Governments send annually to the Opium Section of the League the figures of their requirements in drugs. A central agency would thus be enabled to determine at least approximately what the total volume of trade in drugs should be, as well as the origin and destination of excessive shipments. Thus the beginnings of limitation were to be established.

Unfortunately there were outside factors to interfere with the effectiveness of the scheme. First was the difficulty of securing universal adherence to it. It could not be hoped that the limitation of trade by anything less than all of the exporting countries could seriously hinder the general illicit traffic. In considering the report of the Advisory Committee to the Assembly, in which the difficulty of securing the adoption of the system was noted, Professor Gilbert Murray suggested that, by refusing to purchase from any country not adhering to it, the importing States could force the universal adoption of the system.[1] Great Britain and India enthusiastically supported the plan, but it was referred back to the Advisory Committee for closer study. There the Dutch member, Mr. van Wettum, objected that the arrangement would hamper free trade, create monopolies, and generally increase the illicit traffic. M. Bourgois, the French member, believed that the plan would divide the world into two groups, those adhering to the system and those refusing to comply

[1] 3 A.C. v., p. 10.

with its demands. These two groups would form separate trading units, thereby increasing the total volume of the international trade, and making real limitation impossible. Sir John Jordan, assessor, feared that the plan would result both in an increase in production and in consumption of opium.[1] The plan held obvious advantages for India, which had been one of the first to adhere to the certificate system, and was in a position to supply opium to many markets at the time controlled by Turkey and Persia, neither of which was participating in the opium work of the League. It was, however, the belief of Sir John Jordan that should these markets go to India the production of the countries displaced by her would find its way into the illicit traffic. In replying to the arguments of the assessor, Sir Malcolm Delevingne maintained that the Balkan opium producers would prevent the formation of an Indian monopoly, and that although increased production might be the immediate result of the adopttion of the plan it would ultimately result in a restricted output due to the effect of the boycott. A decision on the issue was postponed at this point because the early adhesion of Turkey and Persia to the Convention was expected, which would automatically have solved the problem, as all other important producing States either had already or were about to adopt the certificate system. However, the expectation was not fulfilled, for, in fact, Turkey did not adopt the system until 1932, and Perisa has not yet accepted it.

The principal defect in the mechanism of the certificate system was that it failed to provide a central organ of control which could collect information and figures on the course and state of the trade, and keep them at the disposal of all the Governments to aid them in administering the certificate system. There was no way of knowing when an order, whether or not accompanied by a certificate of import, would, if fulfilled, bring the total imports of the purchasing country beyond its legitimate

[1] *Minutes Advisory Committee*, 4th Session, p. 23.

bounds. There was in most countries no way of knowing when imports had reached the limits of legitimate medical and trade necessities. There was not even reliable information to be obtained as to what actual quantities these necessities represented. Under these circumstances the actual value of a certificate of import or of export was considerably reduced.

In its 8th Session the Committee recommended that in the case of an administration being called upon to decide on an application for the export of drugs to a country not applying the certificate system, it should attempt to discover whether the order was legitimate. The futility of this recommendation could hardly have escaped the members of the Committee, but no attempt was made to establish the means of obtaining this information which could only have been done through an international body invested with powers of investigation and control. The necessity for a central body of this nature was stressed by the Secretariat in its Progress Report as early as 1923, and its need must have been clearly seen by the Committee as it discussed the difficulties attending the application of the certificate system, but no steps towards the establishment of such a body were taken. It was only as a result of the Geneva Conference in 1925 that an organ with some such powers was created, and then only in the face of active opposition on the part of four out of five members of the Committee who, as delegates, took an important part in the discussions of the Conference. The Convention drawn up at that time contained provision for a Permanent Central Board[1] which was to have certain powers of the kind just mentioned, though they were unfortunately limited to reviewing the past course of the trade without reference to preventing immediate or future excesses. The 1931 Conference for Limiting the Manufacture and Regulating the Distribution of Drugs somewhat amplified these powers by giving the Board the right to pass on all orders for drugs

[1] See Chapter III.

79

destined for States not parties to the Convention, but the attitude of most Governments, not excepting those represented on the Advisory Committee, toward an organ of this nature has always been fear of the alienation of national sovereignty.

The failure of the certificate system to reduce the drug trade to proportions compatible with legitimate needs was not due to technical imperfection, nor even to faulty application, as much as to a misunderstanding of the problem. Whatever the control it might establish over the legitimate trade, it could not prevent the flow of drugs through illicit channels. It was designed to check the use of the regular channels of trade by the illicit trafficker, and in this it was certainly successful wherever it was diligently applied. But it was not designed to deal with the numberless methods of evading the law invented by traffickers, and more especially was it not designed to stop the over-production of drugs which was at the bottom of the trouble. The certificate system, in order to function effectively, needed the complete and organized co-operation of the police to deal with the activities of the traffickers, who threatened its effectiveness on one side, and the control and reduction of the production of drugs, whose excessive output was rendering it ineffective, on the other. If these conditions had been secured, the certificate system would probably have been a completely effective tool against the illicit traffic.

(b) *Exchange of Seizure Information.*—At the 3rd Session of the Advisory Committee[1] it was decided that information about seizures should be communicated directly between the competent departments of the countries concerned, and that only summaries of seizure reports should be sent to the Secretariat for correlation. The burden on the Secretariat in handling all the seizure information was, it was thought, unnecessarily great, and as the diplomatic channel was considered too slow, it

[1] *Advisory Committee*, 3rd Session, p. 11.

was up to the national administrations to bear the responsibility of establishing a co-operative exchange system, reinforced by co-ordinated police action. Mr. Campbell suggested that reports on seizures should be communicated directly to the police and customs authorities in the various countries, as it was brought out in the discussion that practically no central bureaux competent to receive and act on such information existed in any of the countries. It was finally decided that the Secretariat be requested to ask the Governments to designate the responsible departments to which official communications relative to drug seizures might be sent.[1] The general non-existence of such departments was definitely shown in the following year when the report presented to the Committee listed but six countries having a central administrative organ competent to take over this function.[2] However, no change in the system was suggested in the Advisory Committee. The Secretariat continued to receive summary reports of seizure information and to list the cases in detail in annual documents which grew more voluminous each year. No central authority existed, either to act on its own authority or to supervise or co-ordinate the police measures which it was necessary to take immediately on the receipt of any information on cases of illicit traffic. In view of the fact that no such authority existed, the Committee should have recommended the organization of national administrations on lines suitable to the purposes of mutual co-operation. As it was, neither the Secretariat nor the Committee could be sure that the necessary information relative to each case was being promptly communicated to all parties concerned, or that it was being received and acted upon by the competent authorities. This very unsatisfactory state of affairs continued without comment from the Committee, and without any attempt on the part of the Geneva Conference to remedy it. It was not until 1930, when Mr. Sirks, League Assessor on the Advisory Committee, and Chief of the

[1] *Advisory Committee*, 3rd Session, p. 11.   [2] Ibid., 4th Session, p. 79.

Rotterdam Police, again brought up the question, that action was taken.

Mr. Sirks proposed that a central narcotics bureau be established in every country, where the responsibility for dealing with seizure information would be definitely located. After considering the proposal at length, the Committee decided to adopt it in principle, but pointed out at the same time that existing methods of police organization would render the plan impracticable in most countries. Although several national police bureaux have since been established, and international police co-operation been greatly developed in the combat with the drug traffic, the Advisory Committee has not given the work its united and official support.

(c) *Penalties.*—The serious situation which confronted the Advisory Committee in the ever-widening proportions of the drug traffic gave rise to a number of measures aimed against the illicit trafficker. In the 2nd Session of the Committee it was resolved that penalties for smuggling and otherwise illicitly handling the drugs of addiction ought to be made more severe. The Secretariat instituted an inquiry to discover what countries were willing to change their laws in this connection, and at the 4th Session of the Advisory Committee it was able to report that five Governments were considering an increase in penalties against violators of the narcotic laws, and that seven other Governments considered their existing legislation to be sufficient. The severest sentence imposed in any country was in Canada, where serious offences were punishable with seven years' imprisonment. The Committee continued to urge at every session that penalties be increased, and in 1925 at the Geneva Conference the following provision was included in the text of the Convention as Article 28:

Each of the Contracting Parties agrees that breaches of its laws or regulations by which the provisions of the present Convention are enforced shall be punishable by adequate penalties, including in appropriate cases the confiscation of the substances concerned.

However, even the general acceptance of this principle by all the Governments, which Article 28 indicates, was not productive of the desired results. In the 13th Session of the Advisory Committee (1930), M. de Vasconcellos, Portuguese member, said that with regard to penalties the results were poor, and that, in view of the fact that "the criminals had probably made large fortunes while poisoning hundreds of people, the penalties usually inflicted were inadequate."[1] He therefore proposed that the traffic in drugs be considered, with piracy and the counterfeiting of currency, as an international crime. But the Committee could not agree upon the definition of an international crime, and rejected the proposal of its Portuguese member. It suggested, however, that the Council take steps to inform itself as to what measures Governments were taking to increase penalties, though this effort, too, miscarried, for at that time the Opium Section was too heavily burdened with preparations for the Limitation Conference to undertake any special investigations.

But the question of penalties is, after all, subsidiary to the larger question of police control, and will lose much of its importance when effective police surveillance is assured. Mr. Godwin suggests in his study on crime that the certainty of detection is an infinitely greater deterrent to the criminal than the prospect of a heavy penalty which with luck he may escape altogether.[2] It is this chance of escape which must be diminished. Much would be done to effect it by the enaction of the Draft Convention for the Suppression of the Illicit Traffic, drawn up by the International Criminal Police Commission, and submitted to the Advisory Committee in 1931. It provides not only

[1] Document C. 420. M. 229, 1932, XI, p. 9.
[2] George Godwin, *Cain, or the Future of Crime*, Kegan Paul, London. In the year following the institution of the London Metropolitan Police Force (1837) losses from theft decreased from £2,000,000 to £20,000.

for more severe penalties, but for surer methods of apprehending the illicit trafficker both through extradition and direct police co-operation. For two years the project was under consideration by the Advisory Committee, and its general acceptance by Governments was reported in 1934.[1]

(d) *The Black List.*—Sir Malcolm Delevingne, in the 3rd Session of the Advisory Committee, made a proposal for the establishment of a black list of traffickers and drug firms, to be compiled at the Secretariat on the basis of information sent in by the various Governments. It was intended to facilitate the prosecution of cases of infringement of narcotics laws, as well as to set up a moral boycott of firms which had allowed their products to go into the illicit traffic. The proposal was not accepted because of a divergence of opinion among the members of the Committee as to the influence which a black list might be expected to have. Mr. John Campbell was in favour of making the list public, but Sir Malcolm Delevingne was not s'ure that this would not facilitate the escape of traffickers who would thus be informed of their detection. M. Bourgois feared that a black list would involve traders indefinitely in difficulties with the police when actually they may have offended only once. The further discussion of the proposal was therefore postponed until the next session of the Committee. It was not, however, until the 13th Session of the Committee, in 1930, that serious consideration of the question came up again. Meantime the Secretariat had been making up an annual document containing such particulars of seizure cases as the Governments had forwarded to it. However, this document had not the moral effect that Sir Malcolm had intended for his black list, and, especially in view of the large amount of information regarding drug seizu.es which was made available to the Committee during 1929, he again stressed the importance of giving publicity to

[1] See below, p. 117.

the information received and of making it available to the Governments interested. The neglected idea of a black list being thus reintroduced, a long debate on its advisability followed. Mr. Ito (Japan), Dr. Carrière, and M. Bourgois pointed out the danger which the Committee might incur should it condemn any firm without being able to give definite proof of its guilt, or should it name traffickers whose complicity had not been legally established by the courts. Sir Malcolm Delevingne pointed out that what the Committee meant by "illicit traffic" was not necessarily what any national court might mean by "illegal traffic," and the black list was intended for persons engaged in the illicit traffic as understood by the Advisory Committee, that is in the sense of supplying drugs for abusive use. M. Cavazzoni (Italy) wished to make the black list permanent and continuous, adding to it annually the names of firms and traffickers found engaging in the illicit traffic in each successive year. This was warmly contested by Dr. Carrière, Dr. Kahler (Germany), M. de Vasconcellos, and Mr. Ito, who felt that it was unfair to any firm or person to be kept repeatedly before the eyes of the public in this unfavourable light when guilty of perhaps no more than one or two offences. M. Cavazzoni's amendment was defeated by a vote of nine to one, and Sir Malcolm's proposal was thereupon adopted in the following form:

1. A black list of traffickers should be made and kept up to date by a central office.
2. It should be confidential and circulated to Governments only.
3. Information should be sent to the central office by the Governments as soon as it has been established that the persons mentioned have actually been engaged in the illicit traffic.[1]

The Secretariat was made responsible for collecting and

[1] For the complete report of this discussion, see *Minutes of Advisory Committee*, 13th Session, pp. 120–124.

organizing this information as it was received from the Governments.

The police assessor and the representative of the International Criminal Police Commission who sat at the following meeting of the Advisory Committee in 1931 were quick to appreciate the value of the black list to their own work. Mr. Sirks, explaining the importance of the list as a police document, urged that it be made to contain not only undoubted facts, but also assumptions which the police might find valuable as clues. All details were valuable to the police, whether the connections were innocent or not. Dr. Carrière replied that he was unable to accept Mr. Sirks's view, and that, in his opinion, the Governments should be consulted before such a list was drawn up. In spite of the fact that Mr. Sirks protested that the list should not be published Dr. Carrèire maintained his view, which was seconded by M. Bourgois. It was agreed, therefore, that the Secretariat should continue the work already begun in connection with the black list, and that, should it have proposals to make at a later date, the Committee could reopen the discussion at some future session.[1] It had repeatedly been called to the attention of the Committee by the Chief of the Opium Section that the increased staff which would be necessary if the Opium Section undertook the black list work would mean also an increase in expenses. The Opium Section, however, with the rest of the Secretariat, suffered a reduction in appropriations in the Fourth Committee of the Assembly in 1931, and, although Mr. Sirks had proposed that contributions would be made by the various police organizations towards the maintenance of the black list, this may account for the fact that in the 1932 report of the Advisory Committee to the Council the black list was not mentioned. Instead, a recommendation was made to the Governments to communicate promptly "to the authorities of countries concerned, or likely to be concerned," any information regard-

[1] *Advisory Committee*, 14th Session, pp. 155–156.

ing persons "engaged in, or suspected of being engaged in, the illicit traffic."[1] The value of the black list as a permanent and complete document at the constant disposal of the police and Government administrations is thus lost. Fortunately the International Criminal Police Bureau at Vienna is engaged in collecting this type of information, and maintains a file of criminal records of all types, including those concerned with the drug traffic, which substitutes in some measure for the black list. In its 17th Session the Advisory Committee decided that in view of the independent work of the police in this field, the League need no longer be concerned with a black list; but it was recommended that the Secretariat maintain an index of the principal cases and the more important persons involved.[2]

(e) *Free Ports and Zones.*—The Advisory Committee became aware early in its work of the leakage of drugs into the illicit trade at the free ports, and of the weakness which these ports constituted in the control of the traffic. In 1922 the Secretariat circulated a questionnaire among the Governments to discover what measures of control were in practice in the free ports and zones. The results of this questionnaire have already been mentioned.[3] Simultaneously the League Committee on Communications and Transit was asked to suggest practical measures for achieving solid control in these danger-spots, and accordingly a joint subcommittee of the Opium and the Communications and Transit Committees was appointed to study the question. This subcommittee reported in January 1923 that, legally, the regime of a free port allows the sovereign State to exercise the same measures of control there as elsewhere in its jurisdiction.[4] The difficulty of controlling the traffic lies in the fact that there are no customs officers and no regulations such as exist in an ordinary

[1] Document C. 420. M. 229, 1932, XI, p. 6.
[2] *Report of the Advisory Committee to the Council on the Work of the 17th Session,* Document C. 642, M. 305, 1933, XI, p. 18.
[3] See p. 63.   [4] C. 23, p. 355.

port. The usual inspection of freight is therefore not in order, and goods in transit may easily be detracted into illicit trade channels unless a special watch is kept. This is, of course, difficult, unless all merchandise is to be subjected to inspection. Considering that more than thirty of the important ports of the world are free ports, the extent of the danger as well as the difficulty of safeguarding against it are evident.[1] The Geneva Convention of 1925 embodied the report of the Communications and Transit Committee in its 14th Article, which calls for the enforcement in the free ports and zones of all the regulations for the control of the drug trade which apply in the rest of the territory of any country. This provision is also contained in the Limitation Convention (Article 13). But the problem has never received adequate attention from the Governments, and in the 13th Session of the Advisory Committee Mr. Sirks again brought up the subject of free ports in connection with police co-operation. He suggested that valuable results might be obtained by a conference of the Advisory Committee and the police officials of the free ports chiefly concerned in the drug traffic, such as Hamburg, Copenhagen, and Danzig. He pointed out that reports for the previous year (1930) showed that Trieste, Marseilles, Hamburg, and Danzig, had all been mentioned in connection with drugs illicitly exported from Istambul.[2] But the Committee took no action on the proposal of the assessor.

[1] The cities where transhipment can be effected, and where no customs regulations exist for goods in transit, are:

Rio de Janeiro	Stettin	Bilboa
Danzig	Salonika	Cadiz
Copenhagen	Fiume	Santa Cruz
Bremen	Genoa	Gothenburg
Cuxhaven	Naples	Stockholm
Emden	Trieste	Bâle
Flensburg	Sabang	Lausanne
Gustmunde	Tandjoengpinang	Geneva
Hamburg	Sulina	Istambul
Lubeck	Barcelona	Vladivostock

[2] *Minutes Advisory Committee*, 14th Session, p. 159.

(*f*) *The Geneva Convention.*—An indication of the actual progress which the Committee had made in organizing the control of the drug traffic by 1925 may be seen in the Geneva Convention. Six of the provisions embodied in this Convention resulted directly from the work of the Advisory Committee, namely, the certificate system, control of the free ports and zones, increase of penalties, extradition of offenders against narcotic laws, communication to each other by the several Governments through the Secretary-General of all narcotic laws and regulations, and the application of the provisions of the Convention to new drugs, upon the advice of the Health Committee.[1]

The Geneva Conference, in spite of the fact that it succeeded in drawing up a convention embodying a strict control of the drug trade, was actually a failure in that it definitely did not accomplish the task for which it was called. The terms of the Assembly resolution of September 27, 1923, in accordance with which the Geneva Conference met, were these:

The Assembly, having noted with satisfaction that, in accordance with the hope expressed in the fourth resolution adopted by the Assembly in 1922, the Advisory Committee has reported that the information now available makes it possible for the Governments concerned to examine, with a view to the conclusion of an agreement, the question of the limitation of the amounts of morphine, heroin, or cocaine, and their respective salts to be manufactured; of the limitation of the amounts of raw opium and coca leaf to be imported for that purpose and for other medicinal and scientific purposes; and of the limitation of the production of raw opium and the coca leaf for export to the amount required for such medicinal and scientific purposes, requests the Council . . . etc., to invite the Governments concerned to send representatives with plenipotentiary powers to a conference for this purpose. . . .[2]

[1] This article grew out of a list of drugs presented by the French Government, to which it believed the Hague Convention ought to apply. See 4th Session, p. 71.

[2] 4 A.P., p. 101.

This mandate of the Conference cannot in any sense be said to have been accomplished. Instead of providing for the limitation of the production and manufacture of opium and drugs, the Conference provided for controlling the trade in them. In other words, it reflected the attitude of the Advisory Committee, which, since its organization in 1920, had repeatedly rejected the suggestions of some of its members to begin the direct limitation of production, and had persisted in devising measures for controlling the trade.

Indeed, this reversal of the original principle for which the Conference was called may be attributed yet more directly to the Advisory Committee, for the reversal occurred in fact in the Committee itself, when it drew up a set of basic principles for the deliberations of the Conference. The Opium Preparatory Committee, which was composed of the American, British, Dutch, and French members of the Advisory Committee, and two assessors, was first appointed by the Council to draft a plan upon which the discussions of the Geneva Conference might be based. The British and American members supported the idea of direct limitation, but the French member maintained the principle of indirect limitation through control of the trade. The result was a deadlock. Later, to save the situation, the Advisory Committee appointed the above four members, plus the German and British Indian members, to a subcommittee which was to attempt to reach a compromise. This it finally did, but the compromise leaned so heavily toward the side of indirect limitation that when, later, in the Conference itself, the French, Dutch, German, Japanese, and Swiss delegations gave their support to it, the idea of controlling production directly completely vanished, and its originator and last support, the American delegat'on, left the Conference. It is thus not difficult to trace the influence which the Committee exerted on the Geneva Convention of 1925, both in determining the general lines and large principles on which it was based, and in inventing certain measures of control which were embodied in it.

Its influence on the course of the First Geneva Conference which met to consider the opium-smoking problem was of much the same kind. Whereas the American proposals intended the limitation of all production, both of the raw materials and of the manufactured drugs, to a quantity consistent with medical and scientific requirements, the British-Indian member maintained the legitimacy of eating opium, and the British, Dutch, French, German, Japanese, Portuguese, and Siamese members claimed that opium smoking could be suppressed only gradually, as provided in Chapter II of the Hague Convention of 1912. These same Governments, with for the most part the same delegates representing them, attended the First Geneva Conference, and there upheld the opinions already put forward in the Advisory Committee. The object of the American proposals had already been changed by the Assembly from a study of the limitation of opium production to a study of the means of applying the clauses on opium smoking of the Hague Convention. The American delegation was not included in the First Geneva Conference, but it attempted indirectly to influence the discussions there by submitting to the Second Conference a draft convention in which certain clauses relating to smoking opium appeared. These were intended to interpret the original American Proposals in their true sense, and to that end stipulated an immediate reduction of 10 per cent annually of the imports of opium into colonies and territories where smoking was allowed, and the immediate cessation of exports from producing countries except within the limits of the reduction programme. These draft articles were, of course, not considered by the First Conference, which remained well within its terms of reference by studying the means of applying Chapter II of the Hague Convention.

An Agreement was finally reached whereby the interested Powers acknowledged (1) that there was no help for the

·opium-smoking problem until production and export should be checked in the producing countries; (2) that the League, when it judged the time ripe, should appoint a committee to decide whether the production and export of opium was sufficiently in hand to warrant steps being taken toward the abolition of smoking, which should then be effected within fifteen years' time; and (3) that as long as the production of opium remained uncontrolled in China it was useless to seek a remedy for the opium-smoking problem in the colonies. In other words, without denying the obligations undertaken under the Hague Convention, the Geneva Opium Agreement made their performance conditional upon certain very remote developments. The Chinese delegation found itself unable to accept this Agreement and withdrew from the Conference, while the American withdrawal was due as much to this as to the results achieved in the Second Conference.

Here again, in the case of the First Geneva Conference, the influence of the Advisory Committee was seen. It had been clear from the first that the Committee did not wish to discuss the smoking problem, which had been chiefly in mind at the time it was set up. The efforts of Sir John Jordan to have the problems of the Far East discussed were determined, but without success, and the Advisory Committee was very soon completely absorbed with the European traffic in manufactured drugs. In a certain sense the Geneva Opium Agreement and the Geneva Convention of 1925 represented both the temper of the Advisory Committee and the sum of its achievements until that date.

5. Comprehensive Plans for the Organization of Control

The defeat of direct limitation marked the point of departure for the work undertaken by the Advisory Committee following the Geneva Conferences. The Geneva Convention embodied certain administrative measures, notably the certificate system, and provided for co-operation between the Governments, directly and through international organs. But these measures were only imperfectly co-ordinated. The obvious line of continuation of the Committee's work, therefore, was to weld them together into a single system. After the Geneva Conference several definite proposals for organizing control, both national and international, were placed before the Advisory Committee by some of its members, who were beginning to visualize the real nature and scope of the problem and to recognize the necessity for dealing with it in a comprehensive manner.

(a) *Cavazzoni's Plan of Administrative Control and the Model Code.*—At the 9th Session of the Advisory Committee, in January 1927, the Italian Government was represented for the first time, sending as its delegate Signor Stefano Cavazzoni. In his initial speech M. Cavazzoni expressed a firm belief that the purpose of the Committee could never be achieved otherwise than by the direct and quantitative limitation of drug production through rationing. Control, he said, could never replace limitation, but must follow and reinforce any scheme of limitation.[1] However, as the Governments had already committed themselves, by the terms of the Geneva Convention, to the control of the trade, M. Cavazzoni's opinion, as he expressed it in the Fifth Committee of the Assembly a few months later, was that national control must take precedence over international control, for any form of international control must depend upon the efficiency and good faith of national administrations.[2] For this reason M. Cavazzoni developed a plan for administrative control which he presented to the Advisory Committee at its 10th (Extraordinary) Session, held in September 1927.

Briefly, the Plan envisaged a strict and complete application of the certificate system, not only to imports and exports, but to

[1] *Advisory Committee*, 9th Session, p. 113.　　[2] 6 A.C. v., p. 11.

all orders and deliveries within a country. Furthermore, all imports of opium and drugs were to be kept in national warehouses, from which releases could be made only upon presentation of the proper Government certificate, indicating the amount to be released. Thirdly, extensive statistical information was to be required to enable the Government to keep account of every grain of any drug in the country, both the amounts being manufactured, and in the hands of wholesalers or retailers, so that the quantities allowed to leave the Government storehouses should not exceed the legitimate requirements of drug manufacturers and the medical profession.[1]

After a short preliminary consideration of the Plan the Committee decided to refer it to a subcommittee, to which it appointed Dr. Anselmino, M. Bourgois, Dr. Carrière, Sir Malcolm Delevingne, Mr. van Wettum, and M. Cavazzoni. The subcommittee reported at the 11th Session in 1928 that it considered the Cavazzoni Plan to be in effect an attempt to establish a Government monopoly, which would make it unacceptable in most countries. It associated itself with the opinion of Sir Malcolm Delevingne, who believed a careful granting of licenses a better plan. The Advisory Committee adopted this view. The subcommittee further found itself bound to reject the measure, proposed in the Plan, for the limitation of stocks and the suspension of manufacture when stocks became excessive, as well as the measure providing for the control of deliveries of drugs from the factory to the dealer.

In place of the Cavazzoni Plan the subcommittee prepared a Code of Administrative Control which combined various measures gleaned from the administrative experiences of several Governments. The mandate of the subcommittee had, in fact, included the study of administrative systems in general and the drafting of a model code based on such provisions as practice

[1] Document O.C. 666, 1927. Text, *Minutes of the Advisory Committee*, 10th Session, p. 109 *et seq.*

had found useful. In the Code thus drawn up the principles of M. Cavazzoni's Plan were lost. It was based on the less exacting system of licences for all persons in any way connected with the trade in drugs, registration, and report by manufacturers of every transaction and of every lot of drugs manufactured, to the competent Government authority, periodical inspection of factory registers by this authority, and a careful application of the import and export certificate system. The Model Code also stressed the importance of unifying and centralizing drug administration.[1] The water-tight quality of the plan which M. Cavazzoni had envisaged and which lay in the unbroken line of direct Governmental control which it provided, was not to be found in the Model Code. The Advisory Committee nevertheless adopted the latter, finding the Cavazzoni Plan impractical in many of its details and too close an approach to a monopoly system.

(b) *Colonel Woods's Plan for Government Control.*—At the same Session (the 10th) of the Advisory Committee in which M. Cavazzoni's Plan was presented, Colonel Arthur Woods, Assessor, former New York City Police Commissioner, submitted a proposal which, in view of the wide extent of the traffic, and the inability of the police to deal with it unaided by appropriate administrative measures, asked that "all factories manufacturing dangerous drugs should be owned or adequately controlled by their Governments."[2] This, he thought, could be achieved by a system of registry and inspection of all manufacture and trade, and the control of exports, especially to countries which had not adopted the import certificate system. Certain members of the Committee, while agreeing with the principle of Colonel Woods's proposal, found this last measure impracticable owing to the absence of a central organ which would be necessary for the control of shipments to such

[1] *Advisory Committee,* 11th Session, p. 353 *et seq.,* Text of Model Code.
[2] Ibid., 10th Session, p. 72.

countries. However, the Committee resolved to ask the Council to impress strongly upon the Governments the necessity for adopting the measures proposed by Colonel Woods. In 1931, three years after these proceedings, M. Cavazzoni's proposals concerning the control of stocks and the suspension of manufacture if these should become excessive, and Colonel Woods's proposal concerning the special control to be exercised over consignments of drugs going to countries where the import certificate system was not in effect, were embodied in the Limitation Convention.[1]

(c) *Dr. Anselmino's Plan for a Syndicate of Drug Manufacturers.*—One other plan of administrative control was presented at the 10th Session of the Advisory Committee. This was Dr. Anselmino's proposal for a syndicate of drug manufacturers. He suggested that it might work in conjunction with the Permanent Central Opium Board, which, though it was not yet functioning, was provided for in the Geneva Convention. A limited amount of supervisory power was invested in the Board, and it was Dr. Anselmino's belief that it could only function effectively if its control were concentrated on a definitely restricted group of producers. The proposal, however, was not adopted. Mr. van Wettum feared that the syndicate would work for profit instead of control, and M. Bourgois foresaw conflict instead of co-operation between the syndicate and the Board. Sir Malcolm Delevingne, while welcoming the idea because it offered a remedy for the condition of anarchy in production and distribution, nevertheless doubted that the proper co-operation between the syndicate and the Board could be secured. The proposal was therefore not considered further at the time. When, however, three years later, the Committee was obliged to adopt the principle of the direct limitation of manufacture, and to work out a plan for its application, it was at once agreed that the

[1] Articles 16 and 14.

most effective way of achieving this end was to let the existing manufacturers organize a virtually closed cartel.[1]

(*d*) *Colonel Woods's Proposal for the Co-operation of National Administrations.*—A proposal similar to Dr. Anselmino's had been made in the 8th Session of the Advisory Committee in 1926 by Assessor Colonel Woods.[2] His suggestion was that the drug manufacturing firms of all countries should meet in conference with the chairman of the Advisory Committee, and recommend to the Committee the means they might find suitable for limiting the production and distribution of drugs to lawful purposes. He added a further suggestion to the effect that the administrative officials of all countries, in charge of enforcing narcotic laws, should meet to discuss ways and means of carrying out their duties. M. Bourgois, chairman, doubted whether the time was ripe for the first of these resolutions which raised certain delicate questions. Public opinion, he thought, would have to be prepared for it, Governments would not be willing, and the whole question had not in any case been sufficiently investigated. In regard to the second resolution, Mr. van Wettum objected that as the Final Act of the Geneva Convention already provided for direct communication between the competent authorities charged with the administration of the drug laws, Colonel Woods's suggestion was superfluous. He also doubted whether police officials would find it possible to gather from all parts of the world to take part in such a conference, although Colonel Woods assured the Committee that if smugglers found it possible to cross continents and seas the police would also find a means of doing so.[3] On the whole, the Committee did not display much enthusiasm for Colonel Woods's proposals, and urged especially that new measures of this type should not be undertaken until the Geneva Convention had been ratified. The resolutions were

[1] Draft submitted to Council by Advisory Committee, 13th Session.
Advisory Committee, 8th Session, p. 114.   [3] Ibid.

nevertheless appended to the Committee's report to the Council on the work of the 8th Session, and the Council voted that the Secretary-General "take the action arising out of the resolution."[1] What the action was to be neither the Council nor the Advisory Committee specified. The only reference to Colonel Woods's proposals in the Fifth Committee of the Assembly at its next session was made by the British representative, who suggested that they might be applicable to the problem once the Geneva Convention was ratified and had had a chance to function, but that nothing new should be attempted until that time.

6. The Consideration of Monopoly Control

It can easily be seen that in all these proposals for co-ordinating drug control, which were placed before the Advisory Committee after the Geneva Conferences, lay a strong suggestion of monopoly control, Government monopoly within the individual States, and international cartel monopoly. These suggestions were considered by a majority of the Advisory Committee as undesirable, or as impossible of application. Monopoly control over the trade in narcotics was exercised at that time by three or four Governments, two of which, in addition, controlled the production of manufactured drugs. In none of the important manufacturing countries, however, has a monopoly been attempted, or the idea received anything but discouragement. On the other hand, the cultivation of the opium poppy and the production of raw opium are monopolized by the State in India, and since 1927 in Persia. China was believed in 1928 to have made a like move, but the Chinese Government subsequently disavowed it. In all of the colonies of the European Governments in the Far East and the Pacific the preparation and sale of opium for smoking have long been established as Government monopolies. That these monopolies

[1] C. 42, p. 1225.

have for their primary object the increase of the Government revenue is an admitted fact. The use of the monopoly as a system of control is, at best, secondary, and often quite incidental. Nevertheless the possibility of establishing control by this means is in no wise lessened by the fact that it may at the same time be an instrument of revenue. It is important, however, that the emphasis be placed properly. The fact that this emphasis has been shifting steadily from revenue toward control as the motive of monopoly may certainly be placed to the credit of awakening public opinion on the subject. The conditions in the Colonies were first revealed in 1909, and their amelioration was the object of the Shanghai Conference. Revenue from the opium trade at that time not uncommonly comprised 25 per cent of the total revenue of a colony, and was known to reach 90 per cent.[1]

Formerly the sole right to sell opium was auctioned off for a given term of time to the highest bidder. All the advantages of revenue were thus acquired, without any of the cares of administration. An extract from the *Bulletin Officiel de la Province de Macao*, No. 5, of January 29, 1910, gives notice to the effect that at a given date and hour the exclusive privilege of preparing opium and selling it, and of exporting it from Macao, would be auctioned off to the highest bidder for a period of three years. The form in which bids were to be made was the following:

"J'offre la prix annuel de $ . . . pour le privilège exclusif de préparer l'opium, de le vendre préparé à Macao, à Taipa, et à Coloane, et de l'exporter à Macao. Je m'astreins en outre aux conditions spécifiées au Bureau Supérieur des Finances, et je verse pour cautionnement du contrat la somme de $ . . .'"

In the same bulletin series on another date appears a statement

---

[1] At the time of the Enquiry in the Far East, conducted by the League Commission on Opium Smoking in 1929, the average opium revenue in all the colonies and territories was 15 per cent of the total.

that the Government finds it increasingly necessary to take severe measures to control the illicit importation of opium which was threatening the revenue of the State, and prejudicing the control of opium consumption.[1] The farming system in Macao was replaced in 1927 by a system of direct Government monopoly.

Siam and all the territories except the Union of Indo-China, Kwang-Chow-Wan, Hong-Kong, Macao, Formosa, and the Kwantung Leased Territory, completely monopolize the opium trade, being not only sole importers and preparers of the opium, but also maintaining retail shops and smoking establishments. These six, however, permit the retail sale of opium by licensed dealers, whose activity is indirectly encouraged by the fact that they receive a percentage profit on sales, though the total amount that may be sold is limited to a fixed maximum in some cases. The registration, licensing, and rationing of smokers, an essential part of any control aiming at restriction, is not required in three of the Unfederated Malay States, nor in Siam (except for a few hundred smokers who, for reasons of health, infirmity, or social position, cannot frequent the public smoking establishments), nor in the Union of Indo-China, Kwang-Chow-Wan, Hong-Kong, or Macao. In addition to these there are several territories where licensing and registration are required, but where the addicts are not rationed. These are the Unfederated Malay States, the Federated Malay States, the Straits Settlements, and Brunei. Additional licensing or registration of smokers is still being permitted in all the territories except Burma, Sarawak, and Formosa, and in Burma and Formosa the registers have recently been temporarily reopened. In Brunei smoking is permitted only to immigrants.[2]

[1] *Bulletin Officiel*, No. 9, 26 fév., 1910.
[2] Report to the Council by the Commission of Enquiry into Control of Opium Smoking in the Far East, 1930.

THE WORK OF THE OPIUM ADVISORY COMMITTEE

While these obvious gaps in control under the monopoly system are permitted to exist, the monopoly as an instrument for restricting and reducing the consumption of and the trade in opium cannot be effective. As a revenue measure there are no such apparent weaknesses in the system. The sole right of purchase, preparation, and sale belongs to each of the opium monopolies. The contraband trade is, of course, always a danger to the effectiveness of any monopoly, but it is not a weakness inherent in the system itself. Nor can the existence of a contraband trade be blamed on the monopoly system if it is properly operated. Under any form of control a contraband trade will spring up, and its detection is, if anything, easier under a monopoly system of control than under any other.

It is this fact that makes the monopoly desirable in the suppression of opium smoking, but it must be entirely divorced from any idea of revenue before it can be expected to bring results. The Commission of Enquiry into Opium Smoking in the Far East urged strongly that means be found to balance budgets without the aid of opium revenue. The report of the Commission states that the percentage of the total revenue of the colonies and territories made up by opium revenue is as follows:[1]

	1920.	1929.
Brunei (Br.)	16·76	19·51
Sarawak (Br.)	17·86[1]	13·9
British North Borneo	29·1	19·2[2]
Netherlands Indies	12·99	6·35[2]
Siam	23·09	15·81
Indo-China and Kwang-Chow-Wan (Fr.) ..	13·85	4·7
Hong-Kong (Br.)	27·8	9·6
Macao (Port.)	45·49	22·16
Formosa (Jap.)	3·15	2·72[2]
Kwantung Leased Territory (Jap.)	24·1	6·4[2]
Burma (Br.)	2·3	3·14

(¹ 1925; ² 1925.)

[1] Report to the Council of the Commission of Enquiry into Control of Opium Smoking in the Far East, 1930.

	1920.	1929.
Straits Settlements (Br.)..	46·1	15·1
Federated Malay States (Br.) ..	13·9	12·3[2]
Unfederated Malay States (Br.)—		
Johore	29·39[3]	23·0
Kedah	34·55[3]	26·78
Perlis	38·85[3]	30·15
Kelantan	20·0[1]	16·8
Trengganu ..	28·20[2]	17·70

([1] 1925; [2] 1928; [3] 1924.)

In India the Government has exercised complete control over the production of and trade in opium since the eighteenth century. Until 1926 the privilege of disposing of Government export opium was auctioned off annually, but since that date opium for export is sold only directly by the Government, and on the basis of contracts with importing Governments. Opium for internal use in India is also monopoly opium, and is disposed of in excise shops whose proprietorship is purchased from the Government. All opium is prepared in the monopoly factory at Ghazipur. As a revenue measure the opium monopoly, since 1909, has been steadily losing its significance.[1]

In 1927 the Persian Mejlis passed a bill establishing a Government monopoly of opium and narcotics.[2] The monopoly was to cover not only the import, export, and sale of opium, but was designed to restrict the cultivation of the poppy as well. To this end it was provided that the cultivator should be exempt from taxation on all crops substituted for the poppy crop, for a period of five years, and that cultivators undertaking such crop substitution should receive the aid of loans by the Government bank. The use of the monopoly as a restrictive measure was also assured in the provision for reducing the export of opium by 10 per cent annually, and the sale of opium for home use by 5 per cent annually. This advanced policy was adopted in a country where every administrative difficulty

[1] See chapter on India.   [2] Document O.C. 23 (p), p. 16.

exists, three years after the Governments of the European colonies in the Far East had declared it impossible to reduce the consumption of opium there.[1] Whether this willing spirit can be translated into action remains to be seen, but as late as 1934 few measures to implement the ambitious Persian programme appear to have been taken.

This complete monopoly control does not, as has been pointed out already, exist in any of the important drug manufacturing countries, and is not favourably considered by their representatives on the Advisory Committee. The usefulness of the monopoly as a system of control ought not, however, to be ignored. There are three cases of Governments controlling the use of drugs by monopoly, and although the problem is comparatively minor in each of them, the results of their experience cannot be without practical importance.

The Greek Government established a monopoly over the production, import, and sale of opium and all of its derivatives in 1925. This act resulted, not so much from the need to monopolize production, which is small in Greece, but from the difficulties experienced by the Government with regard to Yugoslav opium transhipments to the free port of Salonika. According to the convention existing between the two Governments, transhipments to the port of Salonika are not liable to Greek control. The abuses of this law in the case of shipments of opium were so great that the Greek Government was forced to protect itself by declaring a monopoly. Control consists in centralizing authority in the hands of the Finance Minister, who alone may authorize the cultivation of opium and grant the licenses necessary for it. The Finance Minister is, moreover, charged with obtaining the necessary supplies of opium and drugs for the internal needs of the country. The manufacture of drugs and the preparation of opium may be carried on only by the authorization of the Supreme Health Council in national

[1] See above, p. 91.

factories under three-year contracts. The sale of opium and drugs is confined to the Administrator of the Central State Department for Quinine and Saccharine, and to the Annexes of the Chemical Laboratory of the Ministry of Finance. Only licensed pharmacists may buy the drugs, whose price is fixed by the Government Monopoly Bureau.[1]

In Russia, needless to say, where all production is monopolized by the Government, the manufacture of drugs is no exception. At present the Russian Government produces only enough for its own internal needs, but without prejudice to the future expansion of this industry to supply foreign markets.

In Spain, which is a non-manufacturing country, a State monopoly of the importation and distribution of drugs was established by law in April 1928, but it appears not yet to have been set up. The amount to be purchased annually, as well as the market in which it is to be purchased, is determined in advance by a competent authority.

As these are not important drug manufacturing countries, and their administrative problems in connection with the monopolies are therefore not great, one must be careful in applying their experience in this field to the larger manufacturing countries where a monopoly system would have much greater significance. However, in view of the fact that these systems are sound in theory and can be successful in practice, and considering furthermore that Government monopolies of important manufactured products do exist and are successfully administered, one must look elsewhere for the explanation of the evident reluctance on the part of Governments to take over this particular industry as a monopoly.

After the enforced adoption of the principle of direct limitation of manufacture, the value of the monopoly system as a means of control first began to be emphasized in the Advisory Committee. In its 13th Session the Japanese representative, Mr.

[1] *Advisory Committee*, 8th Session, p. 139.

Ito, stated that in regard to certain classes of goods, wherever a monopoly existed it had been found possible to achieve a certain limitation of production. The problem of limitation was, in fact, rendered easier through a system of monopoly, and he felt that this fact should not be overlooked by the Committee in dealing with dangerous drugs.[1]

In the same session of the Advisory Committee the delegate of Yugoslavia, M. Milicevic, recalled his Government's favourable attitude toward the limitation of manufacture, and said that several attempts to begin drug manufacture in Yugoslavia on private initiative had been repressed by the Government. He could not say whether the Government might find it advisable to set up a drug factory at some future date, but he was positive that no private concern should ever be permitted to do so. He did not believe that a private concern would find it profitable to supply the needs of Yugoslavia alone, but would also depend on exports, which might increase the opportunity for illicit traffic.[2]

Mr. van Wettum, also in the same session of the Committee, stated that the monopoly system of control, which some of his colleagues seemed to favour, presented great difficulties. In the case of a monopoly applied to the manufacture of drugs, he said, it would be almost impossible, at any rate in the beginning, to have Government officials as managers of factories. In many countries, he felt, Parliament would oppose a monopoly system. In the United States there was even a law against monopolies. Governments disliking a system of monopolies in general, and a drug monopoly in particular, would contend that a monopoly was unnecessary because practice had proved that good results could be obtained without it. Furthermore, the expense of a monopoly would be so great that the small countries would find it impossible to establish them. In short, Mr. van Wettum concluded, he believed that "neither the

[1] *Advisory Committee*, 13th Session, p. 38.   [2] Ibid., p. 41.

limitation of manufacture to a definite amount, nor the enforced universal establishment of monopolies could be considered to be practical politics."[1] Mr. van Wettum's argument with regard to the inadvisability of placing an inexperienced Government official in so technical a position as that of manager of a drug factory was of course entirely justified. There would seem to be no difficulty, however, in appointing the experienced manager of a drug concern to the Government service, in the capacity of manager of the Government drug factory. As regards the argument that certain countries, especially the United States, are unfavourable to monopolies, and have even legislated against them, this attitude cannot be said to apply to Government monopolies set up for the purpose of protecting the public from a nefarious trade, but simply to the restriction imposed by strong groups on the free production of innocent goods. Furthermore, it was the general absence of the "good results" to which Mr. van Wettum referred as having been obtained under existing systems that had aroused the Assembly to demand the immediate study of direct limitation. Finally, a general acceptance of the monopoly system would not necessitate the establishment of a monopoly by every Government. Small countries could arrange to be supplied by those large enough to have found it practicable to set up a monopoly, without in any way endangering the effectiveness of the system. Although these objections to Mr. van Wettum's arguments would seem to be simple enough, the latter went entirely unchallenged. No definite action whatever was taken in the matter of monopolies at the 13th Session of the Advisory Committee, in spite of the interest manifested in it by some of the members of the Committee.

It was not until the Committee met in its 14th Session, when its composition was greatly altered by the addition of the representatives of seven non-manufacturing countries, that

[1] *Advisory Committee*, 13th Session, p. 46.

monopolies were discussed at any length. The question had not been included in the agenda, but was brought up indirectly in the course of the discussions. Dr. Chodzko, representative of Poland, declared at one point in the discussions that there was no reason why there should be free trade in drugs at all. Since drugs were necessary for medical use alone the trade in them ought to be confined to the States, or at least to the producers. He expressed surprise that the question of State monopoly had not been definitely considered by the Committee, and felt that sooner or later serious study of the question would have to be undertaken. M. Cavazzoni declared himself to be in entire agreement with Dr. Chodzko in this matter.[1] Later in the same session M. Cavazzoni presented a list of suggestions to the Committee which he desired to have appended to the report to the Council on the Committee's plan for organizing the limitation of manufacture. Among the suggestions was one to the effect that the convention to be drawn up should make provision not only for the trade in, but also the manufacture of, the drugs which were to fall under the terms of the convention.[2] This recommendation was practically repeated in the minority note which six of the non-manufacturing countries,[3] after a struggle, succeeded in having appended to the Committee's report to the Council. In this note was summarized the position of the minority on various questions which had come up for discussion during the session, and in which they dissented from the views of the majority. On the subject of monopolies the minority declared itself in favour of a "system of Governmental monopoly for the trade and where necessary for the manufacture of narcotic drugs falling under the provisions of the Convention."[4]

The Limitation Convention which was drawn up in the

---

[1] *Advisory Committee*, 14th Session, p. 51.   [2] Ibid., p. 63.
[3] Belgium, China, Mexico, Poland, Spain, Uruguay.
[4] *Advisory Committee*, 14th Session, pp. 83 and 241.

summer of 1931 does not contain provision for the establishment of State monopolies, but the Final Act of the Conference, Paragraph IV, reads:

The Conference recommends that Governments should consider the desirability of establishing a State monopoly over the trade in, and, if necessary, over the manufacture of, the drugs covered by the Convention signed on this day's date.

The German delegation stated that it could not accept these recommendations.

The arguments opposed to the monopoly system in the Advisory Committee have not been against the effectiveness of the system itself, but seem rather to show a hesitation to embark on a new and experimental field of administrative method, to leave a known and tried system, in spite of its recognized weaknesses, for a new one, even though it is theoretically sound. There seems to have been a conscious evasion of the subject altogether. It has never figured as a definite item on the agenda of the Committee. Yet whenever it has been brought up in the discussions, as, in the first instance, by Colonel Woods, and later by M. Cavazzoni, Dr. Chodzko, and M. Milicevic, no opposition was made to it as a system except by Mr. van Wettum. The Governments on whose territories no drug manufacture exists have been the ones to support the idea of monopolies, while those which, more tacitly than actively, have opposed it, are the ones which have large manufacturing concerns to deal with. In this fact there may be found some explanation for the position taken on the subject of State monopolies. The power behind the drug industry is so great that the prospect of destroying it as a private enterprise, in favour of State monopoly, is not one which most Governments would face lightly. It is this, rather than any anticipated difficulties in administering a monopoly plant, that is at the bottom of the hesitation with which most of the members of the Committee speak on the subject. Through the influence of the non-manufacturing States on the Committee, who pushed the issue at the Drug Conference in 1931, the paragraph on monopolies just quoted was included in the Final Act of the Conference. It remains to the individual Governments to accept or reject the recommendation, but in view of the terms of the Limitation Convention itself, which provide for a different system of control, its general adoption is not likely to be an event of the near future.

7. *The Work of the Police*

The work of the police, both on the Advisory Committee and independently of it, might well constitute a separate chapter in the history of drug control. But for several reasons it is necessary and desirable to consider the activities of the police together with the work of the Advisory Committee. In the first place the police assessors on the Committee have contributed much to the Committee's achievements; secondly, the international police organization has dealt energetically with the problems of the illicit traffic; and, thirdly, it has made every effort to co-operate directly with the Committee and to establish a recognized and official relationship with it. The fact that these efforts have not been more fruitful gives them greater rather than less significance, for it reveals the grudging resistance of the Committee to them, and contrasts the types of organization that produce action or inaction.

In the 4th Session of the Advisory Committee, in 1923, a resolution was passed to the effect that one of the three League assessors appointed to the Committee by the Council should be a police expert. Colonel Arthur Woods, appointed as assessor to the Committee in 1926, was the first to represent the police. His former position as New York City Police Commissioner, and his scientific knowledge of the problems of crime and policing,[1] qualified him to furnish the Committee with the special assistance wanted in his particular field. His attitude towards his work during the three years of his office as assessor was typified in his introductory remarks to the Committee. He said: "I have not been able to escape the impression in the few days during which I have had the privilege of sitting with this Committee, that there may be too much diplomacy and too little rough-shod direct police action in the fight against these narcotic outlaws. It is not a diplomatic question, Gentlemen, but a pure police task, and in the contest with law-breakers as rich, as powerful, as well-organized, and as far-reaching as these the police must act strongly, and must be free from diplomatic entanglements."[2] The contrast of this clear and fearless judgment of the situation, with the type of statement customarily heard in the Committee, must be evident to anyone who has followed the Committee's work up to this point. It is a conclusive argument in favour of the assessor system that it has permitted the Committee to benefit by the presence of a member who, unshackled by any Government affiliation, and motivated by a strong professional and technical interest, could take so vigorous and uncompromising a stand. There is, furthermore, in the succession of police assessors who have followed Colonel Woods, ample proof that this judgment is not overdrawn.

Colonel Woods's first act was to present the plan which has already been discussed, in which he proposed the holding of an international conference of administrative officials. The objections offered to this idea were made in spite of the fact that there existed already a well-developed international police organization. In 1923 Dr. Shober, Chief of the Vienna Police, had summoned the first International Police Congress. Nineteen national police departments were represented at this Congress,

[1] See Raymond B. Fosdick, *European Police Organization*, Century Co., New York, 1915.   [2] *Advisory Committee*, 8th Session, p. 51.

and ten more have subsequently joined this number. All of the principal European police departments are members, besides China, Japan, Turkey, and the United States. The agenda of the first Congress included the following important points:

1. The organization of direct relations between police authorities (then maintained through diplomatic channels).
2. The extradition of arrested criminals.
3. The suppression of alcoholism and the traffic in morphine and cocaine, within the limits of the sphere of activity of the police.

Resolutions were adopted with regard to these questions, and, what was more important, a permanent international police organ was established. This, the International Criminal Police Commission, a smaller but representative body, has the function of directing and developing the policy set forth by the Congress. At the same time it insures stability and continuity to the organization. The executive body has met annually in the various European capitals, though its seat is officially in Vienna, where its Bureau is housed at the Headquarters of the Vienna Police.

This international organization of the criminal police has extended its work to numerous fields of crime suppression, and to the development of a method and technique necessary to the application of the policies which the quadrennial assemblies of the Congress have formulated. Actually the Commission has directed the work of the organization, while the Congress has maintained its thoroughly representative character.

By 1929 the Commission had so far proved its usefulness that the Council of the League invited it to participate in framing a convention for the suppression of counterfeit currency and the falsification of cheques. This it did, and as the convention demanded the institution of a central international police bureau, the Council named the Bureau of the International Police Commission at Vienna to perform the required function until a separate bureau could be formed. The machinery was in fact already existing in Vienna, where forgery and counterfeiting had for some years been the object of special attention by the Bureau.

The International Police Commission has also attacked the drug problem as one of its chief tasks. In 1926 the Congress, meeting in Berlin, resolved that a central police office should be established in each country to facilitate the campaign against the drug traffic, and that adequate penalties should be provided for offences against the drug laws. In 1928 the Congress, meeting in Berlin, agreed that it would be useful to the police if a member of the Commission were permitted to attend the meetings of the Opium Advisory Committee. This resolution was communicated by letter from the International Police Commission to the Advisory Committee, which voted its consent to the suggestion, but with the reservation that the proposed representative should not have the right to enter into the discussions of the Committee.

The suggestion was to go further than this, however. In the Assembly in 1929 it was resolved that the Council should consider inviting the International Police Commission to suggest ways in which it might help the work of the League's technical committees. The Commission promptly drew up a list of suggestions,[1] all of them based upon its direct representation on the committees of the League. It happened that the same Assembly which passed this resolution also determined upon the necessity of reorganizing the Opium Advisory Committee. Austria, one of the newly appointed members, sent as her delegate Dr. Schultz, Director of the Vienna Police, and Austrian member of the International Police Commission. Dr. Schultz has sat since 1931 in the double capacity of delegate of Austria and representative of the International Police Commission. A most valuable liaison has thus been formed.

Meanwhile, the plan for the comprehensive organization of

[1] Document O.C. 1151, 1930.

the police to deal with the drug traffic, which was mentioned above, was presented to the Advisory Committee at the 13th Session in 1930 by its police assessor, Mr. Sirks.[1] It demanded:

1. The establishment in each country of a central narcotics bureau to unify administration and police control over the narcotics trade.
2. The establishment of co-operative relations with like authorities of other countries.
3. The establishment of a central bureau at the Secretariat of the League of Nations for the international control of the narcotics trade, or the transmission to the International Police Bureau at Vienna of this function.
4. The arrangement for the extradition of offenders against narcotics laws of a certain importance.

At this date a unified police control over the drug traffic had been organized in only three countries, Great Britain, through the Home Office, the Netherlands, through the Interministerial Committee for Opium Affairs, which includes the chiefs of the Amsterdam and Rotterdam police; and Egypt, through its Central Narcotics Intelligence Bureau. These three administrations had shown great efficiency, internationally as well as locally, in controlling the traffic.

The Sirks Plan was discussed at length in the Advisory Committee. The British Indian member, Sir John Campbell, explained as regards the position of India that the centralization of police control in India, desirable though it was in principle, remained impossible of realization because of the autonomy of the Native States. An official report sent to the Secretariat by the British Indian Government in October 1930[2] stated: "When the Dangerous Drugs Act, 1930, comes into force, the control of dangerous drugs will be centralized; international co-operation will be facilitated when the Central Intelligence Bureau is established; the Government of India, however, are unable to

[1] Document, O.C. 1147, 1930.
[2] *Advisory Committee*, 14th Session, p. 105.

reorganize the whole police system in India to suit the needs of the campaign against illicit traffic in drugs, and doubt whether foreign police officers would, in practice, be able to conduct investigations in India; nevertheless the authorities are prepared to co-operate with them where necessary." Dr. Carrière, Swiss member of the Committee, also pointed out that constitutional difficulties stood in the way of centralizing police control in Switzerland, where police and judicial functions still remain in the cantonal domain, thus precluding centralized action. The net result of the discussion of the first point in Mr. Sirks' plan was the adoption of a resolution to the effect:

1. That unified and centralized control is desirable and valuable.
2. That the internal laws of some countries may preclude the adoption of this suggestion.

The Chinese member of the Committee offered the only serious objection made in regard to the second point of the Sirks Plan. China's experiences in "co-operating" with other countries have perhaps taught her the lesson of caution. In any case existing treaties of extraterritoriality present real difficulties to unhampered action, as do also the International Settlements. Moreover, in view of her condition of internal disorganization the proposed measures were entirely impossible of realization. Although China was alone in declaring herself unable to give effect to the second point of Mr. Sirks' plan, its nominal acceptance by the other members of the Committee unfortunately did not mean its immediate application, for, as already shown, only three countries had the administrative machinery ready to carry it out. Following the dispatch of a letter of inquiry by the Secretariat on this subject, replies were received from six Governments indicating that measures had been or were being taken for centralizing control. These were Belgium, Canada, Great Britain, India, Egypt, and Uruguay. A number of replies indicated agreement with the principle in question, while explaining that various circumstances prevented its application, or rendered it unnecessary.

Of particular interest in view of certain attitudes already remarked in the Committee was the decision taken on the third point in the Sirks Plan, the establishment of a central international bureau, either at the Secretariat or at the Vienna International Police Bureau. Mr. Sirks stated in the Advisory Committee[1] that the object of his proposed central international bureau was to bring the various central national offices into contact with each other. He must, therefore, in mentioning the Secretariat as a possible agent, have had in mind a widening of the functions heretofore performed by it in connection with illicit traffic cases. The Vienna International Police Bureau, which he also mentioned, is both a central international repository of police information and a liaison office between national police bureaux. The functions which Mr. Sirks intended the proposed international office to perform were therefore evident. But the Advisory Committee, in reporting to the Council on the Sirks Plan, practically nullified the effect of this proposal, saying:

> The Opium Advisory Committee also suggests that the Governments should refer freely to the Secretariat of the League of Nations all cases of illicit traffic, where it seems probable that information of value could be obtained from them. The Secretariat now possesses a mass of detailed information of value regarding the marks and labels often applied to illicit drugs, the source of supply, and the methods adopted in obtaining such drugs and in disposing of them; it also has in its possession precise details regarding certain international smugglers and their relations with one another.[2]

This statement amounted to nothing more than calling attention to the work of collecting information on seizures which the Secretariat had been performing for eight years. The proposal to develop there an active liaison office was vetoed.

[1] *Advisory Committee*, 13th Session, p. 409.   [2] Ibid., p. 388.

Sir Malcolm Delevingne was of the opinion that better results could be obtained through direct co-operation between the police and administrative authorities of the different countries, and feared that a suggestion for the establishment of an international bureau would not be popular with the Governments, which were not favourable to the tendency towards internationalization.[1] Mr. Sirks pointed out that when a trafficker was caught it was of the highest importance to the police to be able to identify him and to know what his previous record had been. Fingerprints and a file of reports concerning him were indispensable, and while the Secretariat had on hand the particulars about various smugglers, it did not possess the means of identifying them.[2] The Chinese member of the Committee, Dr. Woo Kaiseng, favoured asking the Vienna International Police Bureau to assume this duty, at least for a trial period, but his view was not supported. Although the Committee did not appear favourable to investing the Vienna Bureau with a definite function in connection with the opium traffic work, it supported the principle of police co-operation, and the Vienna Bureau has, in fact, undertaken to insure this as thoroughly as though the Committee had given it a definite mandate. The necessities of the situation have demanded this development.

The presence of another police officer at this session of the Advisory Committee, and his report on the conduct of the police in several cases of drug trafficking, put the Committee face to face with the proof that the Sirks proposal met precisely the needs of the situation. This was the report of Russell Pasha, Chief of the Cairo Police, and Director of the Central Narcotics Intelligence Bureau at Cairo. He said that the energy and ability of the Vienna Police had brought to light an important organization of drug traffickers, and had thus been the means of stopping an immense flow of narcotics into Egypt. Sir Malcolm Delevingne, in acknowledging the report, felt that the Committee

[1] *Advisory Committee*, 13th Session, p. 128.   [2] Ibid.

would benefit by the experience and knowledge of police officials sent to confer with it. His concrete suggestion was that whenever a police official had an account of the drug situation in his country to give, he should be invited to come before the Advisory Committee and make his report. Sir Malcolm's proposal was not adopted by the Committee, and was not mentioned in the report of the Committee to the Council. In spite of the cold reception of this suggestion, however, and of those of Mr. Sirks, the representatives of policing have steadily increased their contribution to the Committee's work.

The International Police Organization meanwhile continued its efforts, and in the Congress held at Antwerp some months later passed a resolution embodying the principles of the Sirks Plan. Meanwhile, too, the Assembly resolution with regard to the co-operation of the International Police Commission with the Advisory Committee took effect in the invitation of the Committee to three members of the Commission to attend its 14th Session and join in the discussions on the illicit traffic. Beside Dr. Schultz, the Commission was represented at this session by the Deputy Chief of the Berlin Police, Dr. Bernhard Weiss, and by M. Mondanel, Divisional Commissioner of the French Police. This delegation urged strongly on the Committee the adoption of a plan for the comprehensive organization of the police as the surest weapon against the illicit traffic, and to this end presented to the Committee the Draft Convention for the Suppression of the Illicit Traffic, which has already been mentioned in relation to penalties.[1] It provided for the strict and uniform application of police measures against crimes committed in connection with the illicit traffic in drugs, defined these crimes, called for the extradition of criminals, or their detention and punishment in whatever country they might have sought refuge, and provided for the centralized organization of the police and periodical conferences of the police chiefs of the

[1] See above, p. 84.

several countries. The same type of organization is provided in the Counterfeit Currency Convention, which has already been mentioned, and in the matter of whose application the Vienna Bureau was invested with the central rôle. The Draft Convention was in fact based, article by article, upon the Currency Convention. Because of the legal technicalities which it was felt might give trouble, it was decided in the Committee to refer the Draft Convention to the consideration of a sub-committee. The subcommittee was composed of Dr. Schultz, Mr. Sirks, Sir Malcolm Delevingne, Mr. van Wettum, and M. Barandon, member of the Legal Section of the Secretariat. At the 16th Session of the Advisory Committee the subcommittee reported its endorsement of the Draft virtually as it was submitted to the Advisory Committee. It was then approved by the 14th Assembly, and the Governments were urged to consider it. By May 1934 twenty-two Governments had attested their approval of the Convention, which may shortly form the basis of a conference similar to that recently held on counterfeit currency.

8. The Control of Opium Smoking

The smoking of opium has been given perhaps less attention than any other aspect of the narcotics problem. There may be a number of reasons for its comparative neglect. It is not generally considered to be as devastating in its effects as addiction to one of the manufactured drugs. It may be, and often is, taken in moderation, though habitually, over long periods of years with no serious ill effects. On the other hand, to abuse it is easy, and the mental and physical degeneration which follows its abuse is certain. Secondly, generations and centuries of practice have established the habit as one to which no stigma is attached, at least among those classes who indulge in it. Thirdly, administration in those countries and territories in which opium is smoked is either not strong enough to deal with the problem or is in the hands of those whose interest in the question is chiefly financial. Except possibly in the case of Hong-Kong, the contention that opium smoking cannot be suppressed until poppy cultivation is controlled is a facile excuse for unwilling Governments, although undoubtedly the problem would be very much simplified if production were controlled. In any case, discussions in the Advisory Committee on the subject of opium smoking, for whatever reason, have been conspicuously absent. It is true that at the time the Advisory Committee began to function, the manufactured drugs problem had become by far more serious than that of opium smoking, which had so largely occupied the Hague Conference. But there were definite provisions in the Hague Convention which the Committee, always basing the extent of its powers upon this instrument, had the unmistakable duty of watching. These articles are the following:

Article 6.—The Contracting Parties shall take measures for the gradual and effective suppression of the manufacture of, internal trade in, and use of prepared opium, with due regard to the varying circumstances of each country concerned, unless regulations on the subject are already in existence.

Article 7.—The Contracting Parties shall prohibit the import and export of prepared opium; those Powers, however, which are not ready immediately to prohibit the export of prepared opium, shall prohibit it as soon as possible.

Article 8.—The Contracting Powers which are not yet ready to prohibit immediately the export of prepared opium:

(a) Shall restrict the number of towns, ports, or other localities through which prepared opium may be exported;

(b) Shall prohibit the export of prepared opium to countries which now forbid, or which may hereafter forbid, the import thereof;

(c) Shall, in the meanwhile, prohibit the consignment of prepared opium to a country which desires to restrict its entry, unless the exporter complies with the regulations of the importing country;

(d) Shall take measures to ensure that every package exported, containing prepared opium, bears a special mark indicating the nature of its contents;

(e) Shall not permit the export of prepared opium except by specially authorized persons.

The inadequacy of these articles themselves is not here in question. But the fact that the Committee neither sought to remedy that inadequacy, nor to ensure that even these meagre undertakings were fulfilled, must be regarded as a serious lapse in the performance of its duties. The First Geneva Opium Conference which met in 1925, thirteen years later, decided that the circumstances were still unfavourable to the conclusion of a convention to suppress opium smoking.[1] It was agreed that when the Council should judge the time ripe, when opium smuggling, that is, should have ceased to be an impediment to the control of smoking, and when a League commission of inquiry should have established this fact, another conference might be called which should aim at abolishing the smoking of opium within fifteen years. It is now more than eight years since this agreement was reached, but the commission of inquiry has not yet been suggested, and the beginning of the fifteen-year period is not yet in sight.

It is true that in 1930 an extensive inquiry by a special commission was made into opium smoking in the Far East, and that in 1931 a conference on the same subject was held in Bangkok by the Powers directly concerned. But neither the inquiry nor the Conference were those foreseen in the Geneva Opium Agreement. Nor, unfortunately, did they further the implied aims of the Hague Convention of 1912, and a considerable expenditure of time and money has left the smoking problem exactly where it was in 1925, if not in 1912. It is true

[1] See above, p. 91.

that the Commission of Enquiry collected a quantity of valuable information on opium smoking in the Far East. But the Bangkok Conference practically ignored its recommendations. The gist of the Agreement reached was as follows:

1. The retail sale and distribution of smoking opium is to be confined to Government owned and managed shops, or to shops supervised by the Government and managed by Government appointees who must be paid a fixed salary by the Government. This need not apply, however, where the system of rationing exists.

2. Minors are not permitted to enter smoking-dens, and any-one aiding or abetting a minor is to be punished.

3. Opium is to be sold for cash only.

4. One Government monopoly may be supplied by another, situated in a different territory, only if it belongs to the same Power.

The Advisory Committee had no part in suggesting or appointing the Commission of Enquiry, or in preparing the Bangkok Conference.

When the Conference had concluded its work, however, its results were gone over at great length in the Committee. Mr. Lyall, League Assessor, expressed his regret that these results were not more considerable. He recalled Article 6 of the Hague Convention, reminded the Committee that the contracting Powers had not fulfilled their obligations under it, and accordingly proposed the following resolution:

The Advisory Committee feels that it is its duty to point out that, whatever difficulties the Governments concerned may experience in suppressing opium smoking, it is incompatible with the above-quoted article (6) of the Hague Convention for a Government to sell opium for smoking to a person who had not contracted the habit of smoking at the time when the Government in question ratified the Hague Convention:

The Advisory Committee therefore recommends that in all territories in which opium smoking is still temporarily authorized, the following measures be adopted if this has not already been done:

(1) That opium for smoking shall in future be sold only to registered smokers;

(2) That a short time-limit be fixed in which opium smokers may register as such, and that, after this period has elapsed, no additions shall be made to the list of registered smokers.[1]

It must be evident that if this simple measure had not long before been taken by all the signatories of the Hague Convention, their duties could not possibly have been fulfilled. But Mr. Lyall's proposal was objected to by the delegates of France, Great Britain, India, the Netherlands, and Siam, on the ground that "it amounted to an unjustified charge that their Governments had failed to carry out their treaty obligations."[2] The proposal was defeated by nine votes to three, with four abstentions. The Final Act of the Bangkok Conference contained a recommendation for research to be undertaken by the Governments on some chemical and physiological aspects of the problem. As the assistance of the Advisory Committee was requested in this matter, that body suggested that the Governments concerned be asked what facilities could be provided for such researches, and what had already been done in this connection. The Italian delegate declared that he would abstain from the vote on this question as a protest against the fact that twenty years after the Hague Convention had been put into force, no advance had been made beyond the stage of research work. This dissatisfaction was shared by a large minority of the Advisory Committee. The Belgian delegate submitted the following resolution:

The Advisory Committee on Traffic in Opium and other Dangerous Drugs, noting that for various reasons the Bangkok Conference has not given the results expected of it, strongly urges all the States of

---

[1] *Report to the Council on the 15th Session*, pp. 11, 12.

[2] Ibid., p. 12.

The Far East to take as quickly as possible more radical measures of all kinds to suppress gradually the opium habit in these regions, reducing both consumption and production.[1]

But the members of the Committee whose Governments were directly concerned rejected the implied censure, voted down the resolution, and were thus responsible for putting the Advisory Committee on record as satisfied that everything possible had been done toward suppressing opium smoking, while all the available facts pointed in the opposite direction.

There was little reason to suppose that the Bangkok Conference might arrive at a constructive agreement for suppressing opium smoking. Since 1925 none of the fundamental conditions had changed. Public opinion was focussed, not on the Far East, but on the manufactured drugs centres of Europe. Again, only the Governments immediately concerned went to Bangkok, thus eliminating from the discussions any fresh or critical opinion. A few months earlier the Limitation Conference had succeeded in framing a convention limiting the manufacture of drugs to medical needs. The ultimate result will be the liberation of large quantities of raw opium, no longer in demand for manufacture, for the smoking market of the East. To reduce the production of the raw material will henceforth be doubly necessary. It was the minimum duty of the Bangkok Conference, if immediate suppression could not be agreed upon, to begin the process by setting a figure representing the present maximum needs of opium for legalized smoking purposes, and, regardless of the illicit traffic, to limit the monopolies to this amount. If Government restriction of smoking is to wait on the decline of the illicit traffic, it will never be begun, but the danger of causing an increase in the traffic has consistently been given as the reason for not tightening Government control. It would seem obvious, however, that only a greatly reduced production of opium can ever effectively stop the illicit traffic, and as such

[1] *Report to the Council on the 15th Session*, p. 14.

reduction presupposes a definite quantitative limit, it becomes the duty of the consuming Governments to agree upon and fix this limit. This first step ought to have been taken at Bangkok. It ought, rather, to have been taken immediately after the Geneva Agreement was signed. There seems certainly to be no reason for the complete lack of policy on the part of the Advisory Committee with regard to this problem, which has been neglected to such an extent that even the most elementary measures mean an advancement toward its solution. In failing to achieve results the Bangkok Conference not merely left the opium-smoking problem as unsolved as before, but it will have made the problem of reducing the cultivation of opium more difficult by its failure to arrive at some quantitative figure of legalized needs. Yet to this meaningless Agreement of Bangkok the Advisory Committee gave the seal of its approval.

9. The Direct Limitation of Drug Production

The year 1929 saw a crisis in the drug situation. The Assembly that year voted for a new approach to the whole problem: new, that is, in the sense that it had not before been tried, for as an idea it was older than the earliest opium convention. Direct limitation of the production of drugs, it was finally determined, offered the only certain solution of the narcotics problem. Although many references have already been made to this Assembly resolution, and to the discussions on limitation in the Advisory Committee, it is impossible to conclude a study of the Committee without considering separately and in its entirety the part it has played in this most significant of the developments in drug control.

In the 1st Session of the Advisory Committee the first definite proposal on this subject was made when Mrs. Hamilton Wright, Assessor, suggested that a conference be called to consider the suppression of poppy cultivation.[1] But the proposal was scarcely given serious consideration. The representative of the Government of India went so far as to state that the suppression of poppy cultivation was beyond the scope of the Hague Convention, and therefore not a subject with which the Committee was competent to deal.[2] In the 2nd Session, it is true, a resolution was passed by the Committee to the effect that the Council should call upon any Government to investigate the production of drugs within its territory when there seemed need for it, but this was only reluctantly adopted as an alternative to immediate general investigation of the situation in all opium-growing countries, and the Committee never called upon the Council to exercise this power with regard to any particular country.

There was an incident also in the 1st Session of the Committee which might have opened the way to a discussion of drug limitation by the most direct means possible. This was the receipt of a letter from a firm of drug manufacturers in England offering their expert services to the League in any capacity which might be needed. The firm was apparently under the impression that the League was about to institute a world monopoly, housed in a League factory, for whose administration the services of experts in this field would be required. It happened that this was not the case. It is not likely that the possibility was even thought of. It was certainly not discussed, and the interesting avenue of possibilities which discussion of the letter indicated remained closed. The suggestion was not, however, entirely fantastic. It indeed presents itself as an almost obvious solution to the observer who sees the results of anarchy in drug production. The establishment of a League drug factory possessing a world monopoly of narcotics manufacture, operated by internationally directed experts, was the subject of a serious proposal made by the Chinese Government to the Committee in its 13th Session in 1930. The proposal emanated from a Chinese

[1] *Advisory Committee*, 1st Session, p. 23.   [2] Ibid., p. 13.

official, a doctor, whose medical and administrative experiences with the opium problem led him to this possible solution. The Committee, however, gave the proposal no notice whatever, although it had been specially directed by the Assembly at this session to consider fully any and all proposals for direct limitation which might come before it.

But the most urgent appeal to the Committee to consider direct limitation was on the occasion of the presentation of the American proposals in 1923. This has already been discussed in some detail.[1] In due course the Council, upon being informed of these proposals, authorized the summoning of an international conference under League auspices to give effect to them. It appointed a Preparatory Committee to draft a plan upon which the Conference could base its work. It has already been pointed out that the Council summoned the Geneva Conference expressly to give effect to the American proposals, and that in framing certain "Measures" which might serve as a guide to the Conference, a task which the Advisory Committee performed when the Preparatory Committee failed to come to an agreement, the chief principle of these proposals was lost. They were defeated, in spite of strong British support, by French opposition. Instead of "the limitation of the amounts of morphine, heroin, or cocaine and their respective salts to be manufactured," and "the limitation of the production of raw opium and the coca leaf for export to the amount required for . . . medicinal and scientific purposes,"[2] the Measures of the Advisory Committee provided for the strict control of the trade in drugs and opium, both through national and international administrative machinery.

These Measures were not, of course, forced upon the Conference. But the Conference, heavily influenced by the same Governments that controlled the decisions of the Advisory Committee, also rejected the idea of direct limitation, and

[1] See above, p. 58.   [2] The American terms.

drafted a convention which went much less far than the Advisory Committee itself had done.

In 1925 the Advisory Committee considered the illicit traffic in opium coming from Persia, which was being carried on in the Persian Gulf. This, it would seem, might have led the Committee naturally on to consider the problem of reducing the cultivation of opium, especially in view of the decision taken at the First Geneva Conference to the effect that the suppression of opium smoking could not be undertaken until the cultivation of the poppy in producing countries had been curtailed. As this indirect reference to production was the closest approach the Conference made to the question, and as no hint of a programme for effecting limitation was contained in the Agreement signed by the Conference, the Advisory Committee did not feel itself entitled to proceed further in this direction. The Conference did include in its Final Act, however, a resolution to the effect that any country desiring it might ask a Commission of the League to collaborate with it in studying the problems of limiting opium cultivation within its borders. In accordance with this resolution the Persian Government asked the Council in 1925 to send a commission of inquiry into Persia to investigate the cultivation of opium. The Commission was accordingly appointed, and at the next session of the Assembly, in 1927, presented its account of the Persian opium situation. The Commission investigated its problem in relation to the special economic conditions in Persia, and concluded that a reduction of the opium crop would have to be accompanied by the scientific substitution of other crops, whose selection and culture would require about five years' time. Careful study was made of the suitability of different crops to the soil. Such related questions as road transport, water supply, taxation, and finance were also studied in conjunction with Persian officials, and a practicable policy for their development outlined.[1]

[1] Document A. 7, 1927, XI.

The report was interesting not only for the valuable contribution it made toward limiting opium production, but as an indication that similar investigations in other opium-producing regions would undoubtedly be profitable. But no other Government has emulated the admirable example of Persia, and the Advisory Committee has taken no action to prompt further investigations. Yet the information to be obtained by this means, and the familiarity with the many phases of the opium problem which could only be gained in this way, were the obvious and necessary basis of any programme which might be undertaken to reduce the production of opium.

With the exception of Signor Cavazzoni, who became a member of the Advisory Committee in 1927 as Italy's first delegate, the whole of the Committee was opposed to limiting the production of narcotic substances by direct means. It was the general opinion that when the trade in drugs was brought under control the supply would naturally limit itself to the demands of legitimate trade. The application of the Geneva Convention was expected to bring about this state of affairs. The statistics of the League actually showed, in the five years following the signing of the Convention, that the conditions of the lawful trade in narcotics were justifying this hope of the Committee. Between the signing and the ratifying of the Convention a tremendous increase in drug production took place. In Germany the manufacture of morphine rose from 14,000 kgs. in 1925 to 20,700 kgs. in 1926. In Switzerland the increase was from 4,680 kgs. to 8,038 kgs. in the same period. The total manufacture of morphine and heroin in the principal manufacturing countries in that year was increased by 11,930 kgs.[1] It was evident that manufacturers felt that the ratification of the Convention was going to have an adverse influence on the trade. And with the coming into effect of the Convention it became clear that their expectations were well founded. Trade and

[1] From statistics contained in Document O.C. 1072, 1930.

manufacture figures fell steadily, if not fantastically, year after year. Under the watch of the Permanent Central Board a measure of certainty and stability with regard to the volume of trade was approached which had not previously been known. But the significant factor in the situation now was not the control of the legal trade in drugs, but the extent of the clandestine traffic. That this was enormous was evident. Both the figures at the disposal of the Central Board and the seizure figures submitted to the Advisory Committee gave ample proof of it. The police were uncovering the traces of vast organizations of smugglers, whose operations were made possible in a number of instances by the deliberate manufacture of drugs for the illicit traffic. Reputable and disreputable firms alike were implicated. Because of the absence of exact figures of legitimate needs in drugs, it was not always possible to tell when a given quantity, supposedly legitimate, might not cover leakage into the illicit traffic. Although the Geneva Convention had not yet had time to function, impatience grew rapidly.

This was the situation when, in 1928, a new proposal for the direct limitation of the manufacture of drugs was presented to the Advisory Committee.[1] It was known as the Crane Scheme,[2] being submitted by Mr. C. K. Crane, through the medium of the State Department of the United States. Its author was actually Mr. A. E. Blanco, at the time a member of the League Opium Section, now head of the Anti-Opium Information Bureau: Geneva. Mr. Blanco, having drafted the Scheme, tried to have it presented by the Secretariat to the Advisory Committee. This failed, but Mr. Crane was interested in the plan and forwarded it to the State Department whence it was sent to the Netherlands Government and to the States members of the League. In brief outline the Crane Scheme proposed:

[1] *Advisory Committee*, 11th Session, p. 123.
[2] Ibid., 12th Session, p. 300. Text: Document C. 251, M. 114, 1931, XI.

1. Notification by each country in advance of the amounts of each of the drugs required for legitimate consumption in the following year, and designation of the country of purchase.
2. Responsibility of each Government for enforcing the quota of manufacture thus automatically established.
3. Economic pressure to be brought against a non-adhering country establishing a "pirate factory." [1]

At the 11th Session of the Committee, the Scheme was disposed of without the benefit of any discussion whatever, on the ground that Mr. Crane was himself not familiar with all the details. The covering letter indicated plainly that the author was not Mr. Crane, but neither that fact, nor the consideration that the Scheme might be discussed on its own merits, carried any weight with the Committee. At its next session a letter from Mr. Crane to the Secretary-General clearing up the question of the authorship of the plan was placed before the Committee, whose Indian member, Sir John Campbell, at once attacked violently the tortuous means which he alleged had been employed in bringing it to the attention of the Committee. This objection, in addition to its irrelevance to the merits or demerits of the plan, was entirely unreasonable. The rules of procedure of the Committee provide that only members of the Committee or Governments shall place a question upon the agenda.[2] If, therefore, a private individual wishes to bring any matter to the attention of the Committee his only approach is through some Government or some member of the Committee itself. He is surely entitled to make use of such connections as he may have with either.

The criticisms of the plan itself were of two kinds. It was generally felt that its consideration was premature, as the results of the Geneva Convention had not yet had time to materialize. But the chief objection was against the substance of the plan, which was styled anything from merely undesirable to iniquitous. Mr. van Wettum opened the discussion by saying

[1] *Advisory Committee*, 12th Session, pp. 288–300.
[2] Ibid., 1st Session, p. 15.

that "he would like to know what the authors of schemes had in mind when they sought to create new international measures at the moment that they had before them a Convention which had given them practically everything they could possibly desire."[1] He intimated, moreover, that economic boycotting was not playing the game. It was not, he said, "the way to the goal sought by the Committee. Moreover, the League had always rejected such proposals."[2] Mr. Sato's objection was that the scheme was contrary to the principle of the freedom of trade, which the Geneva Convention was careful to guarantee.[3] Sir Malcolm Delevingne declared that it was administratively impossible of application, because estimates could never be determined in advance.[4] M. Kahler and Dr. Carrière were equally opposed; but the bitterest attack upon the idea came from Sir John Campbell, who declared at once that he was deeply prejudiced against the Scheme because of the roundabout way in which it had been brought up, and that no country could have any object in adhering to it. The notion of bringing economic pressure to bear on countries which did not adhere was ridiculous. He was extremely impatient with the whole idea, and was anxious only to have all discussion of it over and done with.[5] On the other hand, the Italian and the French delegates defended the plan. M. Bourgois felt that the idea was a valuable one and deserved further consideration. It had the merit of proposing a system of limitation based not on compulsory and arbitrary rationing, but upon ordinary free demand.[6] Signor Cavazzoni welcomed the proposal to study the plan more fully, as all the members of the Committee were representatives of manufacturing countries except himself, and he felt that the plan ought to be laid before other countries with a view to securing a wider set of opinions

[1] *Advisory Committee*, 12th Session, p. 149.
[2] Ibid., p. 150.   [3] Ibid.
[4] Ibid., p. 155. Compare with his statement at the Geneva Conference referred to below, p. 156.
[5] Ibid., pp. 153–155.   [6] Ibid., p. 152.

upon it. The Scheme was, furthermore, a first step in introducing the system of rationing and monopoly which he had so warmly advocated when he first came to the Committee.[1]

But the preponderant opinion was definitely against the Crane Scheme. Without prejudice to future discussion of the principle of limitation of manufacture, the Committee, by a vote of seven to four, adopted Sir John Campbell's resolution, which was put in the following terms: "The Committee, after discussing the Crane Scheme, considered that it should take no action upon it."

But this peremptory treatment of the Crane Scheme did not have the result the Committee intended. Instead of burying the plan, they directed an almost sensational attention to it, and thereby laid themselves open to the charge of ignoring valuable suggestions brought before them, of acting in the limited capacity of representatives of manufacturing countries, and of disregarding their duties as members of an international body. Meanwhile, too, the increase in addiction and smuggling, and the wide publicity given it, had awakened interest in a large number of countries victimized by the drug traffic. These were now convinced of the necessity for limiting the manufacture of drugs by direct methods, and when the Committee made it clear that it would have nothing to do with a plan of this kind, they carried their protests to the Assembly. That body, in its 10th Session, in 1929, passed the following important resolution:[2]

The Assembly,
Impressed by the disclosures made in the report of the Advisory Committee as to the large quantities of dangerous drugs still passing in the illicit traffic;
Recalling the proposals made in the Geneva Conference for the direct limitation, by agreement between the Governments of the manufacturing countries, of the amount of such drugs manufactured;

.   .   .   .

[1] See above, p. 93.   [2] 10 A.P., p. 158.

THE WORK OF THE OPIUM ADVISORY COMMITTEE

(I) Regards the principle of the limitation of the manufacture of drugs mentioned in paragraphs (b), (c), and (g) of Article 4 of the Convention of Geneva by international agreement as now accepted;

(II) Requests the Advisory Committee to prepare plans for such limitation, regard being had to world requirements for medical and scientific purposes and the means of preventing an increase in price which would lead to the establishment of new factories in countries which are not at present manufacturing countries;

(III) The Committee's report will be submitted to the Council which will decide on the convening of a Conference of the Governments in whose countries the above-mentioned drugs are manufactured and the principal consuming countries in a number not exceeding that of the manufacturing countries, and whether certain experts proposed by the Opium and Health Committees should be included;

(IV) Recommends that the Advisory Committee be enlarged in order to secure more effective representation on that Committee of the non-manufacturing countries;

(V) Agrees that the sum of 25,000 Swiss francs shall be included in the budget of the League for 1930 in order to meet the expenses of such a Conference.

In spite of the opinions held by its members, the Advisory Committee was obliged at its next session, in 1930, to act upon the Assembly's resolution. But it was still maintained that the system of control provided by the Geneva Convention, especially the certificate system, was adequate. Mr. van Wettum said that "neither the limitation of manufacture to a definite amount nor the enforced universal establishment of monopolies could be considered to be practical politics. He himself had full confidence in the system of the Geneva Convention. . . ."[1] Dr. Carrière (Switzerland) observed "that his Government had always been, and still was, of the opinion that a method of control by means of export and import certificates, strictly and generally applied, would make it possible to combat the illicit traffic effectively. . . . But these considerations disappeared before the very definite commission that the Assembly had given the Committee. . . ."[2]

---

[1] *Advisory Committee*, 13th Session, p. 46.   [2] Ibid., p. 41.

Dr. Kahler (Germany) was of the opinion that the certificate system had led to a remarkable improvement in the situation. "Considering, as he did, that the import certificate system could be recommended without qualification, Dr. Kahler regretted the desire not to await the ultimate results which the system might yet be expected to yield, especially if more countries ratified the Geneva Convention and thus adopted the system. . . . It was a view, however, which he would not press, seeing that the Assembly had decided in favour of another system—that of direct limitation."[1] On the other hand, the delegates of Great Britain, France, and Japan, considering the principle of direct limitation agreed upon, made no further reference to it, and proceeded to outline plans for its application. The rest of the Committee quickly followed suit.

They decided that three fundamental points had to be considered: (1) the quantity to be manufactured; (2) the allocation of this amount among the present manufacturing countries; and (3) the guarantee that all countries would receive their full requirements.[2] Implicit in this plan was the exclusion of any country not at present manufacturing drugs from that activity. The Japanese delegate was in general agreement with this plan, but he did not feel that any country could be kept from manufacturing its own drug supply if it so desired.[3] It was decided at length that a subcommittee should be named which should study various proposals for giving effect to the Assembly's resolution, not excluding the rejected Crane Scheme.[4]

The Subcommittee on Limitation included Dr. Kahler (Germany), Sir Malcolm Delevingne (Great Britain), M. Ito (Japan), M. Bourgois (France), Sir John Campbell (India), Dr. Carrière (Switzerland), M. Cavazzoni (Italy), Mr. Caldwell (United States), and Mr. van Wettum (Netherlands). Any member of the Permanent Central Board who wished to co-

[1] *Advisory Committee*, 13th Session, p. 43.   [2] Ibid., p. 39.
[3] Ibid.   [4] Ibid., pp. 43, 54.

operate was asked to attend the meetings of the Subcommittee, and Dr. Anselmino accordingly took part in them. Mr. Lyall, member of the Board and Assessor on the Advisory Committee, was also appointed, and a provision made for the attendance of a member of the Health Section.[1]

It was virtually the plan put forward by the British delegate which the Subcommittee on Limitation adopted. Briefly, it proposed (1) the fixation of world production by means of annual estimates of their needs to be submitted by all Governments; (2) the allocation of the world production between the manufacturing countries subject to agreement between themselves, but proportioned approximately on the basis of the present legitimate output, any country in future desiring to begin the manufacture of drugs to give notice to that effect in order to permit a re-allocation of the quotas; and (3) complete freedom of trade within legitimate bounds, the legitimacy of each order received to be determined by a central office before its consignment to the importing country.[2]

The alternative plans considered by the Subcommittee included the Report of the Opium Preparatory Committee which had unsuccessfully attempted in 1924 to draw up a basic plan for the Geneva Conference, the Crane Scheme, the suggestions submitted by M. Bourgois in the present session of the Advisory Committee, letters from M. van Wettum, Dr. Kahler, and Dr. Carrière concerning the existing syndicate of cocaine manufacturers and a projected morphine syndicate, and a letter from the Chinese Government which has already been mentioned, suggesting the establishment of a single international factory under League control.[3]

But for the second time the Committee found its judgment misplaced. Acting in their capacity of representatives of manufacturing countries, they selected a plan which would be favour-

[1] *Advisory Committee*, 13th Session, p. 55.
[2] Ibid., pp. 399, 400. [3] Ibid., p. 399, footnote.

able to their own Governments, failing to take sufficient notice of the interests and possible objections of other countries not represented on the Committee. Two factors worked against the Committee's plan for limitation during the sixteen months between its adoption and the convening of the Limitation Conference. The first was manifested in the Conference of Manufacturers which met in London in November 1930 (at the suggestion of the Council and on the invitation of the British Government). It was the manufacturers themselves who put serious difficulties in the way of the plan by failing to come to an agreement on the allotment of their respective quotas. The second factor was the objection raised by the non-manufacturing countries to what they considered a monopoly of the drug industry to the sole advantage of the large manufacturing countries. Their attitude was expressed in an alternative scheme for limitation, the "Scheme of Stipulated Supply," framed by Mr. Blanco, whose opinion as an impartial but expert observer coincided with their own. In the 14th Session of the Advisory Committee the seven newly appointed representatives of non-manufacturing countries were for the first time present, and this element could therefore express its views directly, as it had never been able to do before.

The chief differences between the two plans was this: whereas the quota system would divide the annual production and export trade among the existing manufacturing countries with the result (a) that no additional countries could be assured of a future share in this activity, and (b) that the consuming countries could not be assured of obtaining their supplies of drugs from the sources which they preferred, the Scheme of Stipulated Supply would secure these privileges to all countries by making it necessary for each Government to state in advance the amounts of drugs to be required by it during the following year, and the country or countries in which it intended to place its orders. The supporters of the quota system maintained that the complete freedom of trade was an essential part of their programme, but the non-manufacturing countries could not be convinced that this was compatible with a quota system of manufacture and export. Later, the Committee's Draft Convention contained a Spanish clause establishing the right of any country to indicate in advance the country or countries from which it wished to secure its supplies. But the mere statement of a principle not implemented with any machinery for its realization remained a paradox in a convention embodying the quota system. The delegate of Yugoslavia also suggested a compromise on the revision of quotas. He suggested that instead of making the quota allocations rigid, or subject to change only by means of a special international conference, some technical body should be empowered to make any changes necessary following the application of a new country for a quota, or for revision of a quota already granted. This would have given the system an elastic quality making it more acceptable to non-manufacturing countries, and at the same time preserving the quota principle to the satisfaction of the manufacturing countries. But the amendment was opposed by the manufacturing countries and lost by eight votes to four, with five abstentions.[1]

The Draft Convention which the Advisory Committee finally adopted after two weeks of deliberation definitely endorsed the quota system. The entire attention of the Committee had been concentrated upon this system of limitation. Occasional attention was necessarily given to alternative principles when they were pressed upon the Committee by dissenting members, but no serious, detailed study was made of any other plans, although several Governments had already informed the Secretary-General of their acceptance of the Scheme of Stipulated Supply. Briefly, the Draft Convention contained the following plan:

[1] *Advisory Committee*, 14th Session, p. 236.

INTERNATIONAL NARCOTICS CONTROL

I. ESTIMATES.

1. Each country shall submit annually to the Permanent Central Board estimates of its needs for consumption and conversion in the following year.

II. QUOTAS.

1. The total world requirements, consisting of the sum of these estimates, minus the quantities manufactured in countries which furnish their own needs alone, shall be divided for manufacture among the following countries . . . (all large manufacturing countries), in the following proportions: . . .[1]

2. Revision of these quotas shall be made by a conference of the manufacturing Governments:

    (a) if any country desires a new quota.

    (b) if the Permanent Central Board reports that a country's quota needs revision due to an increase of orders placed with it, or to declarations of consumers of their intent to increase such orders.

3. If the orders received by an exporting country exceed its quota, transfers shall be arranged between the Governments concerned, or by the Permanent Central Board.

4. Any country may manufacture for its own needs if this purpose is declared when its estimate is submitted.

III. CONTROL.[2]

1. Control shall be vested in a Central Narcotics Office, which shall furnish any estimates which Governments may have failed to submit, and which shall pass on the validity of every order for export before it is filled.

2. The contracting Powers agree to take all measures necessary to carry out the terms of the Convention.

But the Draft did not embody the unanimous views of the Committee. In reporting to the Council on the results of this session's work, the minority[3] added a statement of its own views on the preparatory work for the Limitation Conference. While

---

[1] Left to the decision of the Conference.

[2] Price control was left to be arranged by the Conference.

[3] China, Mexico, Poland, Spain, Uruguay.

138

paying tribute to the endeavours of the Committee which they recognized had resulted in "a considerable step forward," they hoped that the Conference would also take notice of the following suggestions:

1. A system of limitation to be decided upon by the Convention to safeguard the rights of each nation to procure, for its legitimate needs, drugs from the source, and the country it chooses.

2. Each country should make known in advance the quantity of narcotic drugs falling under the provisions of the Convention of which it will be in need for a fixed period as well as the name of the country or countries where it intends to procure its supplies.

.   .   .   .

5. Both the limitation of manufacture and the control of the quantities manufactured should be guaranteed by the action of the Permanent Central Opium Board, assisted, where necessary, by technical authorities.

It was these two opposing plans for effecting limitation which formed the bone of contention at the Limitation Conference. The result was the defeat of both; but if the chief aim of the minority in the Advisory Committee, and of the other non-manufacturing countries whose views they shared, was to keep the manufacturing countries from forming a monopoly, they succeeded in their purpose. And in doing this they served the medical profession well, for a greater danger inherent in the quota-monopoly system was the possibility of price control and dictation, a danger against which the Committee, in the course of discussion, found no safeguard, and which might have had serious results for the medical practice. They also served the interests of free and open production and trade, in the best liberalist manner. But whether the protection gained for the medical profession could not as well have been achieved by a greater stress on control, and on the development of machinery for control, either on a national or on an international basis, but in any case with final authority in an international organ,

is a question which has received too scanty attention. It can
scarcely be denied that the quota system, under the proper
control, would have secured a much more trustworthy safeguard against the illicit traffic than the general freedom of all
countries to engage in the manufacture of dangerous drugs,
even under the same control. But the clash with a system
which, in avoiding its defects, ran the risk of diffusing drug
production over a wide area and indefinitely multiplying the
difficulties of control, to the very possible benefit of the illicit
traffic, did not, unfortunately, result in the drafting of a convention in every respect superior to both. Under the terms of
the Limitation Convention every country undertakes to limit
its manufacture of drugs during the course of a year to the
estimates which it has submitted to the Central Board before
the beginning of that year. These estimates cover the quantities
of drugs to be used internally, and to fill export orders. They are
to be examined by a special Supervisory Body of independent
experts, and revised, if necessary, before the beginning of the
year to which they apply. Thereafter no control whatever of
the manufacture of drugs can be exercised by any central organ
until three months after the close of the year, when the Central
Board will have at hand the annual reports of all Governments,
which include the statistics of manufacture and a summary of
quarterly manufacturers' reports to their Governments. If these
reports reveal an excess of manufacture the responsible Governments undertake to deduct that amount from the estimates for
the following year. The Board, if it is not satisfied with any
country's explanation of an excessive accumulation of drugs
within its territory, may recommend an embargo on drugs to
the country in question, according to the terms of the Geneva
Convention. Trade, also, is not controlled as it was planned
under the quota system. The Central Board is not given any
control over individual orders, except those going to non-
contracting countries, but is confined still, by the terms of the

Geneva Convention, to examining quarterly reports and to making recommendations on the basis of them.

Under the terms of the Convention, then, all distinction between a "manufacturing" or "exporting" and a "non-manufacturing" country disappears. Prices and supply will seek their level according to the laws of ordinary competition, and no particular industry will profit at the expense of another by reason of any imposed restriction. Definite undertakings are given by the contracting parties to control factories by means of rigid inspection, and to organize administrative departments exclusively for the exercise of this control. Quarterly reports from manufacturers are to be required by each Government, and a strict watch kept over the importation of raw materials.

Whether these provisions will be carried out successfully depends entirely upon the efforts of the national administrations. The chief burden of control rests with them. While the Permanent Central Board retains its supervisory powers over the trade, and may keep a remote watch over the manufacture, it is not placed in a position to take an active and effective part in limitation. Part of the success of the Geneva Convention has been due to the efforts of the Central Board to improve national administrative machinery, which is the main implement it has to use in carrying out its own functions. But as an organ established to supervise the trade in drugs it was able to do this, whereas, not endowed with any direct powers over the limitation of manufacture, it will be in a less favourable position for establishing contact with national administrations on this point. It is very possible, however, that in practice, when the Limitation Convention actually comes into effect, this difficulty may melt away. The confidence which the Board has established in its impartiality and efficiency will do much to make it the hub and centre of any new administrative developments. But the chance of this natural continuation of its function does not in any way alter the fact that the Conference, and before it the Advisory

Committee, neglected to secure to it, or to some new central organ, a power of control which past events and developments have proved wise and necessary. It is true that the minority on the Advisory Committee asked that the limitation of manufacture as well as the control of the trade should be in the hands of the Central Board and assistant technicians, but the time and energy which they spent in urging this cause cannot be compared with that spent in trying to defeat the quota system. The Central Narcotics Office proposed by the majority of the Committee, on the other hand, was to have no powers of control over limitation, nor were any measures provided in the Draft Convention for securing national control, as is the case in the Limitation Convention.

In view of the complicated nature of the problem, and of the manifold difficulties which appear on every hand to thwart control under any system, the insistent demands of the victims of addiction, the rich rewards of the traffickers, the ingenuousness of the smuggler, the very difficult problem of policing, it would appear that a complete departure from ordinary methods, a radical change in the policy hitherto followed, would have been given the most serious consideration by the Committee. Such a departure, and such a radical change was inherent in only one of all the plans laid before the Advisory Committee during the discussions on limitation. This was the plan of the Chinese Government for the establishment of a single factory, which, under the control of the League and the management of experts, would supply the total world needs in opiates. Control of the licit output of drugs and the distribution of this output would thereby be reduced to the simplest possible terms, and the work of national administrations would be confined to the policing necessary to prevent all other production of drugs whatever. No doubt could exist that any drugs discovered not bearing official markings, or not, perhaps, conveyed by a special transport service, were of illicit origin; there could be no question that any factory discovered to be manufacturing drugs was doing so illegally. Its suppression would be automatic, and not, as has been the case in the past, bound up with and hindered by its participation in the licit trade. There could be no further danger, for a manufacturer intent on maintaining the integrity of his business, of finding his goods, long after they had passed out of his control, in the channels of the illicit traffic. The large drug manufacturing concerns do not confine themselves to the making of narcotic substances; they supply the chemist with the complete line of his wares. To eliminate from among their products this single item would not in any case ruin any of those firms which were considering the establishment of a cartel among themselves. The number of persons employed in the manufacture of narcotics is extremely small; the contribution of the industry to the national wealth of any country is entirely insignificant.[1] But even though the contrary were true, it could not for a moment outweigh the necessity of establishing a sure control over the production of substances so dangerous to the general welfare. To say, in this age of mechanical and organizational proficiency, that the establishment of a single drug factory under international control is a Utopian notion, technically impossible and impracticable, is obviously ridiculous. It is the argument of those who lack the will to carry out such a plan; the means are not lacking.

For some years the question of reducing the cultivation of the opium poppy and of the coca shrub had been in the background, while the limitation of manufacture was under discussion. But fundamental to the problem of checking the abuse of narcotic drugs is the problem of limiting the production of raw materials from which they are made. Axiomatic as this principle is, it remained unrecognized until 1932, when, in circumstances similar to those in which attention was finally turned to the

[1] Mr. Blanco estimates the value of the world's legitimate drug industry to be $6,000,000 annually.

direct limitation of drug manufacture, the Advisory Committee placed the question upon its agenda for discussion in its 15th Session. In 1930, at the beginning of its discussions on drug manfacture, the Committee's Japanese member, Mr. Ito, declared that the question of raw materials was inevitably bound up with that of manufactured drugs; in failing to include the former in its resolution to limit manufacture, the Assembly had not dealt adequately with the problem; it was the duty of the Committee, therefore, to decide at once upon measures for dealing with both.[1] But Sir John Campbell (India) felt that the opium-producing countries, not being parties to the existing conventions, could not be given the responsibility of reducing their output. It would, moreover, be outside the mandate of the Committee as expressed in the Assembly resolution to discuss this matter.[2] Signor Cavazzoni (Italy) believed that a discussion of opium production at the time would only increase the difficulty of the manufactured drugs problem, which ought to be got out of the way first.

It was perhaps wise to delay the discussion of raw materials for the moment. Limiting the manufacture of drugs, though only part of the whole problem, might well claim the entire attention of the Committee. But it is the neglect of the question in previous sessions, and the failure at this time at least to establish the relationship of the two problems, that raises doubt of the Committee's attitude. Although the Assembly resolution did not mention raw materials, it was the duty of the Committee to call to the attention of the Council that this problem existed, and had soon to be dealt with. Yet there was no mention made in the Committee's report to the Council after the 13th Session of the suggestion of Mr. Ito, nor any hint given that the efforts to limit manufacture would ultimately depend for their success upon the control exercised over raw materials.

The 14th Session was of course taken up almost entirely with

[1] *Advisory Committee*, 13th Session, p. 38.   [2] Ibid., p. 40.

the draft convention which the Committee prepared for the Limitation Conference. Raw materials were not mentioned. But during the course of the deliberations the representative of Turkey stated that the total annual output of Turkish opium amounted to 400 tons.[1] The Yugoslav delegate declared that his country's yield annually was over 100 tons.[2] Both these amounts went to supply the European drug factories. In another section of the report to the Council in which these statements were given, it was explained that "The world's requirements in raw materials for medical needs are, exclusive of the large quantities used by the opium monopolies of the Far East, approximately 350 tons."[3] But the implication of these figures seemed to escape the Committee. It was certainly not made the basis for any remark upon the dangers to the control of drug manufacture inherent in excessive opium production.

If there was ever any intention on the part of the Committee to propose limiting the production of raw materials, the failure to do so in the 14th Session lost for it its last opportunity. Before it met again in the following year three proposals to deal with this problem had been made. The first was made in the Council in its 62nd Session, when a resolution was passed authorizing the Advisory Committee to study the possibility of calling a conference of the Governments of opium-producing countries for the purpose of limiting their production.[4] The second was made in the Limitation Conference when the Soviet delegation moved that raw materials should be limited together with the manufactured drugs.[5] Needless to say the motion received the affirmative vote only of the Soviet delegation. The instructions of the other delegates did not cover such wide ground. And thirdly, the Twelfth Assembly in 1931 adopted a

[1] *Advisory Committee*, 14th Session, p. 234.
[2] Ibid., p. 237.   [3] Ibid.
[4] *Report to the Council on the 15th Session*, p. 14.
[5] *Records of the Limitation Conference*, p. 258.

resolution put forward by the delegate of Panama, asking the Advisory Committee to begin the preparation of materials necessary for the Conference.[1]

It was thus the inescapable duty of the Committee, when it met in its 15th Session in 1932, to take definite action on this question of raw materials. It discussed plans for a questionnaire which was to be sent to the Governments concerned, and noted the proposal of the United States representative for universal participation in the work of the Conference.[2] The principle of reducing and limiting the cultivation of raw materials was accepted by the leading opium-growing States, Persia, Turkey, and Yugoslavia.[3] But two of the chief producers of the coca shrub seem unwilling to adopt it. Peru has not yet replied, and Bolivia has repeated her declaration of 1924 to the effect that she cannot undertake to limit the production of coca leaves.[4]

10. *Conclusions*

The foundations of most of the troubles of the Advisory Committee were laid before its career began. It may be well to review briefly the steps leading to its organization.

The Peace Conference, it will be remembered, in Article 23c of the Covenant, established League supervision over all agreements relating to the control of the narcotics traffic. Accordingly, the First Assembly adopted the British resolution put forward by Mr. Barnes to the effect that the League take upon itself the special work of the Netherlands Government under the Hague Opium Convention,[5] and that a special organ be appointed to assist and advise the Council upon any question and to secure co-operation between the various Governments.[6]

The Committee has always interpreted narrowly the principles

[1] *Report to Council on 15th Session*, p. 14.   [2] Ibid.
[3] Ibid.   [4] Ibid.   [5] 1 A.C. ii, p. 253.
[6] 1 A.P., p. 538, and *Advisory Committee*, 6th Session, p. 104.

upon which it was founded, keeping close to the bare letter of the Conventions in deciding what the legitimate scope of its functions should be. It is unfortunate that the articles of constitution in question have lent themselves to this conservative tendency in the Committee. They could, with greater justice, have been used to support a broader, more enterprising spirit.[1] The Committee did not see that by establishing international supervision over the execution of conventions, the Peace Commission was already going far beyond any provision of the Hague Convention, and that the Covenant, as the later treaty, deserved precedence over the other. If the signatories of the Covenant agreed to establish international supervision it follows that the organ of that supervision was entitled to adopt the powers necessary to its function. But the Committee looked constantly to the Hague Convention for the measure of its powers although its existence was not even foreseen in that instrument. Although the Committee existed by virtue of the Covenant, it consistently failed to recognize in itself the device of a new order.

But this narrow view of the Committee on the scope of its powers must be explained in terms of the composition of the Committee itself. The Assembly agreed that membership should fall to countries directly interested in opium production. Mr. Barnes wisely stipulated that the non-producing countries should be represented by League assessors, appointed by the Council. Actually the Council named as its assessors persons with a special technical knowledge of the situation. While this was also an important qualification, the number of assessors appointed was unfortunately too small to carry much weight in the Committee's discussions, nor have they had the right to vote. Although their attitude has been always alert and progressive, the Council has given too little attention to their views,

[1] See text of Assembly resolution of December 15, 1920, creating the Advisory Committee, above, p. 47, footnote.

which have frequently dissented from those of the rest of the Committee.

Organized as it was, the Committee could scarcely have developed differently. It was necessarily the interests of the Governments they represented which the members of the Committee served. The humanitarian aspects of the problem have not, of course, been forgotten. They are constantly referred to; but in seeking the solution of the drug question as a humanitarian one, each member of the Committee has been especially sensitive to the probable reactions of the Government he represented, to the responses of the administrations which would be affected, and the industries which would feel the restraints of control. These factors in the problem are not insurmountable, but the Committee has not been the body to take the necessary drastic action upon them. And precisely in being too respectful toward these difficulties in its task, the Committee made their solution impossible. It is not in measures to which the drug industry will agree, or which existing administrative departments can apply without upsetting their methods, that remedies are to be found.

It is almost incredible that in the thirteen years of its existence the Advisory Committee has failed to put forward one comprehensive policy for ending the narcotic traffic. It is nevertheless a fact that it not only failed to formulate a plan of action, but actually rejected every such plan that was placed before it, until, in 1929, the Assembly took a hand in the situation. Such proposals were those of the special American delegation in 1923, of Colonel Woods, Dr. Anselmino, Signor Cavazzoni, Mr. Sirks, Mr. Blanco, and the Chinese delegate. Meanwhile, the Committee studied figures and produced numerous inventions designed to check the stream of the illicit traffic at various points. Not that these inventions were poor in themselves. On the contrary. The certificate system fairly stopped the use of the open routes of trade for the illicit traffic. The black list supplied the police with information on the illicit traffic. Uniform labels and etiquettes made it easier to trace drugs found in the illicit traffic to their sources. Careful information on seizures made it possible at length to watch certain ports and trade routes for illicit drugs. These were all excellent measures, but they were not appropriate to the problem. They were aimed at the symptoms of the trouble rather than at its source. In proving the inventive genius of their authors they also revealed their authors' misconception of the fundamental nature of the problem, and thereby explained the failure to produce any comprehensive policy.

These developments may well be explained by another feature in the composition of the Advisory Committee. Most of the Governments elected to membership on it nominated as their representatives either administrative officials or their permanent delegates at the League. The latter are not especially qualified for work on the Opium Committee. Their duties are extensive and general and it is not expected that their knowledge of opium questions will be complete or first hand. The former, indeed, have brought two very great advantages. They have given the Committee the benefit of their knowledge and experience as experts; and they have established a direct and personal connection between the Committee and their respective administrative departments. It is this element which has led in the activity of the Committee, and is responsible for the quality of its achievements. And both the intrinsic merits of these achievements and their fundamental inadequacy may in great part be attributed to one cause, namely, that while the administrator has trained himself to elaborate and adapt a general formula, he has not been trained to create a general policy. It is unreasonable to expect him to perform one type of function at home, and a distinctly different type at Geneva. If this dual qualification was expected of the members of the Committee the Assembly and the Governments which set it up and permitted it to continue in this form are chiefly to blame for its failure to achieve greater things.

If, on the other hand, the Committee had been composed entirely of responsible administrative officials it might have been the means of establishing habits of collaboration and direct contact between the several national administrative departments. But it was scarcely more fitted for this than for the directive and creative work which only an unbureaucratic and independent organ might have been expected to do. But before alternative suggestions for reorganization can be made it is necessary to discuss the form and function of the other organ which deals with the traffic, the Permanent Central Opium Board.

CHAPTER III

THE ORIGINS OF THE PERMANENT CENTRAL OPIUM BOARD

THE Permanent Central Opium Board, whose creation was the most outstanding achievement of the Second Geneva Opium Conference, was in origin a compromise. It was, on the one hand, the least decisive measure of control acceptable to those delegates to the Conference who wished, in any case, to see a plan of direct limitation of drug manufacture replace the methods of control hitherto in use. On the other hand, it was the greatest concession which most of the delegations to the conference would make toward internationalizing control in one central, non-national organ. The powers given the Central Board were the measure of national control with which the various States could be persuaded to part.

The creation of the Central Board was, secondly, a silent admission that a need existed for more drastic supervision of the drug trade than any existing organ had yet fulfilled. Specific powers were given it which the Advisory Committee on the Traffic in Opium had declared itself incompetent to assume. How much more competence the Committee might have taken on without prejudice to the legality of its position is a question which has already been gone into at length. An impartial and expert membership was also given the Board, which made it better able to fulfil certain technical functions that the Advisory Committee, as it was constituted, could perform.

1. The Suggestions of the Opium Advisory Committee

It was not without difficulty that the Permanent Central Board was set up as an independent organ with comparatively important powers. A struggle was involved which brought to light many interesting attitudes toward the opium and drug problem, and by its successful outcome proved how deep the necessity was which could overcome such strong opposition.

In preparation for the Geneva Drug Conference the Council appointed a small body of men to design a draft convention which could be submitted to the Conference when it met, as a basis of discussion. This body, the Opium Preparatory Committee, was composed of Sir Malcolm Delevingne (Great Britain), Mr. Neville (United States), M. Bourgois (France), Mr. van Wettum (Netherlands), and M. Brenier and Sir John Jordan, assessors. It was kept to this limited size for reasons of expense, nor was it found possible to follow the suggestion that other Governments might send members to collaborate informally with the Committee. The efforts of the Opium Preparatory Committee did not result in a unanimous agreement on the plan to be followed at the Conference. The British and American views, holding to the principles of the American proposals which have been accepted by the Advisory Committee, and which were, by the Council's resolution, to be the basis of the Conference, insisted on the direct limitation of production. The French as firmly insisted that the control of the trade was the superior method. As Sir John Jordan later pointed out, the Preparatory Committee had not met as an expert group, but as representatives of Governments, each of which had a definite policy to defend.[1]

In order that the Advisory Committee might present a united front at the Conference, it agreed to appoint a new subcommittee which should attempt to come to an agreement where the Preparatory Committee had failed. Sir John Campbell (India) and Dr. Anselmino (Germany) were thus added to the original membership of the Preparatory Committee, and this subcommittee drew up the draft plan which, with slight modifications, was presented to the Conference as the "Measures

[1] *Advisory Committee*, 6th Session, pp. 7, 8.

Suggested by the Advisory Committee as a Basis for the Deliberations of the Second Conference."[1]

The Measures were a compromise between the French and the American viewpoints. While the proposal of the United States was definitely rejected, and the plan frankly adopted indirect limitation through control of the trade, this was severely modified by the proposal to establish the Permanent Central Opium Board. The merits of this proposed body won the support of the Americans, who did not, however, abandon the principle of the direct limitation of production, which they upheld at the Conference against great opposition. Although the Permanent Central Board was intended to reinforce the system of trade control, it was not unadaptable to the principle of direct limitation, and its support by the partisans of this idea was not incompatible with their position. They were, in fact, more ardent in supporting its establishment than the delegates of the Governments which pressed for control of the trade. These presented the same arguments against it as against the direct limitation of manufacture, namely, that it encroached upon a legitimate field of national activity, and sought to submit national authority to a higher direction.

Briefly, the Central Board proposed in the "Measures" drawn up by the Advisory Committee was to have the following form and function. It was to be constituted of experts chosen by the Council of the League on the advice of the Opium Advisory Committee. It was to require from each of the Governments an annual estimate of its needs in the coming year of raw opium, coca leaves, or of any of the substances derived from them, either for purposes of domestic consumption, manufacture, or commerce. The Board was to receive also from all of the Governments quarterly statistics of imports, exports, and re-exports of each of the drugs, and half-yearly statistics of the amounts manufactured and of the stocks remaining in the

[1] *Advisory Committee*, 6th Session, p. 26.

hands of the wholesale dealers. At the end of each year, finally, it was to receive the figures of the total amount of each of the drugs consumed as such, during that year.

On the basis of these figures the Central Board was to keep a check on the amounts of drugs in each country, and if the estimates of any of them were exceeded, to inform all of the Governments of the situation. These would then undertake not to export any more drugs to the country in question during the course of that year. The Board was also to have the important power of itself furnishing an estimate of the legitimate needs of any country, including non-contracting parties, which did not submit its own estimate, and of revising the estimate of any country which might have submitted, in the judgment of the Board, an excessive estimate. If an exporting country objected to curtailing its supplies of drugs to a country thus "boycotted," it was to have the right to demand a special conference of all the countries concerned to consider whether the imposed limitation, or any other measure, ought to be put into force.

The idea of setting up an international organ composed of nationally independent experts, and endowed with administrative powers was not new. Other technical functions of the League have been carried out by similar bodies, against which the same Governments now in opposition to the proposed Board for drug control had not protested, and by which certain of their national activities already were being ordered. The Communications and Transit Committee, for instance, although its members are Government appointees, is a body of experts, derives its authority from, and is definitely responsible to, the Council and the Assembly, and to the members of the Barcelona Conference. The Commission of Enquiry which proposed the conditions of its organization reported that "the Members of the Committee would be considered not as representing Members of the League by whom they were nominated, but as acting in the name of the Members of the League regarded collectively," and in order to insure this the proposal was made that Governments be invited "to nominate by preference as members of the Committee an expert in any particular specified branch of transport." [1] The powers of the Committee are extensive, and affect deeply important national interests, yet collaboration and co-operation were readily given it on all questions. The objections to submitting drug control to a similarly endowed organ could therefore have been due only to reluctance to entrust this specific problem to international control. Some light is thrown on this point by the debates in the Conference itself.

2. *The Discussions of the Second Geneva Opium Conference*

When the Conference met it was found advisable to form a number of subcommittees to deal respectively with the various phases of the work in hand. In Subcommittee A[2] the question of establishing the Permanent Central Opium Board was brought up at the first meeting by Mr. Neville (United States). M. Bourgois (France) said that his Government did not find itself in a position to supply the estimates which the Board would require, its attention having been drawn to certain difficulties by its scientific and medical associations. M. Hulftegger (Switzerland) stated that it was impossible for the Federal Government to obtain these figures. Mr. van Wettum (Netherlands) felt that, although his Government was able to furnish the required estimates, it was inadvisable to do so.[3] Later he accepted the Board in principle, but as its functioning depended upon the co-operation of all the contracting parties, and as some of these had already declared their unwillingness to

---

[1] See H. R. G. Greaves, *The League Committees and World Order*, p. 145.

[2] Composed of seven manufacturing countries, and five others.

[3] *Proceedings, Second Geneva Opium Conference, Committees and Subcommittees*, p. 89.

co-operate, he suggested that the Board be set up without any active powers, merely to collect and publish statistics, but not to make any recommendation, or take any action, on them.

Against the negative attitude of these delegates Sir Malcolm Delevingne (Great Britain) pointed out that the Board required only approximate estimates which would not be expected, at least in the first years, to be entirely accurate. As to the possibility of calculating these figures, he indicated three methods by which the British Government arrived at reasonably accurate estimates. First, figures were obtained from the National Health Insurance System and from the hospitals. Secondly, manufacturers and wholesale firms were asked to supply the figures of the retail trade. And thirdly, the difference was calculated between imports plus home manufacture, and exports.[1]

Finally, nine Governments agreed to furnish the estimates which would be required by the Central Board, namely, Canada, Great Britain, Japan, Siam, Spain, Sweden, the United States of America, and Uruguay. Switzerland and France definitely declined. M. Bourgois held that fluctuations in trade made it a speculative business, and that therefore it was impracticable to limit it in advance by submitting estimates which would have any binding effect. Much less could the power to impose estimates be given to an international body.

The powers proposed for the Board raised still greater opposition. Mr. Sugimura (Japan) declared that the Central Board could not be given the power to furnish or revise estimates because such a power would obstruct the actions of sovereign States. The Board could be permitted to use only the power of publicity and the appeal to public opinion.[2] Mr. van Wettum agreed with this view, saying that he was willing to grant very full powers to the Board, such as collecting statistics and letting the world know when any country had exceeded

[1] *Proceedings, Second Geneva Opium Conference, Committees and Subcommittees,* p. 90.　　　　　　　　　　　　　　　[2] Ibid., p. 98.

its requirements. M. Bourgois agreed that these were sufficiently wide powers.[1]

As Subcommittee A could not reconcile the various opinions of its members on these important points, it agreed to appoint a Committee of Five, composed of the delegates of France, Great Britain, Japan, Netherlands, and the United States to attempt to reach an agreement.[2]

The discussions of this committee were not long, and resulted in radical alterations of the Measures proposed by the Advisory Committee. The intention of the Advisory Committee had been to create an organ with powers of control. These were replaced in the new proposals, due to the insistence of the French delegate, by powers of general supervision.[3] The fundamental nature of the Board was thus completely altered.

To begin with, the figures to be given to the Board, and upon which it was to base its decisions, were reduced. Instead of receiving estimates of each country's drug requirements for consumption, manufacture, and commerce, the Board was to receive estimates only of the quantities necessary to be imported to fill medical and scientific needs.

Secondly, estimates were not to be binding on the Governments, and might be altered by them during the course of the year as their individual judgments might determine. Nor were the estimates to furnish the Board with the means of regulating the volume and course of the drug trade. No right was now to be vested in the Board of judging the legitimacy of any Government's estimate, of altering such an estimate, or of supplying missing estimates. Instead, the Board was simply to have the right to ask for explanations from any Government in whose territory excessive quantities of drugs seemed to be accumulating, and, in case no satisfactory answer was given, to inform the Council and recommend to the Governments that all exports

[1] *Proceedings, Second Geneva Opium Conference, Committees and Subcommittees*, p. 96. [2] Ibid., p. 98. [3] Ibid., p. 102.

of drugs to that country cease. The obligation undertaken by the signatories to boycott an unruly party to the Convention was omitted from the text of the new proposals.

Thirdly, the immediate supervision of the Board over the course of the trade was made yet less probable by the new provision that, instead of semestrial statistics of manufacture and stocks, the Governments submit figures only annually. All statistics relating to Government supplies of narcotics, moreover, were to be listed separately and not to be subject to discussion by the Board. As the term "Government supplies" included the raw opium handled by monopolies in the colonies of the Far East, this exemption was important.

The one improvement over the Measures of the Advisory Committee was that the statistics of imports and exports should be submitted every two months instead of quarterly. This the British delegate succeeded in introducing against the opposition of the French, who felt that annual statistics of imports and exports were enough.[1]

It was in this form that the proposal for a Central Board was returned to Subcommittee A. Shorn of power and scope of function as it was at the hands of the Committee of Five, its friends in Subcommittee A yet had difficulty in preserving what remained of its useful attributes. The attacks of the Dutch, French, Japanese, and Swiss delegations were at once renewed. M. Bourgois took exception to the proposed power of the Board to act directly in calling the attention of the Governments to excessive imports of drugs, and suggested that the Board ought rather to call the attention of the Council to any irregular situation, and let it, in turn, inform the Governments of the contracting parties.[2] Mr. Porter (United States) pointed out the complete lack of authority the Board would suffer under M. Bourgois's amendment, which would reduce it to a mere

---

[1] *Proceedings, Second Geneva Opium Conference, Committees and Subcommittees,* p. 119.　　　　　　　　　　　　　　　　　[2] Ibid., p. 108.

advisory body of experts and make it difficult to attract competent men to membership on it. As an alternative he suggested that Governments might appeal to the Council against a decision of the Board.[1] Sir Malcolm Delevingne's opposition to the amendment proposed by the French delegate was even stronger. He said that it was the final step in the reduction of the powers of the Board. Originally, he went on, it was to have had the power, through its responsibility for estimates, of determining the amount of drugs to be manufactured each year. This power had been denied it in the proposed Measures of the Advisory Committee, which were themselves the result of compromise. Now the Committee of Five was proposing to deprive the Board of its power to exercise any actual control over the trade, and to leave it bare of all except vague supervisory powers. Already a period of four or five months was necessary, after excessive imports of drugs into any country had actually been effected, before the Board could make any recommendation on the subject. By having first to refer the matter to the Council an additional delay and a possible check was being imposed on the Board which could only further weaken the effectiveness of its action.[2]

Sir Malcolm's arguments won, and Mr. Porter's amendment was passed. But another attempt was made by the French delegate to interpose the authority of the Council in the action of the Board. This was in the discussion of the draft article relating to the Board's right, in case a Government protested to the Council against a recommendation of the Board respecting excessive imports, "to publish a report on the matter, and communicate it to the Council and all the Governments." M. Bourgois desired an amendment to the effect that the Board's report should only be communicated to the Governments after having been submitted to the Council.

Viscount Cecil objected to raising again the principle, already

<hr />

[1] *Proceedings, Second Geneva Opium Conference, Committees and Sub-committees*, p. 109. [2] *Ibid.*, p. 110.

settled, of putting the authority of the Council between the
Board and the possibility of its own action. A compromise was
thereupon reached in the form of a substitute amendment
submitted by Viscount Cecil, namely, that the Board's report
should be communicated to the Council, which should thereupon forward it to all the Governments.[1] Although a period
of delay was thus interposed between the publication of the
Board's final recommendations and their receipt by the Governments, the principle of the independent authority of the Board
was upheld. The independence of the Board's action in regard
to the international trade was thus finally established, and
defined in the Convention itself in Article 24, para. 2. This
says that if a request by the Board for an explanation from any
Government is not answered promptly and satisfactorily, "the
Central Board shall have the right to call the attention of the
Governments of the Contracting Parties and of the Council
of the League of Nations to the matter, and to recommend that
no further exports of the substances covered by the present
Convention or any of them shall be made to the country concerned until the Board reports that it is satisfied as to the situation
in that country in regard to the said substances."

The one improvement made by Subcommittee A in the
draft drawn up by the Committee of Five was in accepting the
British proposal on seizures. It was agreed that seizure statistics
should be submitted to the Board annually, and that an
explanation should be given at the same time of the methods
used in disposing of them.[2] One other change was made which
might have had great significance but for the interpretation the
French and Japanese delegates succeeded in giving to it. Lord
Cecil moved an amendment to the article dealing with estimates,
changing it from "estimates for medical and scientific purposes"
to "estimates for medical, scientific, and other purposes." [3] By

[1] *Proceedings, Second Geneva Opium Conference, Committees and Subcommittees,* p. 114.   [2] Ibid., p. 112.   [3] Ibid., p. 104.

"other purposes" Lord Cecil meant those purposes of manufacture and commerce for which estimates had been required under the Measures of the Advisory Committee. The objections of the French and the Japanese delegations, however, caused the interpretation to be narrowed down to purposes of consumption, and even in this restricted form Lord Cecil's amendment was only passed against the votes of France, Germany, Switzerland, and the Netherlands.

It was thus in a very reduced and humbled state that the proposed Permanent Central Board passed out of the hands of the Subcommittee and came before the Plenary Conference. As it was accepted here without further discussion, it was in this same form that it became a part of the Geneva Opium Convention, and with the powers and functions thus given it that it was set up when, in 1929, that instrument had received the necessary number of ratifications.

The original conception of a Central Board, it can be seen, was completely abandoned during the course of the discussions in Subcommittee A and its Committee of Five. The new concept which succeeded it was well expressed in the statement made by M. Sjöstrand (Sweden) before Subcommittee A. "I think," he said, "it is a distinct advantage that the sanctionary measures contemplated in the Advisory Committee's plan have been dropped. It must be kept in mind that the obligation proposed to be laid upon Governments would have entailed a series of legislative measures in the different countries . . . it seems likely that several countries would have felt reluctant to give up their autonomous powers in these matters." The moral force of the publicity of which the Board would be entitled to make the fullest use was emphasized by the Swedish delegate, who thought that it would prove strong enough to prevail upon "recalcitrant or offending Governments."[1]

[1] *Proceedings, Second Geneva Opium Conference, Committees and Subcommittees*, p. 102.

3. *The Establishment of the Central Board*

The difficulties and differences of opinion out of which the Central Board finally emerged remained to some extent unsettled even after its constitution was fixed by the terms of Chapter VI of the Geneva Opium Convention. The actual establishment of the Board, its relations with the League, its finance, the measure of its independent authority, all these questions were raised and discussed in the Assembly, the Council, and the Advisory Committee, revealing that differences still existed which could only be settled by the Board itself when it was constituted.

The first important discussion dealing with the Board was raised in the Fifth Committee of the Assembly in 1927. Dame Edith Lyttelton, *rapporteur*, read a report on the proposed expense items of the Central Board, and declared that they were not great enough to attract the kind of men necessary to have on the Board. As an alternative, she suggested that the posts be honorary. This was a policy, she held, strongly favoured by the British delegation. It had been gaining favour in the League, and had often been successfully applied.[1]

M. Fotitch (Yugoslavia) objected that, although this type of service might prove satisfactory for temporary work, it could not be hoped that competent men could be secured to hold five-years posts, requiring great technical knowledge and regular and frequent attention to difficult tasks, unless they were adequately paid. The honorarium proposed by the Secretary-General would, he felt, have to be increased if this type of service was to be assured to the Board. The view of the Yugoslavian delegate was fortunately shared by a majority in the Committee.

In the Fourth Committee of the same Assembly the question of including the expenses of the Board in the budget of the

[1] 8 A.C. v., p. 39.

League was discussed and agreed upon. The Supervisory Commission decided that, in view of the facts that the Convention is in line with the terms of Article 23 of the Covenant, that the Conference was called by the League and attended by a large majority of its members, and especially since in many cases specific reference is made to the Council's part in establishing the Board, whose staff, moreover, is to be appointed by the Secretary-General, and whose existence itself depends upon ratification of the Geneva Convention by a definite number of Council members, the budget of the League ought to include the expenditures of the Permanent Central Board.[1]

The importance of this decision is apparent when it is remembered how vital to the real independence of any body is its financial situation. The budget of the League at once supplied the Board with a safe and definite source of income and with the fullest measure of independence from any particular interests.

The discussions in the Assembly concerning the proposed Central Board caused apprehension in some quarters lest doubt as to its exact functions retard the ratification of the Geneva Convention. Accordingly M. Fotitch (Yugoslavia) asked that the question of the relations between the Board and the Advisory Committee be placed upon the agenda of the Advisory Committee at its 10th Session, in 1927.[2] The Advisory Committee referred the question to a subcommittee composed of M. Bourgois, Sir John Campbell, Sir Malcolm Delevingne, M. Fotitch, and Mr. van Wettum. The opinion expressed by the subcommittee was that the Central Board was not independent of the League, but a League organ; that although it had certain judicial powers beyond the competence of the Advisory Committee, it could not go beyond the definite limits of authority imposed upon it by the Convention; and, thirdly, that while any decisions based on facts which the Board might make could

[1] 8 A.C. iv, p. 260.   [2] *Advisory Committee*, 10th Session, p. 7.

not be questioned by the Advisory Committee, even at the request of the Council, lest such an abridgment of independence prevent competent men from giving their services to the Board, any large question of policy determined by the Board might be referred by the Council to the Advisory Committee. The report ended with the hope that mutually helpful relations might grow up between the Board and the Committee, whose respective functions ought not to overlap, but to complement each other.[1]

To this report Signor Cavazzoni raised objections. He felt that the Central Board was a potential source of danger because of the looseness of its connection with the League and its independence from any definite control. He feared that it might develop in a harmful way, that safeguards against arbitrary action by the Board were insufficient, and could only be exercised by the Council with great difficulty and in a limited and superficial way.[2]

Other members of the Advisory Committee felt with Sir Malcolm Delevingne that the Board, if not perfect, was a step in the right direction. They regretted that the proposal for rationing world drug supplies had not been approved by the Conference, as this would have set precise limits to the scope of the Board's activity. In the end Signor Cavazzoni's objections were overruled, but it was agreed that the question should be discussed further in the next session of the Committee.

An interesting proposal was made in the Council a few months later by the Italian delegate, Signor Scialoja. This was that the Secretariat of the Permanent Central Board be made an integral part of the Social Section of the League. The reason for this suggestion, unexpected in view of the discussions at the Geneva Conference, was that States would thus have,

[1] Document O.C. 669, 1927.
[2] *Advisory Committee*, 10th Session, p. 44.

through the League, a means of exercising some control over the activities of the Board.[1]

Signor Scialoja's proposal raised a storm of discussion in the Advisory Committee, which, in its 11th Session, was requested by the Council to give an opinion. Signor Cavazzoni, supported by the delegates of China, France, Germany, and Portugal, pressed for the inclusion of the Board in the organism of the League itself. Sir Malcolm Delevingne, on the other hand, in conjunction with the Indian, the Japanese, and the Netherlands delegates, insisted on the principle of complete independence for the Board, basing his argument on the terms of the Geneva Convention. The result was the acceptance, by a narrow majority, of a compromise resolution put by M. Bourgois, which maintained the propriety of forming the Secretariat of the Board as an integral part of the League's Secretariat, in administrative matters to be subject to the word of the Secretary-General. The implication was that the Board should in no way suffer a loss of technical independence, but that it should gain a certain solidity from the fact of its close association with the League. The implication of the Scialoja proposal, that States would be enabled through the League to supervise the Board, was repudiated by M. Bourgois.[2] In reporting this resolution to the Council the Committee regrettably failed to make clear its own view upon this important matter, and stated simply that it "considers this proposal (Scialoja's) is in complete agreement with the stipulations of Article 20, paragraph 1, of that (the Geneva) Convention, whereby the Secretary-General of the League of Nations is requested to provide for the control of the staff in administrative matters."

The Committee's resolution was non-commital in the

[1] C. 48, p. 130. Also, discussion in 11th Session, *Advisory Committee*, pp. 98 *et seq.*, and Council Document O.C. 744, 1927.

[2] *Advisory Committee*, 11th Session, p. 125.

extreme. But the discussions that preceded it disclosed the fundamentally different conceptions of the nature of the Board which were entertained in various quarters. To Sir Malcolm it was to be an autonomous body acting without reference to any part of the League machinery. To Signor Cavazzoni it was to be part of the framework foreseen by the Covenant of the League in Article 23 (c). Its technical independence, both sides agreed, should be insured, but whereas Sir Malcolm felt that this precluded any form of connection with the existing organization, Signor Cavazzoni insisted that it could be guaranteed only by means of such a relationship. His real fear was that in the absence of any general supervision the Board might be controlled by the Governments whose nationals the Council appointed to membership on it. There can be no doubt, especially in view of subsequent developments, that the Board's relationship with the League has been a source of strength and prestige. Signor Cavazzoni's view was probably right when he said that "there could be no better guarantee of the impartiality and independence (of the Board) than to bring its Secretariat within the framework of the League." [1]

The Geneva Conference had agreed that the Council should appoint the members of the Board, and that the United States and Germany should each name one person to take part in the nominations. The Council elaborated this procedure somewhat, and asked each signatory of the Geneva Convention, each member of the Council, and the United States, to submit two names, and the qualifications which justified the selection of the candidates. In the report in which this procedure was suggested the *rapporteur*, Mr. Dandurand, said that it would be desirable to have every Government name one of its own nationals and a second person of some other nationality as candidates. By this means emphasis would be diverted from the purely national point of view, which, considering the

[1] *Advisory Committee*, 11th Session, p. 105.

nature of the Board, it was desirable to avoid. From the panel of names thus formed, a committee of the Council, consisting of M. Procope (Finland), Mr. Adatci (Japan), Mr. Dandurand (Canada), and a representative of the United States, selected a list of sixteen names. From these the Council, in January 1929, then made the final choice of eight persons. The result was the appointment of the following men: Dr. Anselmino (Germany), M. C. J. J. Bonin (France), Professor Giuseppe Gallavresi (Italy), Mr. L. A. Lyall (Great Britain), Mr. H. L. May (United States), Dr. M. M. Miyajima (Japan), Sir B. K. Mullick (India), and M. Henrik Ramsay (Finland).

With three exceptions the membership of the Board has remained thus. The death of M. Bonin in 1929, and of Sir B. K. Mullick in 1931, led to the appointment of M. Lucide Agel and of Sir Atul Chatterjee. The seat made vacant by the resignation of M. Ramsay in 1932 has been filled by M. Dragan Milicevic (Yugoslavia).

The Board's powers were more clearly defined when it was actually set up. According to the Geneva Convention the Board was itself to arrange the details of its organization. This it did, at the request of the Council,[1] at the same time making certain declarations which helped greatly to define and establish its position. These were noted by the *rapporteur* on the Council, whose report stated:

Though the Council has shown its willingness to make the necessary arrangement for the organization and working of the Board, in order that effect may be given to Article 20 of the Convention, it will be realized that the Board is not an organ of the Council. Being set up in accordance with the provisions of the Convention it will, as I see the position, itself be the judge of the extent of the powers which it derives therefrom. I think, therefore, that the Council need do no more than take note of the passage in the report of the Board regarding its independence and the right which it claims to communi-

---

[1] C. 55, p. 998.

cate direct with Governments. It is clear, I think, that those who set up the Central Board intended it to exercise this right.

The decision taken by the Board to communicate with States that are not parties to the Geneva Convention should also be noted.

At the same time it must be remembered that the Board owes its existence to a Conference called by the League of Nations, that it draws its funds from the League, and that, under Article 20 of the Convention, the Secretariat and staff are to be controlled in all administrative matters by the Secretary-General. It is not, therefore, in my opinion, a completely independent organ, except as regards its technical competence, and its staff should form part of the Secretariat of the League.

The acceptance of this interpretation of the Board's position assured to it at once all the advantages, security, economy, and convenience, of a close relationship with the League, and at the same time guaranteed it complete freedom from delay or interference through the action of any other organ. These conditions were of the greatest importance to the successful functioning of a technical and expert body.

The relations of the Board with the Advisory Committee were especially mentioned in the report of the Board to the Council, but nothing more definite was said than that these relations ought to be as close as possible. In a subsequent session the Board adopted two resolutions bearing on its co-operation with the Advisory Committee, the first offering to place at the disposal of the Committee the annual estimates submitted to it by parties to the Geneva Convention, on the understanding that the Committee secured the consent of the Governments concerned. The second requested that the Committee communicate to the Board the statistics of any narcotics seized for reasons other than illicit import or export, and any statistics in the possession of the Committee from countries which had not sent statistics to the Central Board.[1] To this the Advisory Committee agreed.

[1] Document C. 241, M. 120, 1930, XI, p. 2.

To co-ordinate further the work of the Board and of the Committee, the latter revised the form of the annual reports so that the statistics appended to them might go directly to the Central Board. For countries which were not parties to the Geneva Convention the Committee devised a separate form, but as it provided for annual instead of quarterly submission of statistics, its value to the Board was considerably lessened.[1]

At the same (13th) session of the Advisory Committee it was agreed that any members of the Central Board who might wish to attend the meetings of the Committee would be welcome.[2]

The relationship of the two bodies has thus been cordial, but not close, having been confined for the most part to the avoidance of conflict as described in these measures. Each has gone its way largely independent of the other, neither conflicting in the performance of their work, nor developing any great sense of co-operation. The Board has proposed the study of several questions to the Advisory Committee, which has placed them upon its agenda in the usual manner. The presence of Mr. Lyall at all the sessions of the Committee, both as League assessor and as representative of the Central Board, has assured both organs pursuing similar courses.

[1] *Advisory Committee*, 13th Session, p. 414.   [2] Ibid., p. 10.

CHAPTER IV

THE FUNCTIONING OF THE PERMANENT CENTRAL OPIUM BOARD

ALTHOUGH little more than three years have passed since the first quarterly statistics were received by the Board, and although complete statistics are available only since 1930, the actual work of the Board has been very considerable. Naturally, a longer period will yield more definite conclusions, but its accomplishments have already been well defined. Briefly they are two. It has welded together the various national administrations into something like a co-ordinated system, with itself at the centre; and secondly, it has greatly increased the efficiency of several of these administrative units by direct inspection of their methods. With an active independent organ as a central point, and with the decisive efforts of that organ to make its authority extend as widely as possible, the various national administrations have, one may safely say, begun to feel themselves as parts of a single organization, and to see the benefits to themselves, individually as well as collectively, resulting from common participation in the League plan.

In pointing out these achievements of the Board the question naturally arises: Why did not the Advisory Committee perform these functions long before? The answer may certainly be found largely in the principles on which the Board was organized, in the technical qualifications of its members, and in their undivided service to an international job. However, it must also be remembered that the Governments were better prepared in 1930 to co-operate in this way under the guidance of a central board than they had been in the early days of the Advisory Committee. Already in the Geneva Convention they had recognized the need for more definitely organized international action. Five years later even this was agreed to be insufficient, and a new convention created another organ with yet greater powers than the Central Board, at the same time increasing the functions of the latter. A wider experience and a greater need combined to make the conditions for a successful functioning of the Board better than they had been in 1920 when the Advisory Committee was constituted.

In fact, however, the authority of the Board to command co-operation was small. Under the terms of Chapter VI of the Geneva Convention its greatest power is merely to communicate directly with Governments in making recommendations, and in asking for special information and explanations. Its powers of coercion lie entirely in its prerogative to make public any irregular or dangerous situation. Conformity with its recommendations, while an obligation under the terms of the Geneva Convention, cannot be enforced.

Of these slender powers the Board has made the fullest use.

1. The Establishment of International Supervision

The bulk of the work of the Board was the collection of statistics and the reduction of this matter to an intelligible body of information to be put at once to use. In this latter function lay the chief difference between the statistical work of the Board and of the Advisory Committee. While the Committee merely collected figures, those of the Board were analysed, compared, and annotated, and used as the basis of concrete improvement in the drug situation.

(a) *The Determination of Legitimate Consumption.*—The study of consumption figures has been the most urgent as well as the most problematic of the tasks which the Board has undertaken. Regulation or limitation are words without meaning unless they have a definite objective. That objective could only be to reduce the amount of narcotics used in the world to fit purely legitimate needs. To ascertain this amount was, of course, a first necessity.[1] But the task was difficult. When could a quantity reported as consumed be considered as a reasonable demand of the medical profession, and when did it become evident that a part of it was supplying the illicit traffic? Extravagant and widely varying consumption figures submitted by the Governments in the first year of the Board's functioning gave cause for great anxiety. A comparison of the rates of consumption in countries whose geographical position, racial composition, and medical development were analogous, revealed the fact that extraordinary differences existed. For instance, Esthonia's consumption of cocaine amounted to 12·53 kgs. per million inhabitants, and that of Sweden to 11·92 kgs., whereas the rate for every other Baltic State was between 5 and 6 kgs. per million inhabitants. Australian cocaine consumption was 14·67 kgs. per million inhabitants, whereas for the other Anglo-Saxon countries, the United States, Great Britain, and Canada, it was, respectively, only 7·88, 5·5, and 5·46 kgs. Diacetylmorphine, it was found, was consumed in Italy at the rate of 2·33 kgs., and in France at the rate of 21·6 kgs. per million inhabitants.

Japan and France had consumed respectively seventeen and eighteen times as much heroin, per unit of population, as was consumed on the average in all other countries, excluding India and the United States, whose heroin consumption is abnormally low.[2] A grave situation was revealed in the Kwantung Leased Territory. The enormous amount of morphine reported as consumed there for licit purposes, in spite of the fact that opium

[1] The report of the Health Section, 1929, on consumption (Document O.C. 1112), concluded that reliable figures of medical needs were not calculable under existing conditions, although it indicated methods of reaching approximate figures. This was the only contribution to the problem when the Board began to function.

[2] C. 629, M. 250, 1930, XI, p. 5.

smoking is permitted, left little doubt that drugs were escaping from licit channels to the illicit traffic.

The more glaring of these situations were immediately described in the report of the Board to the Council, and referred to the attention of the Governments. The general comparisons which the Board was able to make pointed the direction for further investigations. The most important question raised was whether the comparatively high rates of consumption in some countries were due to leakage into the illicit traffic, or to peculiarities in the medical practice. The Board felt, therefore, that although its express function was "to watch the course of the international trade," it could not adequately fulfil its duties without inquiring into the internal conditions in these countries. Inquiries were accordingly begun, the results of which showed that medical practices did actually differ widely from one country to another. An apparently excessive consumption figure for one drug might be balanced by a low figure for another.[1] Thus, there was not a great divergence in the total morphine content of the drugs consumed in different countries.

Both the Swedish and the Finnish Governments showed an active sense of duty, for, although the Board had attached no censure to its remarks on the high rate of consumption, they submitted full explanations of the causes for it.[2] The Swedish Government found that its high rate had been due to the large amount of stocks laid up by the pharmacists who were taking advantage of unusually low prices prevailing for opium, and also to the fact that a large amount of opium was used in the preparation of medicines not included in the Swedish pharmacopoeia, and in the making of preparations for the treatment of respiratory diseases, containing 0·2 per cent of morphine. The Finnish Government found that its unusually high rate of consumption of heroin, as compared with other morphine drugs, was due to its low cost. A maximum dose of heroin cost only

---

[1] C.C.P. 78 (1), 1931, p. 20.　　　　[2] A. 35, 1932, XI, p. 6.

15 *pennis*, whereas maximum doses of morphine and codeine cost respectively 75 and 250 *pennis*. In its report to the Council the Board expressed appreciation of the efforts made, on their own initiative, by these two Governments, and suggested that the same procedure followed by all Governments would secure information of the greatest value.

After studying the consumption figures submitted by the Governments for 1930, the Board felt it necessary to ask the Japanese Government for an explanation of the situation in its territories. The total world consumption of heroin in 1930 was, with the exception of Russia, Turkey, and the Japanese territories, 620 kgs. In the same year Japan reported a consumption of 1,351 kgs. "This astonishing fact," said the Board, "is thus explained by the Japanese authorities":[1]

In Japan, owing to the climatic and regional conditions, there are large numbers of diseases of the respiratory organs. There is a large demand for preparations containing morphine for cough remedies. Furthermore, in Japan there does not exist a distinctly separate practice for consultation with the medical practitioner and the preparation of medicaments by the chemist, so that cough remedies are dispensed both by medical practitioners and chemists. For this reason the number of those who prepare and dispense the medicaments is much larger in Japan than in other countries. The result is that there is much waste, and this accounts for the larger consumption of drugs in the country. Again, there is no restriction in Japan against qualified persons prescribing preparations containing opium derivatives, and there is a tendency for medical practitioners to prefer prescribing heroin, because of its efficacy and price. This may be the principal reason for the consumption of a larger quantity of heroin and of smaller quantities of morphine and medicinal opium.

The conditions in the Kwangtung Leased Territory, both as regards morphine and heroin, was infinitely worse even than in Japan, and had not improved since the Board's recommendation to the Japanese Government in the previous year to take

[1] C.C.P. 78 (1), 1931, p. 22.

measures against the danger. In the report of the Board for 1930 this recommendation was repeated. Comparison was made between Kwantung and Hong-Kong, which are in the same region, have similar populations, and in both of which opium smoking is still permitted. While Hong-Kong in 1930 consumed no morphine or heroin, Kwantung consumed 33·33 kgs. of heroin and 91·67 kgs. of morphine per million inhabitants. "The Board deeply regrets," said the report, "to find that no material change has occurred in the situation with regard to morphine and heroin. Kwantung is a territory leased by China to Japan for a certain number of years. Japan is therefore in the position of a trustee, and her responsibilities towards the alien subjects entrusted to her care are even greater than those towards her own subjects."

As for the situation in France, which was also specially commented on in the report of the Central Board for 1929, it was reported in 1930 that the consumption rate for coca leaves amounted to 1,561 kgs. per million inhabitants, a figure which the Board considered to be "entirely abnormal." The next highest consumption figure reported was that of Belgium, whose rate was only 55·83 kgs. per million inhabitants. In answer to a request for an explanation of this excessive amount, the French Government replied that previous to the Decree of March 20, 1930, coca leaves had not been subject to the control applied to other substances. French chemists therefore took advantage of this immunity to lay in a supply of coca leaves before the new regulations should come into effect. They also induced the Government to alter the new law in order to allow them to sell a limited quantity of coca leaves without complying with ordinary regulations. By a new decree they were therefore authorized to stock and sell 5 kgs. of the leaves annually without restriction.[1]

The abnormally high rate of consumption of coca leaves

[1] Roughly 114 kgs. daily of pure cocaine for each chemist.

dropped in 1931 to about a third of the previous year's figure, although it was still high. "A relatively high consumption of coca leaves," the Board's report stated in 1932, "in Switzerland and Belgium—the populations of which are partly French by race—might be accounted for by a general tradition of using tonic wines with a basis of coca leaf. It might perhaps be possible to trace back to some ethnical origin the utilization of several tons of essence of coca leaf revealed by the examination of the commercial statistics of the Peruvian exports to Canada."[1] The French Government explained to the Board in 1931 that some 14,000 kgs. of coca leaves were used annually in the preparation of wines, of which 240,000 bottles were made each year.

At the close of 1931 Dr. Anselmino completed a memorandum on the methods of calculating consumption figures. On the basis of this valuable work the Board concluded that "its study of this question should be confined, for the present, to the consumption of such opiates as fall under the Geneva Convention, and may be considered up to a point interchangeable for comparative purposes." It was confirmed in its previous opinion that comparison was only possible between countries whose medical practices were similar. The method, previously employed, of comparing countries whose medical practices differed, by reducing the amounts of drugs consumed to terms of their opium content, was found to be of questionable validity due to the varying therapeutic powers of the different drugs. It was thought that a safer mode of comparison was the reduction of the quantities of opiates consumed to the number of doses contained in them, and the combination of this figure with the number of practitioners, clinics, and dispensaries per unit of population in each country. By grouping the countries into six divisions according to their medical development, a fairly reliable method of comparison was worked out. For the present

[1] A. 35, 1932, XI, p. 12.

it is only by such comparison that any decisions can be reached as to the quantities of opiates needed for legitimate consumption, and the probable deflection of drugs from licit to illicit channels. This method of calculation has now been submitted for approval to the Health Committee, and the analysis of consumption reports meanwhile is pursued "within the limits of such supervision as it was possible to lay down empirically."[1]

It was found necessary to explain to the Governments, reports the Board in 1932, the exact meaning of "consumption figures," in order that the information which it is necessary to glean from them might be had. Misinterpretations have caused the Board considerable difficulty. It was pointed out, therefore, that "the Board can strike no balance for any given country if the consumption is figured on any other basis than the quantities delivered by wholesalers to retailers." Wholesalers are defined as those "persons or firms (including producers and manufacturers) holding substances for sale or supply (including export), or conversion, other than retail dealers." A clearer definition of the term "Government purposes," so convenient for disguising any questionable disposition of drugs and so confusing in view of frequent socialization of medical services, was adjourned for further consideration.

The question of consumption, of such cardinal importance to the task of limiting drug production, has, it can be seen, been tackled with vigour by the Board. The results of its work must depend largely upon the response of Governments, whose activity has been stimulated directly and indirectly by the Board. Methods of calculating consumption within a country have been worked out and presented to the Governments; equally have methods been studied to adapt the information received to the international problem. Unhesitating comment and condemnation have been passed on special situations. The report of the Board

[1] A. 35, 1932, XI, p. 10.

to the Council on the consumption figures in 1932 was prefaced with the following unequivocal remark: "The fact that a number of States have failed to fulfil international obligations which they have voluntarily assumed must be a matter of grave concern to everyone who is interested in the future of the League of Nations or the fulfilment of international obligations . . . the Board believes the Council will desire to know to what extent the absence of the missing statistics interferes with the work of the Board."[1] Such a statement creates a refreshing sense of progress when compared with the scrupulous regard for political sensibilities manifested in the earlier days of the Advisory Committee.

(b) *The Illicit Traffic.*—While attempting to reach at once an estimate of medical needs, and of the size of the illicit traffic, by studying consumption figures, the Central Board also attacked the illicit traffic more directly by studying seizure statistics. These have, on the whole, been less fruitful of results than indirect approaches to the problem through the examination of discrepancies in trade reports and consumption figures. The annual reports from Governments on the seizures effected during the year were the only statistics made available to the Board by the terms of the Geneva Convention. It was at once evident that these were inadequate to a thorough investigation of the illicit traffic. In its report to the Council on the work of the 6th and 7th Sessions, the first report based on a full year's statistics, the Board pointed out that the seizure figures obtained gave no information as to the origin of the confiscated goods, nor of the method used in disposing of them. They were not supplied often enough, furthermore, to enable the Board to take effective action. The more detailed information in the hands of the Advisory Committee was only unofficially at the disposal

[1] A. 35, 1932, XI, p. 5.

of the Board, which could not make any real use of it until the Committee had discussed it and the Governments concerned had commented on it. The Board therefore asked the Advisory Committee to furnish it with quarterly summaries of its seizure information, in order that the Board might be better able to uncover the sources and routes of the traffic. This request the Advisory Committee promptly granted.

But the inadequacy of seizure figures, however complete, for determining the extent of the illicit traffic, was apparent. From a study of trade figures the fact was discovered that some ten tons of morphine and heroin passed into the illicit traffic in 1930.[1] Seizures for the same period amounted only to some two and a half tons.[2] Thus, as the Board said, "Seizures depend, in the first place, on the efficiency of the preventive service and, seondly, on luck. An absence of seizures does not necessarily show an absence of illicit traffic."[3] The problem was therefore attacked from the side of demand, which, if it could be calculated, might give an idea of the extent of the illicit traffic, allowance being made for the addicts who get their supplies legally. Already in the Assembly in 1930 a resolution had been passed in the Fifth Committee asking the Advisory Committee "to study and report to the Council on the question whether Governments should be asked to indicate, as far as it is possible for them to do so ... the approximate number of persons in their country addicted to each type of drug, the approximate amounts of such drugs consumed, and the methods of treatment employed."[4]

Upon the motion of M. Garcia-Oldini (Chile) this resolution was included with another, proposed by the Chinese delegation, to the effect that a comprehensive inquiry into the illicit traffic be undertaken by all Governments for the three years past, by which means it was hoped to effect a final exposure of the sources,

[1] C.C.P. 78 (1), 1931, p. 30.　　[2] A. 35, 1932, XI, p. 13.
[3] Ibid.　　[4] A. 11, C. 5, p. 113.

routes, and centres of the traffic. In spite of the Dutch delegate's objection that the proposed resolution cast reflection upon the Advisory Committee,[1] it was passed by the Assembly, and communicated to the Governments by the Secretary-General in November 1930. The proposed inquiry into addiction was discussed in the Advisory Committee in its 14th Session early in 1931, and the decision reached that certain questions connected with it should be referred to the Health Committee pending whose report the Governments might be asked "without undertaking a special inquiry, to supply any information they may have on the matter, so far as this is possible."[2] There have not been any results of this inquiry. The Central Board attempted to make a study of the possible relationship between drug addiction and seizures of drugs in a given country, but lack of information made any definite conclusions impossible,[3] and it was obliged to await the results of the investigation instituted by the Assembly in 1930. In its 15th Session in 1932 the Advisory Committee decided to postpone the consideration of this question to the next session, pending the collection of the required information.[4]

It seems not improbable that the results hoped for will never materialize, and this for two reasons. First, the information required has never existed. And second, the method of "recommending to Governments" is, as has often been proved, ineffective for instituting prompt action on new and untried lines. Even the limited measure of supervision and direction which the Central Board has used has been productive of infinitely better results than the "recommendations" of the Advisory Committee, which, while pointing out an objective, have not been concerned with the machinery for its achievement. Action on the question of addiction might well be accelerated by informal communication between the Central Board and the chiefs of

[1] A. 11, C. 5, pp. 79, 80. [2] *Advisory Committee*, 14th Session, p. 261.
[3] C.C.P. 87 (1), 1931, pp. 4, 5. [4] C. 420, M. 229, 1932, XI, p. 16.

national administrative departments. If the Board is to fulfil its duties under the two Conventions it ought to be empowered to direct the collection of the information which is essential to watching the course of its international trade. Under any other arrangement, in view of the difficulties, hesitations, and uncertainties which prevent efficiency when many separate administrations engage in the solution of a common problem, the Board must fail. This fundamental fact has repeatedly been recognized by the Board itself.

Alternative to, or, perhaps, co-ordinate with, such action by the Central Board, the International Criminal Police Commission might be called upon to make this most important investigation into the illicit traffic. In any case, such information as will be collected by any of the Governments will come largely from police sources. The installation of central national police bureaux, a plan long advocated by police assessors on the Advisory Committee, and embodied in the Draft Convention for the Suppression of the Illicit Traffic in Dangerous Drugs drawn up by the International Police Commission,[1] would be a vital aid to the work. Meanwhile, as has already been shown,[2] the Commission has proved itself entirely capable of performing this type of work with competence and success. It awaits recognition, authorization, and direction by the Governments to which its several members adhere, or, better, by an international political body. If such authorization and direction is not forthcoming the Commission, if it remains the alert and efficient body it is, will find itself forced automatically, by the necessities of the situation, to proceed without it. Such a course is neither wise nor desirable from the standpoint of good government. To allow, or worse, to make it necessary, for a bureaucratic body to take the initiative and to direct its own functioning, is to put an end to far-sighted, comprehensive, representative, policy making. And the fault cannot be placed at the door of

[1] Document O.C. 1369, Art. 10.   [2] See above, p. 117.

the bureaucracy. The case of the Criminal Police Commission is one of a competent organism ready to perform services whose need is urgent, and which fails to find anywhere the hand whose proper tool it may become. Its use in connection with the opium work of the League, in particular in the present question of uncovering the illicit traffic, is only one of many possible functions it might fulfil.

(c) *The Regulation of Trade and Manufacture.*—It was the study of the manufacture and trade statistics which the Board found yielded the largest amount of information. Even before the completion of the full report on the first year's statistics the Board said that it felt "very strongly that a necessary step towards the suppression of the illicit traffic is the gathering of reliable information for the whole world about the licit trade in narcotics." The results have borne out this judgment. At an early session the Board decided to append to its annual report to the Council a table of the statistics received by it during the year. The publication of this matter was considered most important to the full dissemination of facts concerning the traffic which it was necessary for each Government to know for the better conduct of its own affairs.

The first year's full statistics revealed several important factors in the drug situation. The most important was probably the discovery that during 1929 some twelve tons of morphine were manufactured and used for conversion into substances not coming under the terms of the Geneva Convention. With the exception of diacetylmorphine, the esters of morphine were not subject to control in 1929, and as large quantities of these substances were known to have been manufactured in the course of the year, the Board concluded that they were produced from these twelve tons of morphine. As the esters have no known medical or scientific use, it seemed inevitable that they had gone into the illicit traffic. In 1930 the esters of morphine were placed under the restrictions laid down in the Geneva Convention, through the action of the Health Committee. Although it was too late to remedy this situation, the Board determined to prevent its recurrence in the future. It recommended to the Governments, therefore, that in their annual reports to the Board they state how much of each kind of drug not covered by the Geneva Convention was manufactured during the year. By this means a watch could be kept over these substances. A warning was given also against the danger of stocks of the esters manufactured in past years, which might still be in the hands of dealers. Only strict Government control over them could prevent a country from becoming a centre of the illicit traffic.

Although the Geneva Convention provided in Article 10 for the progressive inclusion of new substances under its terms, the machinery for effecting this was extremely slow, so that before a newly invented drug could be brought under control vast quantities could be manufactured and spread over the world. After the appalling disclosure just described, the Board prepared a memorandum which it presented to the Advisory Committee in January 1930, suggesting a new procedure to replace Article 10. It was proposed, in brief, that any drug subsequently discovered should automatically be considered as falling under the terms of the Convention, unless and until the Health Committee, together with the Office International d'Hygiène Publique at Paris, should declare it harmless.[1]

The suggestion was considered by the Advisory Committee, but, in spite of the support of the assessor from the Central Board, and the delegates of China, Spain, the United States, and Uruguay, the Committee as a whole did not favour it.[2] Instead it referred the question to the Health Committee, with the hope that some means could be found to accelerate the procedure under Article 10.

[1] Proposed by Mr. May (United States). See Document C.C.P. 70, 1931.
[2] *Advisory Committee*, 11th Session, p. 240.

Although the draft convention for the limitation of manufacture, drawn up at the same session of the Committee, contained no such provision as that proposed by the Board, a similar measure was included in the Limitation Convention itself, in Article 11. This provides that no new drug may be manufactured in any country unless it has medical or scientific value. The manufacture of any new substance shall be limited to such quantities as are needed in the home market, and as are required to fill orders for export, and shall be controlled by the terms of the Convention. The Health Committee in conjunction with the Paris Health Office shall determine, meanwhile, under which group of drugs the new substance shall be included. The provisions of the Convention already cover every known narcotic substance.

The Board has subsequently asked the Advisory Committee to consider whether the amendment of Article 10 of the Geneva Convention might not be effected to conform with the new article in the Limitation Convention, but the Committee is of the opinion that efforts should rather be expended toward securing the ratification of the new Convention than the modification of the old.

A second very definite recommendation was made by the Board after examining the first year's statistics. This referred to the situation in countries where both the production of raw materials and the manufacture of drugs takes place, a circumstance which enables them to escape the punitive effect of a drug embargo, planned under Articles 24 and 26 of the Geneva Convention against an offending country. The Board urged that against such a country it be empowered to recommend a boycott as well as an embargo, for only by striking at its exports would a measure have sanctionary qualities. The proposal was considered in the Advisory Committee, which, with the exception of the Dutch and the Swiss delegates, agreed upon its desirability. The Yugoslav delegate to the Advisory Committee even suggested the boycotting of all States which did not adhere to the Convention. It was pointed out, however, that the effect might be to turn the production of a boycotted country directly into the illicit traffic. Furthermore, as India and Yugoslavia alone of the opium-producing countries adhered to the Convention, and as these two countries could not supply the needs of the world, the application of a boycott might leave the consuming countries in a difficult position. The question was referred, therefore, to the Limitation Conference, but no measures were taken there to embody it in the Convention.

It has been found very difficult, upon the basis of statistics, to arrive at any clear understanding of the situation with regard to raw materials, both opium and coca leaves. Some of the opium-exporting countries have neither supplied statistics to the Board, nor issued export authorizations to accompany consignments of opium. The importing countries have thus been unable to say what the country of provenance was, especially when trans-shipments had taken place *en route*. When the Persian Government did submit statistics of export it was found that entries were made as to "the British Empire," a designation sufficiently vague to make it entirely useless for the purposes of the Board. The statistics collected by the Advisory Committee in the past years showed the same inaccuracy and discrepancies in the Persian figures, so that the Board felt convinced that a large amount of opium was finding its way thence into the illicit traffic. The establishment of monopoly control of opium in Persia happily holds out the promise of greater co-operation in the future. Turkey, although the opium regulations were reported to be revised in 1931, enforced the Geneva convention only in 1933. Export figures for Turkish opium are still inaccurate. Imports of Turkish opium, however, have been notified to the Board by the manufacturing countries, so that some information on this subject has existed. The 1932 report of the Board to the Council states the conclusion that the total surplus opium production of Persia for the year 1931 went to the Far East, both to supply the gap left by the reduction of Indian exports and to the so-called "Vladivostok" trade, whose destination is the illegal Chinese market. This surplus was discovered by the fact that whereas in 1930 some 109 tons of opium were imported from Persia into the manufacturing countries, only one ton was imported by them in 1931.

A discrepancy of 13 tons of raw opium was reported by the Board in 1932. It was declared by the German Government for Kwantung, but apparently did not reach that destination.[1]

The situation with regard to manufactured drugs has been revealed much more satisfactorily than that of raw opium by the annual statistics and the quarterly reports submitted by the Governments. The failure of France to send in quarterly figures of imports and exports on time at first prevented the Board from making complete comparisons of trade figures, but since the first quarter of 1931 this has been remedied. A general lack of statistics covering the drugs needed for Government purposes has also troubled the Board. For a time the outstanding source of illicit drug manufacture was shown to be Turkey. Statistics of exports from the Turkish Government, it is true, have been highly incomplete, and though recently more satisfactory from this point of view, they have not tallied with the import figures of other countries. A comparison of Turkish heroin export figures (no manufacture figures have ever been sent) with those of the other manufacturing countries also showed this country to be supplying more than all the others, except Russia, together. In combination with the valuable work of the Egyptian police authorities in uncovering an enormous illicit traffic with sources in Turkey, these indications gleaned by the Board from its statistical information pointed conclusively to Turkey as a black spot on the map of drug control. The Board's energetic measures for giving publicity to the situation, coupled

[1] A. 35, 1932, XI, p. 14.

with activities of the Opium Advisory Committee, and pressure of individual Governments, have resulted in the reform of the Turkish drug control system and the closing down of the factories in question.[1]

But it is evident that in spite of discrepancies and abnormal figures frequently found, the total reported world manufacture decreased progressively with the wider application of the Geneva Convention. How much of this improvement in the situation was due to the vigilance of the Board is difficult to prove, but the many direct and continuous contacts which the Board established with various national administrations is one indication that it was largely instrumental in achieving the result. Furthermore, the results of many investigations and inquiries made when statistics showed discrepancies, led the Board to say that it was completely satisfied that no case of falsification of the facts had ever been discovered.

In its report to the Council for 1931 the Board was able to show that figures submitted by the Governments for manufacture did not seriously exceed those set down by the Final Act of the Limitation Conference as a guide for limiting licit manufacture until the Convention should come into effect. These figures were as follows (per year):

Morphine	9 tons
Diacetylmorphine	2 tons
Cocaine	5½ tons[2]

Actually there were manufactured in 1930:[3]

Morphine	9·2 tons
Diacetylmorphine	3·9 tons
Cocaine	4·7 tons

---

[1] The *Manchester Guardian* announced on April 27, 1933, that the expulsion of these firms from Turkey only resulted in their transfer to Bulgaria.

[2] A. 35, 1932, XI, p. 9.   [3] L.N.P.O. 25, 1932, XI.

and in 1931:[1]

Morphine	..	..	..	8·3 tons (plus 0·3 ton Turkish)
Diacetylmorphine	..		..	1·2 tons (plus 1·4 tons Turkish)
Cocaine	..	..	..	4·0 tons (plus 0·6 ton Russian)

The Russian figures are calculated from the figures of other countries which have exported crude cocaine to Russia during the year.

These figures of manufacture do not show an alarming difference between the quantities of drugs which it is calculated are needed for medical use, and the quantities which have actually been produced. It must be remembered, however, that in 1931 at least ten tons of drugs were known to have passed into the illicit traffic. Turkey admitted the manufacture of seven tons, France of five. These facts can only point to an enormous illicit production of these drugs beyond the control of the responsible Governments. But as it is obviously easier to elude detection when transporting drugs than when making them, the new Limitation Convention, with its control over manufacture clauses, should achieve better results.

The experiences of the Board with securing figures of stocks were among its most difficult ones, and illustrated at the same time the efficaciousness of its methods. After the receipt of the first statistical returns the Board was obliged to report to the Council that the lack of adequate figures on this subject made it impossible to say whether a dangerous accumulation of drugs existed in any country. In the following year eight Governments again failed to submit these figures, while several that did showed discrepancies into which the Board had to inquire. Canadian figures failed to balance by the amount of 384 kgs. of raw opium. The Board's inquiry revealed that the cause lay in errors committed by the wholesale dealers in calculating their stocks. A system of regular inspection of books and stocks was thereupon

[1] L.N.P.O. 25, 1932, XI.

installed by the Canadian Government to prevent recurrences of such errors. A similar procedure was followed with Czechoslovakia and Greece, while the failure of the United States to give figures of stocks for 1929 was pursued until that Government admitted that the figures required were not known. Since then they have been supplied.[1]

Inquiry into the reasons for the abnormal supply of heroin and cocaine accumulating in Belgium drew from that Government the explanation that trade fluctuations were largely responsible for unusually large imports, as was also the fact that foreign exporters were stocking the Belgian market as a result of the declared intention of a Belgian firm to supply all the medical needs of the country. The Health Department, however, was proposing to prohibit the import of any drug unless the necessity for them could be adequately proved. The same assurance was given the Secretary of the Board during his visit in Belgium.[2]

In the same report to the Council an account is given of the South African situation. The Government of the Union stated that records of stocks had not been kept by the competent department, and hence did not exist; whereupon the Board "decided to request that Government to take such steps as might be necessary to fulfil the obligations with regard to stocks which it had undertaken under the terms of the Geneva Convention. The example of the Canadian Government, which had appointed inspectors for the purpose of investigating the stocks and records of licensed wholesalers, was cited in support of the Board's request."[3] This action had some, though qualified, success. The Government pleaded that financial reasons prevented the establishment of a system of inspection, but promised to attempt other means of securing the required information. Subsequently returns, completed "as far as possible," were received for the year 1930.

[1] C.C.P. 94 (1), 1932, pp. 4–6.   [2] Ibid., p. 9.   [3] Ibid., p. 8.

An interesting and significant discovery was made by the Board, when it examined the manufacture statistics for 1930, in the French figure for morphine. This was given as exactly 10 per cent of the amount of raw opium imported for the purpose of making morphine. The Board therefore concluded that the morphine figure was not an exact calculation, but was based simply on the percentage generally accepted as representing the average morphine content of opium. The statistics of other countries, however, showed that during the same year and from the same kinds of opium, 11 per cent and 12 per cent of morphine had been obtained. This larger percentage, when applied to the 124,950 kgs. of raw opium used in France for the manufacture of morphine, indicated the production of $1\frac{1}{2}$ tons more of this drug than the French Government reported. As this quantity does not appear in any of the figures of the licit trade it must have passed into the illicit traffic.[1] An important source of contraband drugs was thus established by the Board in examining the second annual statistics submitted to it. At about the same time an inquiry was begun by the Health Section, at the instance of the Advisory Committee, to discover a standard method for determining the morphine content of raw opium, and a proposal of the Japanese delegate to consider collecting statistics of the alkaloid content of all raw materials was postponed by the Committee pending the end of this investigation.[2] The Limitation Convention embodies the results of this activity in Article 17, which provides that manufacturers must submit to their Governments quarterly statistics, which shall include the percentage of alkaloids contained in the raw materials used. The Governments in turn are to submit to the Central Board annual summaries of the manufacturers' statistics.

[1] C.C.P. 78 (1), 1931, p. 30.
[2] *Advisory Committee*, 13th Session, p. 176, and *Advisory Committee*, 14th Session, pp. 192, 193.

The Central Board has had a brief but active career. It has acquired data on drug consumption, showing how much and in what manner legitimate use of narcotics differed from country to country, and worked out a formula by which it may be possible to judge the medical needs of any country in spite of these differences. It has discovered that huge quantities of drugs have been consumed or collected in Japanese territories since 1929, and that comparatively large amounts of coca leaves are apparently used by Latin peoples for making tonic wines. It has found that a large stock of coca leaves has accumulated in the Netherlands, and by calling attention to the fact has insured the Government's responsibility for its control. The illicit traffic has been shown to distribute at least ten tons of drugs and hundreds of tons of opium among addicts each year, the chief victims being China, Egypt, and the United States, and some of the origins Turkey and Persia; sources of the traffic have been discovered in the manufacture of drugs not coming under the Geneva Convention, in the use of raw opium whose morphine content was not known, in the absence of control over exports, and in manufacture directly serving the illicit traffic. To meet these situations Articles 11 and 17 were included in the Limitation Convention, and an attempt was made by the Board, though unsuccessfully, to secure power to take measures against a Government that did not control its exports. The general volume, extent, and course of the legitimate production and trade in drugs has been regularized, so that departures from the normal are easily detected. It was found that in 1931, Sweden, Belgium, Yugoslavia, and Czechoslovakia began to manufacture morphine, and that Poland and Bulgaria intended soon to do the same.

These have been, so far, the results of the Board's labours with statistics. Of less importance so far, but of very considerable significance, have been its activities in organizing national administrative units.

2. *The Development by the Board of National Administration*

It was apparent from the first that difficulties of an administrative nature were preventing the efficient co-operation of Governments with the Board. The same difficulty had long nullified many of the recommendations of the Advisory Committee. The new duties and responsibilities incurred under the Geneva Convention, it has been seen,[1] caused the reorganization of several Governmental narcotics departments on entirely new lines. Since 1928, at least fifteen countries have instituted reforms of greater or less extent, Portugal, Spain, Japan, the Netherlands, Persia, Turkey, France, Greece, Poland, Roumania, Hungary, Yugoslavia, the Union of South Africa, Australia, and the United States. Some of this reform had been accomplished when the Central Board came into existence. But much remained to be done both in extending such reforms to other countries and in ensuring full co-operation with the Central Board. The case of Roumania offers an excellent example of the work the Board has done in this connection. Although the Roumanian system of administration had been reformed in 1928, before the Board began to function, it was not until the last quarter of 1930 that quarterly statistics of imports and exports were sent to the Board, and as late as 1931 no annual report on manufacture, stocks, consumption, etc., had been submitted. The one table received was not drawn up in such a manner as to be of any great value to the Board. A telegraphic request to the Roumanian Government brought the quarterly statistics for the first quarter of 1931, but again much data was missing and the report was practically useless for the purposes of the Board.

It was then that the Government of that country asked the Board to send one of its members to Bucarest to go over the administrative organization and offer suggestions for its improve-

[1] See above, pp. 69 *et seq.*

ment. The Secretary of the Board was accordingly sent, and his account of the proceedings in Roumania is of real significance in the record of international administrative development. It is worth quoting in full.[1]

The Secretary's efforts . . . met with the most helpful personal assistance from the Minister of Foreign Affairs, and especially from the Minister of Public Health. The latter, Dr. Jean Cantacuzene—who is a doctor of medicine and a member of the Health Committee and of the Permanent Committee of the Office International d'Hygiène Publique—is familiar with the work of the League in connection with opium, but having been a member of the present Roumanian Cabinet at the time of the Secretary's visit less than a month, could hardly be expected to have been *au courant* with the situation outlined above. His intervention greatly facilitated the Secretary's task, and his immediate action can be summed up as follows:

The carrying out of all obligations under the Geneva Convention, such as international control, preparing of statistics, etc., has been entrusted exclusively to the Director of the Institut Chimico-Pharmaceutique of the Ministry of Public Health, whose staff is already budgeted for. Instructions have been given that a comprehensive plan for a radical reorganization of all control over narcotics within the country, liaison with the Customs, etc., shall be submitted to the Minister direct at the earliest possible date. For this work the Director was instructed to accept whatever suggestions the Secretary of the Board might make, and especially to acquaint himself with every detail concerning the statistics required by the Board. The delivery of import certificates and/or export authorizations is, however, to be left to the Committee which already exists, as both the Minister and the Director of the Institut are of opinion that a Committee consisting of independent and highly placed officials is better fitted to go into the merits of every single application for a certificate or authorization than any one department.

As a result of the Minister's decision, in the course of daily conversations with Dr. Konya, Director of the Institut, every statistical form was discussed with a view to anticipating every possible difficulty that might be encountered in filling it up. Further, with the assistance

---

[1] C.C.P. 77 (1), 1931.

of Dr. Konya, the necessary steps were taken to secure better co-operation on the part of the Director of Customs.

The particular points discussed with the Customs and on which an agreement in the sense desired by the Board was reached are summed up in a letter to the President from the Minister of Public Health received subsequent to the Secretary's return to Geneva. This communication (Annex 3) confirms officially the various decisions taken by the Roumanian Government which are intended to strengthen the internal control over the trade in narcotics as reported above.

The contents of the letter referred to in the report of the Secretary are equally of the greatest significance, both as an indication of the results obtained by the Board's methods, and as a manifestation of the spirit of willing co-operation with which a Government could respond to the directive function which the Board was assuming. It read as follows:[1]

July 2, 1931.

SIR,

We have the honour to thank you for your valuable assistance in allowing Don Ugo Theodoli, Secretary of the Permanent Central Opium Board, to visit Bucarest, in order to explain to our Ministry the statistical data which the Roumanian Government has undertaken to send to the Committee at fixed intervals.

Dr. Konya, Director of the Chemico-Pharmaceutical Institute, was appointed by this Ministry to consult with the Secretary of the Central Board, and has now submitted his report, showing the methods adopted and the valuable information which he received.

Statistical Forms A, B, C, and D were discussed and gone into in detail, with special reference to the data to be supplied by the Roumanian Government.

The two experts had an interview with the Director-General of Customs at the Ministry of Finance, the object being to determine the essential points of a scheme to ensure means of maintaining close contact between the Ministry of Public Health and the General Customs Administration.

These points were as follows:

---

[1] C.C.P. 77 (1), 1931.

FUNCTIONING OF PERMANENT CENTRAL OPIUM BOARD

(1) All customs offices are to draw up, immediately after the end of each quarter, returns showing the narcotic drugs actually imported and exported during that quarter.

These returns must give the date and number of the import authorization, a description of the narcotic drugs, the quantity imported, and the country of origin. In the case of exports, the country of destination must be shown.

(2) Under the terms of the Geneva Convention, any Party to that Convention is responsible for narcotic drugs deposited in a free port or free zone bonded warehouse, and narcotic drugs from abroad deposited in a bonded warehouse are to be treated as imports and must be reported as such to the Central Board at Geneva. The removal from the country of the whole or part of any quantity of narcotic drugs deposited in a warehouse is also assimilated to an export, and must be reported as such to the Central Board. This means that narcotic drugs reported as having entered the country at the time of warehousing need not be reported a second time, upon their removal from the warehouse to a destination within the country. The same applies to export. (See Article 14 of the Convention.)

(3) In the case of a quantity of narcotic drugs to be conveyed through the country (Transit) to another country, the date of entry and exit, a description of the drug and the quantity must be reported, unless the goods are accompanied by a diversion certificate. (See Article 15 of the Convention.)

(4) Although the Geneva Convention contains no stipulation to this effect, from a practical standpoint and further to simplify operations, the number of customs offices through which the entry and exit of narcotic drugs is permitted should be reduced to the lowest possible minimum.

In order that these provisions may be introduced without delay, we approached the Minister of Finance (letter dated June 16th last).

The organization by the Ministry of a special section for the control of narcotic drugs and the plan of action of that section were also discussed with your representative.

As regards the State monopoly of narcotic drugs, to be established by the Ministry in virtue of our Health Laws, nothing definite can be settled for the moment, as we are waiting to consult laws and regulations—which the Secretary of the Central Board is sending us —in force in countries where such a monopoly already exists: we have a plan which can if necessary be adapted.

Your delegate was most ready to give us the necessary explanations and information, and we have thus derived the greatest benefit from your delegate's advice.

Thanking you again,

We are, etc.,

(Signed)   Dr. CANTACUZENE,
                    Minister.

Dr. P. KONYA,
           *Director of the Chemico-Pharmaceutical
           Institute.*

The Board was not unconscious of the fact that in performing this type of work it was, in a manner, acting outside the strict rôle planned for it in the Geneva Convention. But its opinion was that the ends for which it was constituted not only justified, but demanded, employing the methods which have been followed. In connection with the Roumanian situation the Secretary of the Board said:

"That he fully realizes that to discuss the question of internal control with the competent departments of Governments he is brought in contact with may be considered as being outside his competence. However reluctant he may feel to go outside this particular field, which is, of course, strictly and solely statistical in character, he has realized, as the result of experience gained after visiting the offices of various Governments, that accurate statistics are and can only be the result of strict and efficient internal control. To visit a country with the sole purpose of criticizing that Government's statistical returns without making any suggestions as to the best way of obtaining accuracy would be in his opinion sheer waste of time and money.[1]

It is of the greatest importance to note that the Central Board was at once able to achieve results here which the Advisory Committee, in spite of frequent resolutions asking for more complete co-operation from the Governments, had been unable

[1] C.C.P. 77 (1), 1931.

to secure in the course of ten years. The reason should not be far to seek. The Board commanded the confidence given only to disinterested experts. Personal efficiency can rarely prevail entirely over the fact of national affiliation, to enable the representatives of a Government to command the confidence which is readily given to the expert whose interest is manifestly the League's, or that of his particular technical work. The framers of Chapter VI of the Geneva Convention fortunately maintained the independence of the Board, although they deprived it of much of the power it was originally intended to have. This independence was further assured in the Assembly which determined finally that the finances of the Central Board should be borne by the League, and not by any group of Governments or by a private fund. The valuable attribute of independence which the Board thus acquired was the first essential for an organ which should successfully dare to touch the tenderest of national sensibilities by attempting the reform of internal administrative departments.

The important factor in this instance of the reform of an administrative system, and which is equally present in each of the efforts of this kind which the Board has made, is the development of a sense of co-operation, not only within individual departments, but with the League, and through it, with other countries. This development was, and remains, of the first importance in any system of control. It is merely to assert an obvious fact that here, as in other instances of international administration, while the formation of policy and general direction may come from a central, non-national organ, the machinery for carrying it into effect is still national. Its use as an instrument of international organization depends, therefore, upon the acceptance by Governments of responsibility for carrying out their respective obligations in international affairs, and upon the reform of their administrative departments to fit a new scale of needs. This is not to say that international tasks will continue to depend upon this system for their execution. It is merely the stage which has been attained thus far in the development of a more truly international civil service.

3. *Extension of the Board's Powers by the Limitation Convention; The Supervisory Body*

Another stage was reached in the Limitation Conference in 1931 when the Supervisory Body was established. It will be remembered that in 1925 the Geneva Conference would have nothing to do with the proposal contained in the draft of the Advisory Committee that the annual estimates submitted by the Governments to the Central Board should provide that organ each year with a definite standard by which to measure and limit the volume of the trade in drugs. Still less would it concede the proposed power of the Board to supply the estimate of any country which failed to submit its own, or to revise an estimate that seemed excessive. This very important power was reduced during the course of the Conference to one merely enabling the Board to use the estimates it received as an indication of the volume of the legitimate trade, on the basis of which it might make recommendations for the future. The estimate clause of the Convention was thus vitiated.

But in 1931 the Limitation Conference recognized that some standard was imperative if the manufacture of drugs was to be limited to a quantity determined upon at the beginning of each year. Such a standard could obviously be found only in the aggregate of national estimates for medical needs. Obviously, too, the estimates, in order to be effective, had to be definitely binding for the year in respect of which they were made and to be based on a universally accepted standard of legitimate needs. To insure this, it was seen, some technically competent body would have to examine them and be empowered to alter them if they appeared excessive.

To accomplish this function the Supervisory Body was established. It might appear that the Central Board was the natural organ to be entrusted with this duty, if only to avoid the necessity of establishing another body. Under the new Convention the statistical reports of the Governments should conform to the estimates. It is the duty of the Central Board to see that this conformity exists, and it must base its judgment of the state of the international trade largely upon the relations which it finds the statistics bear to the estimates. As the Board depends upon the Supervisory Body for estimates, it is essential that harmonious relations be established between the two bodies. The Convention provides, to this end, that the Secretary-General, who is to appoint the Secretariat of the Supervisory Body, shall "ensure a close collaboration with the Permanent Central Board."[1] The Central Board, moreover, appoints one of the four members of the Supervisory Body, the other three being the candidates respectively of the Opium Advisory Committee, the Health Committee, and the Office d'Hygiène at Paris.[2] In effect, the new provisions with regard to estimates, even though their execution devolves upon a new organ, clearly increase the powers of the Board, making them in greater measure compatible with its responsibilities. Functionally, if not organically, the Supervisory Body is a committee of the Permanent Central Board.

The Limitation Convention has also widened the powers of the Board in other respects. Again with regard to estimates, it is the Board which receives them and which may request any country which is not a signatory of the Convention to furnish

[1] Article 5, para. 6.
[2] The following have been appointed to the Supervisory Body: Dr. Carrière, Sir Malcolm Delevingne, Mr. Herbert May, and Professor Tiffeneau.

estimates. It is to prescribe the form upon which the estimates are to be returned, and the Convention details carefully what the estimates are to include. Whereas the Geneva Convention of 1925 asked only for estimates "of the quantities of each of the substances covered by the Convention to be imported into their territory for internal consumption during the following year for medical, scentific, and other purposes,"[1] the Limitation Convention asks for estimates of the quantities of each of the drugs covered by the Convention, in whatever form, necessary for use for medical and scientific needs, for purposes of conversion for domestic consumption or export, the amount of reserve stocks it is desired to maintain, and the amount required to establish and maintain Government stocks.[2] Every estimate has also to be accompanied with a description of the method of its calculation.[3] These provisions will immensely facilitate the work of the Board and do away with the necessity of pursuing the long inquiries which have hitherto taken up so much time. It is obvious that the Limitation Conference intended to make estimates a real tool in the hands of the Board.

Several of the suggestions of the Board made from time to time in its reports to the Council have been embodied in the Limitation Convention. For instance, the Board will henceforth receive annual statistics of the drugs used in the preparation of substances which do not require an export authorization. These are substances containing less than a certain minimum amount of one of the drugs. In the past they have sometimes furnished a screen behind which large quantities of narcotics could be spirited away into the illicit traffic. The alkaloid content of the raw materials used must also be reported annually to the Board.[4] Several substances, such as codeine, ethylmorphine, and their salts, which are not themselves capable of producing addiction, but which may be turned back into dangerous drugs, will in

[1] Article 21.
[2] Article 5, para. 2.
[3] Article 5, para. 3.
[4] Articles 17 and 22.

the future be submitted to partial control, and the Board is to receive annual statistics of the imports, exports, manufacture, stocks, and seizures of these substances.[1] Codeine, especially, there is reason to suppose, has been used in great quantities to cover the passage of drugs from the licit into the illicit trade.

But the most important of the powers which the Board has acquired under the terms of the new Convention, with the exception, perhaps, of those regarding estimates, are two which again suggest the original plan for a Central Board as it was envisaged by the Advisory Committee before the Geneva Conference. The first is the duty of notifying the contracting parties when any country is exceeding its estimates with regard to imports, and the obligation of all Governments thereupon to cease exporting to that country[2] during the year in question, or until the Board is satisfied that no further danger exists. The Geneva Convention, it will be remembered, allowed the Board merely to recommend, after asking for explanations from the Government concerned, that exports to that country cease. Any Government which was not inclined to follow the Board's recommendation could simply inform the Board and the Council of its intention not to comply with it. Although the new provision is undoubtedly an improvement on the old, it falls short of the full power which the Board finds necessary to the proper execution of its function. It may act only when the imports of any country are excessive, but not if its exports, or its manufacture, or its stocks, are too great. It may be found, for instance, that one country is being flooded with the drugs of another. Its imports will thereupon be stopped, but the exports of the other, which is more likely to be the offender, may continue in other directions when the certificate system can be evaded. A reference has already been made to the Board's request that its powers be amended so as to permit it to take action against this

[1] Article 13.   [2] Article 14, para. 2.

danger. But the new Convention does not appear to have adequately met the situation.

The other new function which the Board is entitled to perform is that of stopping the export to any country not party to the Convention of any consignment of drugs weighing more than 5 kgs., if there seems to be danger of that country's estimate being exceeded. Every authorization for such export must be submitted to the Board for approval before the consignment it covers is shipped.[1] A complete control would, of course, make this excellent provision applicable to every export and to any country.

4. Conclusions

The Central Board has been functioning since January 1929. Four years is not too short a period to allow a reasonable judgment to be made of its activities. Reviewing the whole history of opium and drug control, the installation of the Central Board seems to mark the beginning of effective action. Control of the drug traffic was not to be achieved by the payment of lip-service to the idea of international action. It waited upon the positive application of that principle. This was clearly seen and accepted in the Geneva Conference. But it is difficult to pass from the adoption of a principle to its application. The hesitancy with which the Board was endowed with any effective function and the clipped and tied state in which it was finally allowed to materialize, give evidence of this.

But if the Central Board deserves merit for its energy and success in dealing with the drug situation, it must also be recognized how much the strength of public opinion has increased in the past years, how much attention police activity has called to the drug situation, how the growing seriousness of the problem itself has called for action. The Conference for the Limitation of Drug Manufacture was the outcome of the

[1] Article 14, para. 1.

insistence of certain delegates to the Assembly, notably the representatives of Governments victimized by the drug traffic. The attitude of most Governments has been altered of late, and especially has the increasing interest of Governments which were once apathetic been effective in improving the situation. In some measure it is now understood that the primary object to be attained is not the retention of a maximum amount of national authority over the drug trade, but the greatest measure of immunity from the social depredations of the traffic. To assure this end it has been seen that authority must be concentrated in a central, and therefore international, organ. The measure in which this principle has been allowed is the measure of the Board's success, which, in this relative sense, is unquestioned. Its greater achievements wait on wider powers. That these may in time be forthcoming is not a groundless hope. Although a less advanced opinion prevailed in the Limitation Conference, it was the view of some of its members that:

Both the limitation of manufacture and the control of the quantities manufactured should be guaranteed by the action of the Permanent Central Opium Board, assisted, where necessary, by technical authorities.[1]

The next drug conference may take this step.

[1] *Advisory Committee*, 14th Session, p. 241.

Part Two

THE CONTROL OF RAW OPIUM PRODUCTION

Introductory

THE vital necessity in narcotics control to-day is the reduction of the cultivation of raw materials. Of these opium is for the present the most important. The effective limitation of manufacture, while it still remains to be attained, is at least agreed upon, and the method and machinery for its achievement have been established. The Convention for the Limitation of Drug Manufacture was ratified within twenty-one months of its signing by thirty-three Governments, a record among international conventions. It embodies, moreover, by far the most advanced methods of international administration yet adopted. But the limitation of raw material production must of necessity be the foundation of any effective control of manufacture. The recent experiences of Turkey and of Bulgaria demonstrate the futility of attempting to control manufacture while the opium poppy can be freely cultivated. The tightening of control over manufacture in Europe shifted illicit enterprises to Turkey. Driven from Turkey, they began operations in Bulgaria. Effective restrictions there will remove them to some other part of the world. In the Near and Far East there is still enough space for the establishment of similar factories as long as the raw materials they require are available. The control of the production of these materials in the areas where they are now openly cultivated will result in their transfer to uncontrolled regions, as has been the case with drug manufacture. For this reason any future agreement on limitation must include provisions for control in potential opium-growing areas. For the moment China is the most serious menace to any scheme of universal control, either of drug manufacture or of opium cultivation. Both the Advisory Committee and the Permanent Central Board are endeavouring to secure an undertaking from the Chinese Government that definite measures of control will be adopted.[1] But the tragic condition of that country may make it for years to come at once the victim and the refuge of the lawless. In all the other countries the Governments have declared themselves ready, and can be held responsible, for limiting and controlling opium production. The situation in China is not an argument for putting off the assumption of that responsibility.

The Opium Section of the League Secretariat has made an invaluable study of the present state of raw opium production and its relation to the quantities used for drug manufacture and for smoking.[2] That document reveals the extreme urgency of beginning limitation at once. A brief review of its conclusions will demonstrate the importance of control of opium production to the success of the Limitation Convention as well as to the reduction of opium smoking. The statistics used as the basis of the study are for the six years, 1925–30, inclusive. The average annual importation of raw opium into the manufacturing countries for this period was 396 tons, according to the figures submitted by these countries to the Secretariat. In the same period other, i.e. non-manufacturing, countries imported 33 tons of raw opium annually for use as medicinal opium, making a total for medicinal purposes of 429 tons annually. This figure must be compared with annual legitimate requirements. The authoritative League document on this subject is the Analysis of the International Trade in Morphine, Diacetylmorphine, and Cocaine, which gives as the maximum world requirement of morphine (including that used for the manufacture of diacetylmorphine) the figure of $32\frac{1}{2}$ tons per annum. As the opium manufactured into morphine contains from 10 per cent to 15 per cent of morphine, and is, in fact, chiefly of the higher grade, it is reasonable to take 12 per cent as the basis of calculation in deducing the quantity of raw opium represented in these

[1] Document C. 495, M. 250, 1933, XI, p. 10.
[2] Document Conf. L.F.S. 60, 1931.

32½ tons of morphine. By these means the figure of 272 tons of raw opium is obtained. As for medicinal opium, the Health Section of the Secretariat has calculated annual legitimate requirements to be between 50 and 56 tons. Taking the larger figure and adding it to the above 272 tons used for the manufacture of drugs, one arrives at the figure of 328 tons as the maximum amount of raw opium needed annually for the satisfaction of legitimate medical demands. Comparing this with the figure, previously ascertained, of 429 tons of raw opium imported into various countries in each year supposedly for medical purposes, a discrepancy of 101 tons is revealed, which must be taken as the quantity, the morphine content of which has passed annually into the illicit traffic in the period under discussion.

But this is only half the story. The average imports of raw opium into the Colonies for smoking was reported to the League as 617 tons per year.[1] Of these some 8 tons are estimated to have passed into illicit channels. Furthermore, all of the 237 tons known to have been exported annually from the Persian port of Bushire to Vladivostok may be assumed to have gone into the illicit traffic. At least 245 tons of raw opium has thus passed into illicit channels annually from legitimate sources of supply. This is, of course, a highly conservative figure. Illicit consumption in India, Persia, Turkey, and China, and most of the illicit consumption in the Colonies where smoking is still permitted, is not included in this figure.[2]

By adding together the two figures, therefore (of *known* excess opium used for manufacture and for smoking), it may

[1] This average agrees approximately with the legitimate consumption figure given by the Commission of Enquiry into Opium Smoking for 1928–29.

[2] The Commission of Enquiry estimated illicit importation of opium to be equal to legal importation, i.e. about 600 tons annually. The 1925 Opium Conference had before it the figure of 15,000 tons as the estimated annual illicit production of China.

be concluded that a minimum of 354 tons of raw opium are produced annually in excess of medical and other legitimate requirements.

The case for immediate reduction needs no further argument. Its urgency has been recognized both by the Commission of Enquiry into Opium Smoking and by the Conference for the Limitation of Drug Manufacture. The Bangkok Conference on opium smoking also included the principle in its Final Act. From each of these sources came the recommendation that an international conference be held to discuss the control of raw opium and coca production. The League Council, therefore, in January 1931, and the Assembly in its 12th Session, resolved that preparations should be begun. Since its 15th Session the Advisory Committee has been engaged in preparing plans for the coming Conference, while the Opium Section is compiling data on the basis of answers to questionnaires sent out to the producing countries. When the Conference meets, therefore, it will have a wide basis of authority. Its membership, furthermore, thanks to an American amendment of the original motion, will be universal, and not, as first proposed, confined to the producing countries.

The opium-growing countries, meanwhile, are producing plans for domestic limitation, partly, no doubt, in anticipation of international action, and partly as the result of the pressure of public opinion concentrated in the Assembly and in the Limitation Conference. Both the strict forms of control generally being adopted and the readiness of Governments to discuss international action have the greatest significance for the success of the Conference which the Secretariat and the Advisory Committee are now preparing. In order to understand the problems with which this Conference will have to deal it is essential to study the developments which have taken place thus far in controlling the production of opium. India occupies a special position, because control there has advanced to the point of bringing complete elimination of poppy cultivation, at least for export, within sight. It is, moreover, the only country able to provide abundant statistical information on this subject. For the other three of the four chief opium growers such scattered information and figures as exist must serve as the basis of a survey which, while lacking the fullness of the Indian account, will still indicate the general outline of the present position and the point from which international action must begin.

CHAPTER V

INDIA

THE opium problem in India has a past. It is impossible properly to understand the situation as it exists to-day, or to appreciate the changes in policy that have been made, unless one looks back into the last centuries in which to-day's problem has its roots. India's popular reputation with regard to opium is an heritage from earlier times. But whatever room for improvement still exists, there is no longer any comparison possible between the conditions that marked the opium trade a hundred years ago and the conditions that mark it now. It is in order to realize fully the magnitude of the change that we must glance at least briefly at the pages of history.

1. *The Opium Traffic*

When Portuguese, Dutch, and English traders began to penetrate into the Far East in the Middle Ages they found among the articles of commerce in which the people dealt a medicinal plant called *afyam*. The name is Arabic, bearing out the theory that the plant originated among the Arabs and was transported by them to India and China. Opium is still known by this name in parts of the East. The word, furthermore, means "medicine," and would seem to indicate, therefore, the original use made of the plant by the Eastern people. In the letters and records of European travellers in the Orient in the Middle Ages reference is sometimes found to opium as a drug used by the people to overcome fatigue or to cure certain ailments. The almost entire absence of any mention of its abusive use must be evidence that this was unknown, for a foreigner would have been particularly interested in chronicling a custom that was strange to him. It should be noted especially that the smoking of opium seems to have been entirely unknown at this time.

Not until the beginning of the seventeenth century do records show that any considerable consumption of opium was developing, and according to Rowntree the date coincides with the introduction of opium smoking in China.[1] From that time on there was a rapid increase in the demand for opium, trade in it assumed capital importance, and gains from it grew enormously. The fact that opium could be imported into China legally as medicine made its prohibition for smoking purposes difficult to enforce. Increasingly large quantities were brought into the country in spite of the many edicts issued against it. It appears that the cultivation of opium in China was of no importance, indeed was practically unknown at this time. Opium came from Bengal, the headquarters of the East India Company, in Portuguese, Dutch, and English carriers.

As the seventeenth century wore on the English gradually superseded the traders of other nations, and although the East India Company did not itself export opium it monopolized production and was thus responsible for supplying the Chinese market. Several of the Indian States, over which the East India Company had not extended its control, raised opium, and also helped to supply the Chinese market. Their product was known as Malwa or Bombay opium, while that of the East India Company was called Bengal opium, a distinction which is still made.

Official control over the opium trade in India began in 1773 when Warren Hastings, director of the Company, organized the Opium Monopoly. Under this arrangement the Company annually invited bids from private individuals for the exclusive right of buying the opium crop, stipulating that the entire produce had to be bought, and at a fixed price turned over to the Company. The terms of the opium contract provided also a penalty of 300 rupees for every chest short of the number

[1] *The Imperial Drug Trade*, p. 16.

contracted for. In 1775 Cornwallis mitigated this rigorous rule to some extent by removing the fine when the shortage could be shown to be due to natural calamities. It was then provided, also, that *ryots* (Indian peasants) were not to be forced to cultivate opium against their will as had hitherto been the case.[1] Within a few years, however, the contract system threatened to ruin the opium industry. Presumably the contractors offered such low prices that the cultivators found it more profitable to give up opium growing or to sell clandestinely to the illicit traffickers. In order to save the opium trade from complete ruin, therefore, the Company gave up the contract system and formed the State monopoly agency, which from that time forth employed its own agents to buy up all the opium cultivated in the states under the Company's rule. The middleman thus eliminated, the cultivators were paid directly by the Government and received a price which encouraged them to continue to grow opium. At no time, however, did the Company engage directly in the exportation of opium. When all the opium was bought and collected in Calcutta, auctions were held, merchants bidding for the opium which they then exported on their private accounts. In this way the Company absolved itself from all connection with the importation of opium into China which, being prohibited by the Chinese Government, the Company's London directors deprecated as clandestine.[2]

Until 1818 Bengal opium practically ruled the market, for the Native States which grew Malwa opium were disrupted by internal strife, and the East India Company managed to place a cordon around the ports to which Malwa opium might be sent for export, forbidding British subjects to deal in it. But in 1818 the regions producing Malwa opium came into political relationship with Great Britain as allied and protected states, and it was no longer possible to deny them trading rights. Consequently the Company made an agreement with them whereby Malwa

[1] Sinha, *Economic Annals of Bengal.*   [2] Ibid.

opium, too, should be bought by the Monopoly, which thereby secured control over the entire Indian production. But opium was commanding a high price abroad, and this fact, together with the facility of smuggling, rendered the arrangement ineffective and it was soon abandoned.

The opium revenue was now dangerously threatened, and in order to save the price of Bengal opium in the foreign market the Company levied a road tax on Malwa opium going to Bombay for export. But the price could be raised by this means, it was found, only at the cost of evasion of the law and an increase in the illicit traffic. Bengal opium continued to suffer from Malwa's competition and the situation finally forced a complete reversal of the Company's policy.

Until 1830 that policy had been to keep the supply of opium fairly steady, and by keeping down competition to control the price in such a manner as to assure to the Company a dependable revenue. With Malwa opium getting out of hand, however, and forcing Bengal opium to sell at ruinously low prices, the Company attempted to save itself by increasing the supply of Bengal opium at Calcutta. In order to do this it encouraged opium cultivation in Benares and Behar where it had hitherto been prohibited. The results were astounding. The quantity of Bengal opium put up for sale at Calcutta almost doubled at once, and within a few years it quadrupled. At the same time the exports of Malwa opium increased and for the next fifteen years equalled the exports of the Bengal product. Only the excessive demand from China permitted the continued prosperity of both Malwa and Bengal opium on the market.

But the policy of the Monopoly was to bear its inevitable fruit. The China trade was illegal, and it was the struggle between British opium dealers and Chinese Government and customs officials which resulted in the famous "Opium War." This unfortunate chapter might have been omitted from the history of British foreign relations had the political fortunes of some of the statesmen of the time been different. Cobden and Gladstone bitterly opposed the prosecution of the war and the terms of the peace made at its conclusion. In the House of Commons in April 1840 Gladstone said: "I do not know how it can be urged as a crime against the Chinese that they refused provisions to those who refused obedience to their laws whilst residing in their territory. I am not competent to judge how long this war may last, nor how protracted may be its operations, but this I can say, that a war more unjust in its origins, a war more calculated in its progress to cover this country with disgrace, I do not know and I have not read of."[1] Believing that Peel was considering him for a Cabinet position, Gladstone wrote in his journal: "I considered and consulted on the Chinese question, which I regarded as a serious impediment to office of that description, and I had provisionally contemplated saying to Peel, in case he should offer me Ireland with the cabinet, to reply that I would gladly serve his government in the secretaryship, but that I feared his Chinese measures would hardly admit of my acting in the cabinet."[2] When Peel approached him with a view to making him Vice-President of the Board of Trade, Gladstone wrote: " 'I cannot,' I said, 'reconcile it to my sense of right to exact from China, as a term of peace, compensation for the opium surrendered to her.' "[3]

Palmerston, on the other hand, in a speech before Parliament in 1843, "observed that exception had been taken to his China policy; but on that head he said he would appeal to the Duke of Wellington in the House of Lords, merely observing that if a satisfactory arrangement of commerce with a nation of two hundred millions of people was the consequence, a greater benefit to British manufacture could hardly be conceived.[4]

[1] John Morley, *Life of Gladstone*, i, p. 398.   [2] Ibid., p. 244.
[3] Ibid., p. 242.   [4] Ashley, *Life of Lord Palmerston*, i, p. 398.

But opposing the Government's Chinese policy was not aiming at the root of the trouble. That was to be found in India where the opium trade had become not merely important but almost indispensable in balancing the budget. Nor was it profitable from that angle alone. The report of the Select Committee of Parliament which studied the question in 1832–33 had stated that the Monopoly was run for "the profit of those who were in the hope of being concerned in it."[1] The Committee considered substituting a heavy export tax for the existing monopoly system, but the risk of loss was too great to be faced. During the first three-quarters of the East India Company's rule the revenue derived from opium amounted to one-third of the total revenue of the Company. Thereafter it rose to one-half, and at the time of the Company's dissolution in 1857 some £5,000,000 annually came from this source.[2] It is not remarkable, under these circumstances, that the Finance Minister in 1882, discussing the opium policy, said that though there was room for a difference of opinion the problem ought to be treated primarily as a practical one, for it would be utterly impossible to make up from any other source a loss in the revenue of £5,000,000.[3] Again in 1893 Sir David Barbour, a former Finance Minister of India, said that without the revenue derived from opium the Indian administration could not be run, while additional taxation of the people was too heavy a burden to be thought of.[4]

The situation aroused great indignation in the country. In the House of Commons the motion was debated to abolish altogether the production and trade in opium and to grant the Indian Government £3,000,000 annually to recompense it for loss in revenue. The motion was lost by only thirty votes, the division being 130 to 160.[5] Finally, on June 30, 1893, the

---

[1] Banerjee, *A History of Indian Taxation*, p. 316.
[2] Ibid., p. 321.   [3] Ibid., p. 328.   [4] Ibid., p. 333.
[5] *Hansard*, Ser. 8, CCCLII. 285.

House resolved to have a Royal Commission appointed to investigate and report upon the opium situation in India.[1] But the main issue was only put off, for the Commission was not concerned with the problem of the China trade and even with regard to the conditions in India it had only the feeblest recommendations to make. It was left to China itself to find a way out of its difficulties, which it proceeded to do by drastic methods. In September 1906 a decree was issued abolishing the production of opium by successive stages covering ten years, and prohibiting its use. Two months later proposals were made by the Chinese to the British Government regarding the importation of Indian opium into China, and early in 1908 an agreement was reached by the two Governments whereby the exports of Indian opium to China should at once begin to be reduced at the rate of 5,100 chests annually for three years. If at the end of that period the Chinese should have succeeded in reducing their cultivation of opium to a similar extent the reductions were to be continued at the same rate, and the trade would thus be brought to a close in 1917. But Chinese opinion was so inflamed during this period that it was possible to proceed with reduction even more quickly than this. By 1913 the position was such that the Government of India decided to stop exports altogether.

A definite period in the history of Indian opium was thus ended. Since that time the problem has been to keep production down to the comparatively low requirements of the colonial possessions of the Far East, and at the same time to maintain as much as possible of its revenue-earning power. The efforts of the Opium Monopoly to achieve this result form the subject of the following pages.

[1] *Hansard*, Ser. 4, XIV, 1893, 634.

2. *The Opium Monopoly* [1]

The Opium Monopoly has performed its work with a high standard of efficiency, adapting itself on the whole readily to the changes produced by the policy of reduction. A survey of the work done by the Department in the course of a year should give a useful picture of the opium industry.

The sowing of opium occurs in India in the autumn, in October and November. Before that date the Government of India announces the area which it will be necessary to cultivate in the coming season, and fixes the prices to be paid to the cultivators. In this it is advised by the officers of the Department who are in close touch with the peasants, or *ryots*, as they are called in India, and know what compensation they are likely, for one reason or another, to demand. The task of the Department is then to secure the area set by the Government. The ease or difficulty of this task depends upon the popularity of the crop at the moment. In good years the officers are able to select the best lands and the most efficient cultivators, weeding out the less desirable ones, while in poor years it is necessary to accept all offers that are made, and even sometimes to resort to special encouragement and propaganda, usually through native land-owners or by the Agents of the Department, in order to secure the required area. The cultivators then present themselves for seed and advance payments, and the season's cultivation begins. The work of the Department officers during the winter months consists largely in tours of inspection covering the greater part of the area where poppy is grown, measuring the exact number of *bighas* under cultivation, estimating the output, and examining licences. In 1910 the Opium Agent reported having spent one hundred and eighty-three days on his annual tour of inspection, much of the time in rough camps and on

[1] The figures in this section are found in the Annual Reports on the Operations of the Opium Department.

difficult routes. The system of inspection is essential to the control of production as there is no other means of keeping it within the fixed limits. The months of May and June are harvest-time. The *ryots* at this time collect the sap from the poppy heads, sometimes under the supervision of an Agency officer. At one time, for instance, it was remarked that a better quality of opium was secured from first than from second cuttings, and instructions were given the peasants in the new method of collecting the poppy juice. The peasants are responsible for transporting the opium to the headquarters of the Agency. There it is weighed and graded, and further payment, if any is due, is made to them. The average produce of an individual cultivator is approximately two *seers* (a *seer* is equal to 0·93 kg.) of raw opium, and at the period under discussion he was receiving anything from five to nine rupees (seven to twelve shillings) per *seer*. In later years payment was raised to eleven, thirteen, and fifteen rupees, and since 1927 it has remained at ten rupees per *seer*. As this represents the return to the peasant for six months' labour, it is obvious that he must also depend upon other crops for his livelihood.

The work of the Monopoly plant begins when the opium harvest has been gathered. The opium goes through one of two processes, slightly different methods being employed to prepare it for exportation and for domestic consumption. Damaged and adulterated opium has first to be eliminated, although the previous inspection insures a fairly reliable product. The opium purchased from the Malwa States is more often found to have been adulterated. The opium for export is packed into chests of sixty *seers* each, while that intended for sale to the excise departments of the provinces, and thus for domestic consumption, is packed into forty-*seer* chests. The first is known as "provision" opium, and the second as "excise" opium.

The Opium Agency runs with a definite profit. Its income is derived from three principal sources. The first and largest is the sale of provision opium. It was this item which was so drastically cut down after 1908–09 and which has been progressively reduced ever since. From 1900 to 1910 the Agency was exporting from 42,000 to 52,000 chests[1] of opium each year, receipts on this account reaching from 54,000,000 to 76,000,000 rupees. By 1912–13 less than 18,000 chests were sent out, but due to a large increase in price the receipts from exports totalled still almost 50,000,000 rupees. In the next decade, during the years of the War, exports did not surpass 14,000 chests in any one year, and receipts from them varied from 18,000,000 to 36,000,000 rupees. The last available figure for export receipts (for 1930–31) is just below 18,000,000 rupees, although only 4,481 chests were sold. In spite of the enormous shrinkage in the activity of the Monopoly indicated by these figures, its income from the sale of provision opium has remained on a comparatively high level.

The second source of income to the Monopoly is the sale of medicinal opium and opium alkaloids. It was during the War that these began to be important, although they have since lost much of their prominence. These substances are produced as by-products. The damaged or adulterated opium, and the scrapings from the vats in which it is boiled are not fit for consumption as opium, but their morphine content can be utilized for medical purposes. Medical opium was first supplied by the Monopoly factory at Ghazipur in 1911–12. In 1914–15 the report of the Opium Department stated that a special feature of the year's work had been the demand for medical opium coming from Europe and America in consequence of the stoppage of Persian and Turkish opium caused by the War. Six hundred chests were dispatched to London in that year for disposal as medical opium. In the following year 2,050 chests were supplied. This figure was not reduced at the close of the War, and the report for 1917–18 stated that the manufacture of alkaloids was double that of pre-War years. The next year saw

[1] A chest contains 51·1 kgs.

another great increase in the production of alkaloids; £10,546 was realized on the sale of 520 lb. of morphine and codeine to English firms, while 2,000 chests of medical opium were again disposed of. But in 1919–20 the Dangerous Drugs Bill was passed in England and importation of drugs was thereby curtailed. Simultaneously Turkish medical opium began to force out the Indian product, having a higher morphine content, and for a time none of these products was manufactured at Ghazipur. In 1924 the manufacture of alkaloids and medicinal opium was revived to some extent, but only fifty-odd chests of the latter were exported, although more than 5,000 lb. of alkaloids were sent to England. For some time this level was kept, but recently the export of medicinal opium as well as of alkaloids has fallen off. India is supplied with her domestic needs by the Monopoly factory, but English firms depend mainly upon Turkish or Balkan opium. As a profit-making factor the sale of these substances is of little importance to the Monopoly.

The third source of income to the Monopoly is the sale of excise opium to the provinces. Between 1912 and 1920 the general level of sales was highest, its record point for the first thirty years of this century being the year 1912–13, when 9,487 chests were issued. Since 1920, however, this branch of the Monopoly's work has dwindled. It was announced by the Opium Agent in 1925 that no profits are made from the sale of excise opium by the Monopoly, the permanent policy being to issue it at cost price to the provincial excise departments. The price has risen by leaps and bounds, however, particularly since 1920. In 1925 it was at nearly five times the pre-War level. And as the statistics show that receipts from the sale of excise opium to the provinces have actually exceeded the total expenses of the Monopoly since 1927, these expenses covering all the costs of provision as well as of excise opium, there appears to have been some deviation from this policy.

The expenses of the Monopoly, on the other hand, are also

of three kinds. The largest item is payments made to cultivators. Purchases of Malwa opium are the next in importance, while the cost of running the Agency is the third and smallest item. The total expense account has always been far below income, leaving in every year a substantial margin of profit. In spite of vast reduction in output since the Chinese Agreement went into effect profits are still, on an average, half as great as in the time of the China trade.

3. *Provision Opium*[1]

The opium policy of the Government of India has resulted in the reduction of opium exports from 45,000 chests in 1900 to 4,481 chests in 1930. The consumption of opium in India, on the other hand, is greater now by 700 chests per year than in 1900 (5,260 chests in 1930–31). The policy of reduction has, therefore, been concerned chiefly with exports, and a discussion of the measures of reduction thus becomes a discussion of the history of provision opium.

(a) *The Effect of Reduction of Exports on the Peasant.*—After the China trade was stopped district after district was closed to the cultivation of the poppy. In 1910–11 there were 383,000 acres of land sown in poppy. By 1913–14 there were only 170,000 acres. The yield of opium during this period fell from 44,000 chests to 18,000 chests, and the number of cultivators was reduced from some 700,000 to less than 500,000. This overwhelming reversal of an ancient policy destroyed the confidence of the peasant in opium as a profitable crop. The Opium Agency had great difficulty from this time forth in inducing the cultivators to grow the requisite amount of poppy. Even the increased demand caused by war needs was not a

---

[1] All figures in this section are taken from the Finance and Revenue Accounts of British India.

sufficient inducement to the *ryots* to undertake opium cultivation again as in former years. Each successive report of the Agency, from 1910 until 1920, complains of the necessity of offering new inducements to cultivators in order to get them to engage the land specified by Government.

Until 1914 the price paid to the cultivators for raw opium was not greatly enhanced, rising only from 5 rupees 3 annas to 6 rupees per *seer*, but the danger of falling short of war demands thereafter, in the event of peasants refusing to engage for poppy, made a material rise in the rate of payment essential. During the years of the War, therefore, the *ryots* received up to 9 rupees per *seer* for their opium. But in 1917 the Monopoly's report to the Government explained that the fall in the price of poppy seed due to its restricted output during the War had practically neutralized the effect of the enhanced prices offered for opium. The *ryots* were finding other crops more profitable, and it was the opinion of the Monopoly Agent that unless the Government regulated the prices of poppy seed the cultivation of opium would suffer seriously. Seed values had been falling steadily, as the following table, giving the prices per *maund*, shows:

1912–13	..	..	.. 7 rupees 10 annas
1913–14	..	..	.. 8 rupees 4 annas
1914–15	..	..	.. 6 rupees 13 annas
1915–16	..	..	.. 4 rupees 13 annas

As the yield per *seer* averages about 3 *maunds* per acre of poppy, and as each peasant was cultivating, on the average, half an acre of poppy, the importance of the seed crop is clear. The efforts of the Monopoly Agent to secure larger sales of poppy seed during the following year, and the reopening of markets after the War, resulted in a rise in price from 5 to 11 rupees. A further decline in engagements for poppy cultivation was thereby prevented, although no increase occurred, and it was still found difficult to obtain the acreage required by the Government.

Meanwhile, the competition of other crops was increasing. Cotton, wheat, and sugar were in high demand during the War, and were bringing in better returns than opium, being at the same time more easily cultivated. Under these difficult circumstances the chief factor in saving opium-growing from complete ruin was the inducement offered to the *ryots* in the shape of money advances. Both for the purchase of seeds and for the construction of wells, essential for crop irrigation, very substantial advances were made each year. Even this inducement, however, was often of little advantage to the Monopoly in the end, as the peasant was inclined to give over his best land to the more remunerative crops and to reserve the poorest portion for opium. Another factor, in the opinion of the Agent in 1918, which helped to maintain poppy in spite of adversities, was the opportunity the cultivators had of keeping a little of their product for themselves and their friends. The Board of Revenue, however, was rather of the opinion that the continued cultivation of the poppy was due to the attractiveness of the cash advances and to the habit which the peasants had formed through long years of cultivating it.

The alleged popularity of opium as a crop and the peasants' dependence upon it are seriously challenged by these facts. It does not appear from the reports of the Monopoly that any difficulty was ever felt in cutting down the area of cultivation, or in turning the peasants from opium to some other crop. Whatever element of habit or of tradition there may have been appears to have ceded quickly to the economic advantages offered by other crops. Its popularity may further be questioned in the light of the statement made in the Monopoly report for 1922, to the effect that the regular tour of inspection of the opium fields by the Agency officers was made impossible by the antagonism of the political non-co-operators. In some places officials were boycotted, and in others mobbed and placed in serious danger. In the same report a vote of thanks is accorded to the Special Managers, Court of Wards, Nanpara and Sitapur, for their help in inducing the cultivators of their estates to grow poppy.

It was not until about 1923 that opium seems to have become a popular crop. By this time the restrictions on cultivation imposed as a result of international action had reached a point where their effect was felt by the *ryots*. In 1924–25 it was reported that 24,941 cultivators had to be dispensed with. In the following year 54,810 cultivators were forced to abandon poppy for another crop, and nearly 10,000 more in the next. This drastic elimination of opium growers was bound to be severely felt and numerous petitions were received by the Monopoly begging for the reopening of some of the closed areas. The period of transition seems to have been short, however, for as soon after this as 1927 it was reported that once again difficulty was encountered in securing the requisite number of cultivators, who had been frightened away by the reductions of the past years and had turned definitely to more promising crops. Meanwhile, too, the Agricultural Department was preparing supplies of better wheat and cane seed, to be used by the peasants in these districts as poppy substitutes. The reduction in area from 122,000 acres in 1921–22 to 54,000 acres in 1927–28 thus appears to have been made with a negligible amount of hardship. A 10 per cent decrease in area each year since that time has been announced in advance so that the peasant has been warned in time to be able to turn to another crop. The adaptability of the soil and the climate to other crops and the availability of scientific advice, good seed, and markets, combine to make the problem of further reduction of the simplest.

(b) *The Effect of Reduction of Exports on Revenue.*—There has been a continual interplay of measures of reduction on the one hand and of financial recouping ,on the other. Because revenue both from the sale of export opium and from excise opium have contributed importantly to the total revenue of India, it is best to discuss them together, although actually they fall under separate heads. The receipts and expenditures of the Monopoly and the returns from the sale of export opium belong to the Government of India. The profits from retail sales within the country on the other hand, and the income derived from the levy of various licence fees in connection with retailing opium belong to the several provincial governments. These two divisions, however, will be dealt with together in this section in order to indicate the real importance of the opium trade, whether foreign or domestic, to the wealth of India. The budget of the Government of India, moreover, includes the receipts and expenditures of the provincial excise departments.

The significant fact in the financial aspect of the opium question since 1913 is that in spite of restricted output, reduced exports, and an even rate of consumption at home, revenue has been very greatly increased. After the China trade was ended opium revenue came to some 30,000,000 rupees annually. At that time the total annual revenue of India was between £85,000,000 and £90,000,000, opium furnishing 2·3 per cent of this amount. By 1920 Indian revenue had jumped to £150,000,000 a year, but the opium revenue, having increased to roughly 54,000,000 rupees annually, still furnished over 2·5 per cent of the total. After 1920 further measures were taken to cut down the opium trade, and revenue from this source fell for the next five years to an annual average of 45,000,000 rupees. But since 1926, in spite of further reductions, it has soared to 60,000,000 rupees yearly, the average for the decade being, therefore, practically the same as in the War years. The increase in the revenue from opium, in other words, very nearly kept pace proportionately with the enormous increase in the whole revenue of India since the War, and its percentage contribution to the total income of the country is therefore little less at the present time than it has been at any time since the close of the China trade definitely altered the scope of the problem.

The question is naturally asked: How has it been possible, in the face of a production diminished by one-half, to keep revenue not only from diminishing but on an upward trend?

The most important source of the higher returns was from the first the increased price both of provision and of excise opium. When exports to China began to be reduced the price per chest rose from the neighbourhood of 1,500 rupees to over 2,000 rupees. Gradually exports recovered and prices worked up to 3,000 rupees. In 1920 for the first time several chests were sold at 4,000 rupees. In 1917 a new system had been instituted of selling opium direct from the Monopoly to the importing Government by order. Previously the Monopoly had sold all its opium at auction to merchants in Calcutta, but the fluctuations in price and the uncertainty of returns consequent upon this system indicated that a change would be advantageous. By means of direct sales the double benefit of a known revenue and of a higher return was assured. It was possible to divert a part at least of the profits formerly reaped by the private merchants into the Government coffers. Thus the Monopoly was able to fix its price at 4,000 rupees per chest, and, since 1926, when the auction was abolished altogether, this has been the standard price for export opium.

The price of the opium sold by the Monopoly to the provincial excise departments has likewise been increased. The established price from 1900 or earlier until 1916 was 510 rupees per chest, but in that year it was raised to 660 rupees. In 1918–19 it was again raised to 780 rupees. From 1921 until 1925 the rate leapt from 1,076 to 2,465 rupees per chest, but it has gradually subsided since that date and in 1931 had reached the comparatively low level of 1,352 rupees. This, combined with the policy of "maximum revenue and minimum consumption," which governed the retail sale of opium in India, resulted in a swift and general rise in the retail price of opium in all the provinces. In 1918 the average retail cost was 70 rupees per *seer* (a chest contains 40 *seers*). By 1920 it had risen to 106 rupees, to 127 in 1922, and to 137 in 1931.

During the War years, though not after, increased prices were combined with increased production, and the profits of the Monopoly were further enhanced by the lucrative trade in medicinal opium and manufactured drugs. Expenses as well were of course greatly increased during this period. More cultivators were engaged, and the rate paid them was raised from 7 to 9 rupees per *seer*. With production increasing from 16,000 to 21,000 chests the total sum paid to the cultivators rose from 8 to 12 million rupees. Old districts of cultivation, closed when the China trade ended, were reopened, and a new department of research was instituted for improving the quality of the opium produced, the medicinal opium and morphine manufactured for war purposes required expensive new machinery, and all of these developments meant a large increase in staff. Another source of increased expenditure was the policy adopted in 1913 of purchasing opium direct from the Native States. At first some 7,000,000 rupees were spent in this way each year. But in 1915 it was decided that special tracts in the Malwa territory should be cultivated for the purpose of supplying the Agency, and until 1920 this seems to have had the effect of reducing payments for Malwa opium to approximately 2,000,000 rupees per year. But the total result of this increased activity was to increase operating costs from 9,800,000 to 19,600,000 rupees between 1914 and 1918. Receipts, however, were so much higher than expenses that the total opium revenue was 21,000,000 rupees more in 1918 than in 1914. Five millions were due to the increased receipts from the retail sale of opium in India, and 16,000,000 to the profits of The Monopoly on exports.

After the close of the War, and in particular after the beginning of the direct sale policy, further reductions in the quantity of opium exported were undertaken. Direct sale to the importing Governments was doubtless a means of control as well as a source of greater revenue. And the establishment of the League's Opium Advisory Committee concentrated attention upon the opium traffic, although the Committee declined to deal with the raw opium question. The period 1921–26 saw a reduction of 43 per cent in opium exports, while excise issues were only a little higher than before 1928. The increase in price of provision opium, however, counteracted the fall in exports so that returns dropped only 20 per cent, while the enormous rise in the wholesale issue price of excise opium increased the returns on that account from 7,000,000 to 13,000,000 rupees, or by 85 per cent. But this again was swallowed up in higher payments to the *ryots* and increased expenditure for Malwa opium. Indeed the demand of the cultivators for 15 rupees per *seer* as compared with 9 and 11 rupees in previous years made it cheaper for the Government to buy Malwa opium. Purchases of Malwa actually increased by 77 per cent, and production there was so encouraged that the area sown in poppy increased by 20 per cent.

The Monopoly, for these reasons, was reaping exactly half the profits which the more prosperous years of the War had brought in. Instead of the substantial gains of these years, reaching in one year 33,000,000 rupees, it was possible to make only some 17,000,000 rupees on an average each year, the highest figure being 20,000,000 rupees, earned in 1925. Only the retail sale of excise opium, in spite of the fact that consumption remained practically unchanged, brought in a larger return, being responsible for 27,000,000 rupees annually instead of, as in the previous period, only some 22,000,000 rupees.

The Government of India embarked upon a new policy in 1926 as a direct result of the First Geneva Opium Conference. This policy was voiced by Lord Reading at the opening of the

Council of State in February 1926 when he said: ". . . we have come to the conclusion that in order at once to fulfil our international obligations in the largest measure and to obviate the complications that may arise from the delicate and invidious task of sitting in judgment on the internal policy of other Governments, it is desirable that we should declare publicly our intention to reduce progressively the exports of opium from India so as to extinguish them altogether within a definite period, except as regards exports of opium for strictly medical purposes."[1]

The opium of the Indian Monopoly had been no menace to the control of smoking in any of the colonial possessions, but the adoption of the 10 per cent reduction policy was a guarantee that no further difficulties need be feared from this source.[2]

That policy has been pursued steadily since its adoption in 1927. It is unfortunate that it was not the export figure for 1926 which was taken as the starting-point, but the new and larger figure for 1927. In 1926, 6,792 chests were exported. It was then decided that reduction should begin as from 1927. But instead of maintaining the level of the preceding year, 8,012 chests were exported in 1927, and reduction begun upon that basis. As a result the exports of opium since then have totalled 31,718 chests, whereas they should not have exceeded 25,000 chests. Some 6,600 chests, worth 26,700,000 rupees, in other words, have been exported beyond what might have been necessary. Nor can the fact be ignored that if reduction had continued at the rate set up soon after the War, that is, at an average of 2,000 chests per year, the death-knell of the export trade would have sounded some years sooner. Whereas the total exports of the years 1921–26 were 43 per cent lower than between 1916 and 1921, there was a further reduction of only 14 per cent in the next five years.

[1] Exports were to be reduced by 10 per cent each year.
[2] The opium-smoking colonies have unfortunately not embarked upon a corresponding programme of reduction of imports.

The necessity of disposing of a large accumulation of stocks may have been an important preventative of continued reduction at the earlier rate. The figures given in the official reports of the Government of India show that from 1921 until 1928 the quantity of opium produced in British India and purchased from the Native States exceeded the quantities sold for export and for consumption in India by some 50,000 chests. This is a very considerable quantity, being, at the present rate of consumption and export, a ten-year supply. Since 1928, however, 11,000 chests out of the total accumulation of stocks have been absorbed by an excess of export and consumption over production and purchase. The sale of these stocks of opium has undoubtedly been an important reason for the recent financial prosperity of the Monopoly. Their expense to the Monopoly was incurred in past years, allowing the return on sales now to be counted as clear profit. Expenses have been cut drastically since 1926. In that year payments to cultivators came to over 14,000,000 rupees. In 1930 this item had fallen to less than 3,000,000 rupees. Purchases of Malwa, it has already been seen, cost less by one-half than in the first five years of the decade, while the other expenses of the Agency were reduced at the same rate. On the other hand, material reductions in exports did not begin to make themselves felt until in 1929–30, thanks to the abnormally high figure on which the reduction policy was based. The export price has, of course, remained constant at 4,000 rupees. The result has been that the profits of the Monopoly have been larger than at any time since the very prosperous years of the War.

Meanwhile, consumption in India itself has diminished slightly, but the rise in retail prices and vend fees have caused a slight increase in receipts. The combined returns from export and excise opium have provided a yearly average of 53,600,000 rupees revenue between 1926 and 1931, as compared with 42,000,000 rupees in the five preceding years. But the significance of opium in the total revenue of India has not increased in the same proportion. It has, in fact, grown less due to the rise in revenue receipts on other accounts. The following table will indicate the financial position of opium in the last decade:

(In millions of Rupees)

Year	Monopoly Profits	Gains on Retail Sales	Total	Per cent of Total Revenue
				Per cent
1921–22	12·7	25·4	38·1	2·0
1922–23	19·2	26·2	45·4	2·2
1923–24	16·6	27·4	44·0	2·0
1924–25	14·4	26·9	41·3	1·9
1925–26	20·3	23·0	43·3	1·3
1926–27	33·2	26·4	59·6	2·1
1927–28	30·7	26·5	57·2	2·0
1928–29	27·1	28·2	55·3	1·9
1929–30	25·5	27·8	53·3	1·7
1930–31	17·8	24·8	42·6	1·6

The indications are that the rest of India's transition from the status of an exporter of opium to that of a non-exporter will be passed without any appreciable disruption either in the economic or in the financial sphere. The position of the Malwa States as producers of opium, and the debated question of Indian excise policy will then remain the two important phases of the opium policy in India.

4. *Excise Opium* [1]

It has been indicated that the Indian opium problem has two aspects, the foreign and the domestic. Although the exportation

---

[1] The statistics in this section are taken from the Finance and Revenue Accounts of British India, and from the annual reports of its provincial Excise Administrations.

of opium has been the more important from the quantitative standpoint, the domestic problem in recent years has aroused considerable interest both in India and abroad. Opium smoking is prohibited in Assam, and is in process of ultimate abolition in the rest of India. The eating and drinking of opium, on the other hand, is tolerated everywhere and is governed by the following official policy: "The Government of India have always held that it is neither practicable nor desirable to depart from their traditional policy of tolerating the moderate use of raw opium, and of hemp drugs (*charas, ganja,* and *bhang*), while using every possible measure to prevent abuse."[1]

Medical experts, however, and the informed public, have a different opinion, and one against which the Government of India will not much longer be able to contend. Their view is, first, that the quasi-medical use of opium is entirely superstitious as opium, except for the relief of diarrhœa, has no medical value beyond the temporary alleviation of pain or discomfort, and, second, that its moderate use for narcotic effects which is condoned by the Government as a harmless and time-honoured practice, has the most pernicious consequences. "The social effects," says H. G. Alexander, "as I must insist again and again, are very bad. Everyone I spoke to in the East who had real knowledge of the homes of the people agreed with this. The opium addict himself may be little the worse, physically at any rate; but his character is undermined, and his family is often ruined. And this may be true even of the moderate consumer. As to the confirmed addict, he is a wreck, morally and physically, within a year or two. It is surely significant that if any soldier in the army of British India is found to be an opium taker he is instantly dismissed; so, at least, I was told by a staff officer at Delhi, but I could not confirm

[1] *Annual Report on Opium of the Government of India to the League of Nations,* 1929.

the statement. The explanation given is that any man who takes opium is unreliable."[1]

The total legal consumption of opium in British India in 1929 was 252 tons, to which must be added another 7 tons of hemp drugs. Illicit consumption, and consumption in the Native States, whose area is nearly equal to that of British India, is not included in this figure. But illicit consumption has dropped steadily since 1920, when 8,638 chests of opium were issued for domestic consumption, as compared with 5,030 chests in 1929. There are various causes to which this may be assigned.

Certainly there has been a decided development of public opinion against the use of opium in India which has considerably affected reduction of consumption. Gandhi is said to be responsible for a 20 per cent decrease in consumption in Assam, one of the worst areas in India. His campaign was, unfortunately, stopped by Government on the ground that his methods amounted to an incitement to civil disobedience. Also, between April and December 1930 eighty-three persons were convicted for picketing drink and opium shops in the Manbhun and Hazaribagh coalfields of Bihar and Orissa.[2] Another factor has doubtless been the watchfulness of outside opinion. It will not again be possible, since the concentration of interest in the narcotics problem at Geneva, for any phase of it to escape public notice for long. The Government of India is very sensitive to this opinion, for it has had a long struggle to overcome the evil reputation gained through its Chinese trade. A third important factor in reducing opium consumption in the last decade was the transfer of the control of excise policy from the Central Government to the Legislative Councils of the provinces. In the decade 1910 to 1920 the issue of opium to provincial excise departments averaged some 8,000 chests

[1] H. G. Alexander, *Narcotics in India and South Asia*, 1930.
[2] See *Bihar and Orissa Legislative Council Proceedings*, vol. xxiii, p. 83.

a year. In the following decade this average was reduced to some 5,000 chests. Policy in the first period was controlled entirely by the Central Government. In 1919 the Montagu-Chelmsford Reforms made excise a subject of provincial control; policy was henceforth to be determined by the elected Legislative Councils. But the exercise by the provincial Councils of their powers in this matter has not been free from conflict either with the Central Government or with the Executive branch of the provincial government. What success they have gained has been won only with a struggle, and but for opposition might now be very much greater.

To understand this, four important factors in the situation must be considered. In the first place, the Central Government is responsible at the League for its internal opium policy, and it has never ceased to pronounce as its policy, and to urge upon the provincial governments the policy of "maximum revenue and minimum consumption." That this policy has been strongly condemned and held responsible for the fact that consumption has not been more drastically reduced is beside the point for the moment, but it is an important question which will be discussed later.

In the second place, excise policy cannot be divorced from general financial policy, and in a conflict between them it is the latter which must prevail. Under the Montford Reforms all questions of finance are controlled by the provincial Executive. If a conflict arises between finance and excise policy, as it inevitably must, it is the prerogative of the Executive to overrule the decision of the Legislative Council. The Executive may be influenced by it, but the question will in the end be decided according to its discretion.

Thirdly, the Legislative Councils, even supposing that they will be able to make their desires effective, are not thereby effecting certainly the will of the Indian people. Some of the members of these Councils are appointed by the Executive, and the election of the rest is far from being held on a basis of universal suffrage. The Indian Ministers moreover, whose responsibility to the Legislative Council is merely nominal, are appointed and may be dismissed by the Executive.

Finally, the provincial Executive, which thus dominates the situation, is actually only a division of the Central Government. But this may best be expressed by quoting from the introduction to the Proposals for Indian Constitutional Reform of 1932:

> British India is a unitary State, the administrative control of which is by law centred in the Secretary of State in whom are vested powers of control over all "acts, operations, and concerns which relate to the government or revenue of India" ; and such powers as appertain to the provincial governments in India are derived through the Central Government by a species of delegation from the central authority, and are exercised subject to his control. It follows that the provinces have no original powers or authority to surrender.

In view of these considerations it is difficult to maintain that the Government of India has lost all responsibility for the control of excise policy since the introduction of the Montford Reforms. The words of the Indian delegate to the Geneva Conference in 1925 are not convincing. A memorandum submitted by him states:

> The control of opium has, under the Constitution introduced in 1919, been transferred to the Legislative Councils of the various provinces, except in one instance, and further restriction of consumption is a matter for those Councils to deal with, and is no longer within the powers of the Central Government. The possibility of further advance in the direction of the suppression of the use of opium depends upon public opinion among the electorate to those Councils, and the Government of India has made it known that it will not interfere with the discretion of the Councils in this matter.

Whether or not this discretion has been interfered with, as it is constitutionally possible to do, must be considered next.

The debates in the Legislative Assembly, where Government

policy on opium is frequently explained, and debates and resolutions in the provincial Councils, give a good indication of the situation. It is clear from the former that not only the production and export of opium have been the concern of Central Government, but also the consumption of opium in India and hence excise policy. The responsibility of the Government at the League for opium consumption in India, and the necessity for a measure of uniformity and co-operation in the administration of excise, have made the interest of the Central Government in this "transferred" subject necessary. It is not, in fact, possible that some single, central authority should not have a general supervisory or advisory power over the various provinces in a matter which is subject to international regulation and treaty obligation.

In 1926 the Government called a conference of provincial ministers to discuss the co-ordination of excise policies. As a result of the findings of the Conference the Government of India framed a general programme of activity which was adopted by the provinces. It suggested the investigation by local committees of conditions in the industrial areas and the "black spots" of consumption, and the registration and rationing of consumers. Government also suggested forming a liaison between Central and Provincial Governments to facilitate investigations, but this proposal was rejected in favour of holding a second Conference which should collate the material gathered by the investigating bodies. This second Conference was held in 1930, and on the basis of the reports which were submitted the Central Government proposed that reduction of consumption could be effected by pursuing the following general policy in all the provinces: high prices, reduction of the number of shops, reduction of the limit of sale and of personal possession, rationing of shops and registration of consumers, and education and propaganda in areas where such special problems as the administration of opium to children were found. This programme has been adopted by most of the provinces, with the result that opium smoking is now the subject of legislation in Assam and Burma, which aim at its ultimate abolition, while Bombay and Madras are considering similar legislation, and in Bihar and Orissa, Bengal, the Central Provinces, the United Provinces, the Punjab, Baluchistan, and the North-west Frontier Provinces smoking is permitted only to licencees or to lone smokers—not, that is, in company. This appears to aim at the root of the evil, as smoking has been seen to be serious only when it is practised in groups.

In addition to these conferences the Government has made other attempts to co-ordinate opium control in India. At Simla in 1930 it proposed the formation of a Central Narcotics Bureau for the purpose of collecting, collating, and disseminating information regarding the illicit traffic, especially in its inter-national and inter-provincial aspects.[1] In 1926 the smuggling problem was considered by a conference held in Ajmer, where it was decided to establish a special preventive staff under the control of the Government Railway Police to stop smuggling from Rajputana and Central India into British India. The Central Narcotics Bureau has not yet been created because of a lack of funds (despite the considerable revenue collected by the Government on account of opium), but the policing of the district around Rajputana was an important step, as it is the base for smuggling operations in Malwa opium and the principal source of the illicit opium which is found in British India.

Another, and probably the most important Conference to be called by the Central Government was held in 1927. On this occasion the princes of the Native States were invited to discuss the opium problem with officials of the British Indian Government in order to reach an agreement on the subject of Malwa and the large accumulations of stocks. This Con-ference decided to send out a Committee of Enquiry to in-

[1] *India*, 1930–31, p. 441.

vestigate conditions in the Native States and to propose remedies. The Committee was composed of three members, Mr. J. A. Pope, I.C.S., Excise Commissioner for Central India and Adviser for Opium Affairs for Central India and Rajputana; Mr. G. S. Henderson, Imperial Agriculturist at Pusa; and Khan Bahadur Qazi Azizuddin Ahmed, Dewan, Datia State. The report which the Committee presented in 1928 has not yet been published.[1]

The conflict resulting from combining the policies of revenue and reduction was apparent both in national and provincial legislatures. In the Legislative Assembly in 1921 the Hon. W. M. Hailey, Finance Member, said: "For some years the cultivation of opium has not been as attractive to the cultivator in the United Provinces as in the past. No doubt the fact will rejoice the hearts of those people—perhaps there are not so many in this country as there are in the United States and England—who desire to see the total abolition of our opium supplies both to the outside world and to India. But it is not a point which could be expected to rejoice our hearts at Budget time, because it may imply a very considerable loss of revenue."[2]

In Bombay there has been considerable conflict between the Excise Department and the Legislative Council. Since 1925 the Legislative Council has adhered to a policy of reducing the number of shops selling liquor and opium. But in 1933 it was discovered that without consulting the Council the minister had been prevailed upon to allow an increase of 50 per cent in the number of shops selling liquor and opium. The excise minister explained that the increased number of shops was not increasing consumption, but was necessary to stop the growth of the illicit traffic which was threatening the revenue.[3] Members of the Legislative Council pointed out several sources of revenue

[1] See below, pp. 289 et seq.
[2] *Legislative Assembly Debates*, 1921, p. 855.
[3] *Bombay Legislative Proceedings*, March 1933.

which might be tapped when excise revenue began to decline seriously, and that the Government had only to ask the Council to vote the necessary money to meet any deficit due to excise. Plans for such substitution of revenue had already been studied. Instead of this, and contrary to the vote of "every Maratha and every Moslem" in the province, the Government had authorized the opening of many additional excise shops. There are many other instances of this tug-of-war between revenue and reduction in the debates of other provincial Councils which need not be detailed here. The policy of the Central Government, which has been generally adopted in the provinces, with regard to prices has been subject to much criticism.

In spite of the decrease in consumption in recent years there is no doubt that the rate of decline has been checked by combining revenue with reduction. The policy of maximum revenue and minimum consumption amounts, in fact, to a pace of two steps forward and one step back. It means steady progress, to be sure, but it is not a pace to be adopted for the purpose of arriving at a given point in the shortest possible time. Smuggling is admittedly widespread in the Punjab and in other territories adjacent to the Rajput States, but the policy of raising the price of licit opium, which encourages smuggling, is persisted in for the sake of the revenue. The theory is that high prices discourage consumption. In fact, they merely replace licit with illicit opium. It is likewise claimed that reducing the number of shops and the quantity of opium for sale would encourage the illicit traffic, as it undoubtedly would under the present system. The only possible means of dealing with the smuggler, since the addict will have his opium at any price, is to cut the ground from under his feet by supplying consumers at a rate which he cannot possibly afford—if necessary, gratis. If the Government were to announce that all consumers registered before a certain date would henceforth receive the amount of opium they required daily on these terms, smugglers would find their activity limited in the future to new addicts. But here they would be more easily defeated by the methods of education and propaganda than is possible at present among confirmed addicts. Direct agitation against the use of opium is a method which Gandhi and his followers used with extraordinary results in Assam. The Excise Department of Assam explains the reduction in opium consumption from 64,000 *seers* to 42,000 *seers* between 1921 and 1922 as due to the picketing of opium shops by non-co-operators.

But it has not been the policy to take such decisive action in the matter. The number of shops and the quantity of opium issued each year is, on the contrary, determined by sounding the popular demand. In Bengal in 1925–26, for instance, seventeen new shops were opened, according to the report of the excise administration, in response to a "genuine demand." This does not appear to be a means of reducing consumption. It belongs to the "maximum revenue" part of the policy, persistence in which must logically set bounds to "minimum consumption."

Clearly the control of opium consumption must be divorced from all idea of revenue. It is evident that it is not enough merely to separate the functions of controlling consumption and of collecting excise. This results only in conflict between the two organs respectively so empowered. The fact of any dependence upon revenue derived from opium can only serve, if not to defeat, at least indefinitely to retard, the ultimate object of control.

It will be necessary, moreover, to remove opium from the field of excise if it is to be centrally controlled. Although the current of reform in India is in the direction of decentralization, and although this seems the part of political wisdom, there is no necessity for extending this tendency to the field of narcotics control. Developments in India itself, as well as in other countries, clearly show that centralization of control and responsibility are essential. And it is evident, in spite of objections which may be taken to the specific policy of the Central Government, that it has been useful and is becoming increasingly necessary as the one agent which can act for India as a whole in international circles, as a co-ordinator of the policies of the various provincial administrations, and as a possible supervisor in any plan for general control.

5. *Malwa Opium*

There is a final aspect of the opium problem in India which has only indirectly been touched upon. This is the question of disposing of Malwa, or Native States, opium. The greatest uncertainty has attended this question from the first. In 1913 the purchase of Malwa began, according to the report of the Agency at Ghazipur. From that time excise opium was prepared on the basis of three parts Malwa opium to one part Benares opium. Shortly thereafter the special cultivation of Malwa opium for the Monopoly was begun. But it has never been possible to discover how much land is given over to poppy cultivation in the Native States. The figures given in the official agricultural statistics apparently bear no relation to the actual area, as they can account for only a third to a quarter of the opium used by the Monopoly alone. It has already been pointed out that a considerable extension of poppy acreage in the Native States resulted when the Monopoly increased its purchases towards the end of the War. What became of this area when purchases were later reduced is uncertain. In 1921 the Hon. W. M. Hailey, speaking in the Legislative Assembly, made the astounding statement that there was an agreement with the Native States to purchase 40,000 *maunds* (about 26,600 chests) of their opium each year. This was in explanation of an unusually large item of expense put down for the purchase of Malwa. Although this figure represents more than double the quantity handled by the Monopoly in any year since 1920, no explanation for the excessive amount was given. The quantities reported as purchased from 1921–23 until 1931–32 are, in round numbers of chests, as follows: 7,000, 8,200, 10,900, 6,800, 6,300, 2,300, 5,100, 2,200, 800, 4,000, 4,700. The irregularity of these figures suggests that production in the Native States cannot be based on any known demand. One can only conclude that there is a very large and indeterminate pool of Malwa opium always on hand.

Whatever may have been the conclusions of the Native States Enquiry Committee on the subject of regulation and control, only two developments have been apparent. In 1930 it was announced that the contractual amount of Malwa to be purchased annually by the Monopoly was 6,500 *maunds*, or 4,300 chests. In that year 4,020 chests were bought, and 4,700 in the next. The second development was to take over, at the rate of 800 chests each year, the stocks of opium held by the Mewar State. These are both important steps toward control. But as no known measures for controlling production have been taken in the Native States, as no system of regulation placing any responsibility upon the Government of British India, which alone is responsible in international circles, seems to have been evolved, and as whatever decisions the Committee of Enquiry may have arrived at are still unrevealed, the Malwa opium situation remains as nebulous as before.

The important aspect of this problem is not so much that control is difficult or even impossible at the present time to establish. That may be deduced from the facts that are known. It is rather that at the moment when the machinery of international control is extending its scope to include the production of raw materials, it is impossible to get at the most elementary information concerning the conditions in an important area of production. China is the only other region which offers these difficulties. Neither the extent of cultivation, nor the disposition of the opium which is raised is known, except perhaps to the Indian princes. Their ability or their willingness to restrict or control are also not known. Between this silent and unresponsive area on the one hand, and the organization for international control on the other, the Government of India offers the only point of contact. It will not be able for long to guard the secrets of the Indian princes, in spite of the political difficulties and delicacies which it now pleads, if it is to maintain its reputation for ready co-operation in international control.

CHAPTER VI

OPIUM PRODUCTION IN THE NEAR EAST

APART from India, the important opium producers are Persia, Turkey, Yugoslavia, and to a lesser extent Bulgaria and Greece. Russia, for the purpose of this survey, may be left out of account, both because, so far as statistics now show, it supplies only its own needs for drug manufacture,[1] and because Russian opium and drugs have not been seized in the illicit market.[2] Bulgaria and Greece are important chiefly as potential producers of opium, and Greece in particular for its position on an important trade route leading to the port of Salonika. Control is, therefore, of the utmost importance in these two countries. But in Yugoslavia, Turkey, and Persia production is the important problem. Control here is more than a question of policing. It presupposes the ability of a government to do a certain amount of economic planning, to give financial and technical aid to its agricultural classes, and to take the financial measures that may be necessary if limitation affects revenue. Such a programme obviously can be worked out only if the wealth and administrative organization of a country are fairly well developed. Both these important factors differ in the three countries which are considered here.

1. *Yugoslavia*[3]

In its comparatively brief period of existence the Yugoslav

[1] Germany reported to the Permanent Central Board in 1932 imports of Russian opium, but these are the first recorded in League documents.

[2] Some reports, however, indicate a large organized traffic from Russia into Manchuria.

[3] Sources: Supérficie Productive et Rendement des Plantes Cultivées, Ministère de l'Agriculture et des Eaux. Economic Yugoslavia, Ministry of Commerce and Industry, 1930.

Kingdom of Yugoslavia, 1919–29, published Central Press Bureau of the Presidency of the Ministerial Council, 1930.

Government has carried out an extensive programme of agrarian reform. In this region before the War a system of feudal land-holding kept a large part of the population (76 per cent were engaged in agriculture) in great poverty. The first act of the newly established monarchy was to confiscate the large estates, for a definite compensation paid in the form of rent, and to redistribute the land among poor and landless agriculturists. The distribution was made on the basis of need, and at the rate of 5 *hectares* of land per head for families of ten, with an additional 2 *hectares* per head above this number. Together with the land houses, implements, cattle, and money loans were given. The special Ministry created to carry out this immense programme established Government stations throughout the country to give advice, information, and instruction to the peasants. Eighty-six large seed stations with six hundred smaller substations have been set up, which furnish the farmers with selected seeds either as loans or at half price. Warehouses for the sale of artificial fertilizers, which are sold at cost price, have also been built, and special Government instructors are sent out to explain modern agricultural methods. Thirty-one preparatory schools for the study of agriculture have been established. The emancipated farmers have united themselves into 6,500 Agricultural Associations on the co-operative plan, which number in all some 550,000 members. The new Agrarian Bank, founded in 1929, has a capital of 700,000,000 *dinars* (something over £2,800,000). It supplies long and short term loans to the peasants on easy terms of payment.

Of the total area of 24·6 million *hectares*, 13 million *hectares* are cultivated and 7 million are forested. Of the total population of 11·9 million, more than 9 million are farmers.

The life of the nation is thus obviously in its agriculture. The significant fact for the purposes of this study, however, is that administration is well established in this most important part of the economic life of the country. The Government is equipped with the means for carrying out such measures of reform and restriction as may be necessary for limiting its share of the world production of opium to medical and scientific needs. The organization of its agriculture may even make it desirable at some future time to locate special controlled areas of poppy cultivation there.

Opium growing has not gained the hold on the peasant cultivators of Yugoslavia that it has gained, for instance, in Persia. Yugoslavia's chief crops and chief exports are maize and wheat. Cereals occupy 5·7 million of the total of 13 million *hectares* of cultivated land. No other class of crops takes up so large an area, but hemp, flax, cotton, hops, and sugar beet rank with opium as important crops. The poppy occupies about 0·1 per cent of the total cultivated land, although in the South Serbian region where it is chiefly grown it occupies about 5 per cent of the area under cultivation. There has been a steady increase in the area under poppy cultivation in the past few years. In 1924 25,000 acres were sown in poppy, and yearly increases raised this figure to 32,000 in 1929. Eighty per cent of this land is in the districts of Bitolia, Skoplie, and Bregalnitza in the valley of the Vardar, and smaller areas are given over to poppy cultivation in the northern districts of Belgrade and Zagreb. Ossek, Maribor, and Srem also contribute a smaller share to the opium output. In all of these regions other important crops are grown, and although the peasants receive a high price for opium they are far from being dependent upon it for a livelihood. But the demand is sharp, due to its rich morphine content. It yields from 14 to 17 per cent morphine, whereas the next best quality, which is Turkish opium, gives only a maximum of 15 per cent. It is thus of greater value to countries like the United States which assess tariff rates by unit of weight rather than of value.

Opium constitutes about one-tenth of 1 per cent of the total export trade value of Yugoslavia, and from the standpoint of the country's trade balance cannot be considered of any importance. In South Serbia, however, the Skoplie Chamber of Commerce is seriously concerned with opium exports. This organization brought the attention of the Government to the fact that discrimination was being practised against Yugoslav opium by foreign importers since the adoption by Yugoslavia of the import certificate system. They suggested as a remedy that the Government denounce the Geneva Convention. Fortunately, the Government took the more progressive view that every effort should be made instead to secure the adherence of all civilized countries to the Geneva Convention.[1]

Yugoslavia ratified the Geneva Convention in 1929, and immediately thereafter established a special Advisory Committee in the Ministry of Labour to deal with problems arising in the opium industry. At the end of the year a law was promulgated regulating the traffic in opium and narcotic drugs. During the course of the year a strict control over exports had been established by the customs authorities, so that every detail of each transaction—the quantity, the name of the exporter, and the name of the consignee—was known and recorded. The Secretariat of the League was put in possession of this information at the beginning of 1930.[2] In the preparation and work of the Limitation Conference the Yugoslav delegate took an active part, having two interests to defend, first the existing opium-growing industry, and second a potential manufacturing industry. The limitation of manufacture directly affects the opium growers, as Yugoslav opium is used exclusively for the manufacture of drugs. The Yugoslav Government, however, has declared itself ready to limit the production of raw opium. There will undoubtedly be opposition from the Skoplie Chamber of Commerce, but the economic and administrative development of the country is such that reduction should not present any serious difficulty.

[1] *Advisory Committee*, 14th Session, pp. 183 and 235.
[2] Ibid, 13th Session, p. 58.

2. *Turkey*

The most important producer of the opium used for the manufacture of morphine and its derivatives is Turkey. Of the 390,000 kg. of opium reported used by the manufacturers in 1930, Turkey supplied 226,000 kg., and Yugoslavia 140,000. The quality of Turkish opium, while not as good as that of Yugoslavia, is, nevertheless, excellent, containing about 14 per cent morphine. It enjoys high favour in the European markets.

Important as it is to the drug industry, it is still more important to the economic life of the Turkish people. Like Yugoslavia, Turkey is predominantly an agricultural country, but a large part of it is without the natural fertility of the former. Productivity, except in the rich coastal regions, is the fruit of incessant labour to overcome the disadvantages of soil and climate. Grazing and the simplest forms of agriculture have formed the economic life of the people for many centuries. For these reasons any product of the soil which has proved its adaptability to the difficult conditions of the country has an especially strong hold upon the peasant. It is difficult to convince him of the desirability of innovations, and perhaps yet more difficult to effect innovations adopted in principle. Because poppy is one of the few crops which can be relied upon, these factors are particularly relevant to the problem of reducing the cultivation of opium.

The total cultivated area of Turkey is some 10,000,000 acres.[1] More than 20 per cent of this is wheat land and another 20 per cent is sown in other grains, chiefly in barley. Tobacco, cotton, fruit, and vegetables are the remaining important crops. Opium occupies only 70,000 acres,[2] or 0·7 per cent of the arable land, and is very much less important from this standpoint than

[1] Figures are from the Turkish Government publication, *Recensement Générale de l'Agriculture*, 1927.

[2] Turkish Government's statement to the Opium Advisory Committee; League Document O.C. 1337, 1931.

from that of the value of the crop. In the five vilayets[1] where opium can be raised to the greatest advantage it is, on the basis of value, second only to wheat. Some £T43,000,000 worth of wheat is grown in these regions annually, while opium brings in a return of £T10,000,000, tobacco £T9,000,000, barley £T8,000,000, and cotton £T3,000,000. Poppy compares very favourably with the other important crops in the return which it offers per unit of land. Whereas both wheat and barley bring in something over £T1 per acre, opium realizes more than £T5, and cotton and tobacco £T14 and £T10 respectively. Poppy seed constitutes a very important by-product of Turkish opium, and as the demand for it is high in the European markets it enhances the attraction of the crop. Although even in the poppy-growing regions opium occupies only some 63,000 of the 3,000,000 acres planted in these five principal crops, it is clear that its value is out of all proportion to the area given over to its cultivation.

The coastal sections of the vilayets under discussion, Manisa and the border regions of Konya and Kutahia, are more especially adapted to the culture of fruits, which grow near the shores of the Black Sea, and to cotton and citrus fruits which grow readily near the Mediterranean. In the hot, dry, central sections of Denizli, Buldur, Kutahia, and Konya, and in Afyonkarahisar, which lies in the heart of the peninsula, opium grows most successfully. Flourishing crops of forage which can be made to grow without the help of expensive irrigation schemes, are the only important alternative crop.

The new Turkey which arose after the War under the leadership of Mustapha Kemal Pasha has had to face formidable obstacles. In 1920 Turkey was war-wasted. The new start had to be made with a ravaged land, a decimated population, an

---

[1] Afyonkarahisar, Manisa, Kutahia, Buldur, and Denizli. Konya and Balikesir also give over large areas to poppy, but chiefly for the production of seed.

enormous public debt, and a complete lack of industrial equipment. The first need of the country was to develop its natural resources, and to build up a sufficient home industry to supply the national needs and to secure independence from foreign supplies. Budgetary difficulties necessitated the imposition of heavy direct taxes, which, while indispensable under the circumstances, hindered the free development of industry which was the Government's chief concern. As a remedy high import duties have been imposed on products capable of being produced in Turkey. Agricultural and industrial machinery, however, has been admitted free of duty, and several industries have been generously subsidized by the Government.

Several banks have been established in the last few years, in addition to the Agricultural Bank which has been functioning since 1880, and which has branches in most of the towns of Turkey. These are the Business Bank, established in 1924, the Industrial and Mining Bank, 1925, and the Banque Immobilière, 1926. The first two are for the development of industry and have interests in sugar, rice, canning, and silk factories, and in coal, copper, silver, and lead mines. In 1931 the Central Bank of the Turkish Republic was established. It is the sole bank of issue and carries out all the Treasury operations of the Turkish Government.[1] Although these measures have resulted in a considerable development of home industries, the shrinking market for exports and the fall in prices have for the present brought expansion to a standstill.

In such a situation the products which maintain their position in the market assume a double importance. The demand for Turkish opium has not faltered, although the price has dropped considerably in the last two years. In addition to shipments of raw opium, manufactured drugs also have been exported in large quantities. The total production of opium has therefore

[1] Department of Overseas Trade Report, No. 519, 1932.

increased since 1929, before which date no drug manufacture was known to exist in Turkey.

Nor has the competition of Yugoslav opium caused a decrease in Turkish exports, although it is probably this factor which has been mainly responsible for the fall in price of the Turkish product. This may be inferred from the fact that prices have been falling gradually since 1926, the year in which Yugoslavia began to be an important exporter of opium. The total value of Turkish opium exports has fallen greatly for this reason, while the quantity exported has remained fairly level. One must also take account of the fact that more opium is exported from Turkey than the reports of that country show. These are the official Turkish figures since 1928:

Year	Opium Exports	Value
	kgs.	£T
1928	313,000	5,600,000
1929	368,000	6,600,000
1930	226,000	2,800,000
1931	358,000	2,800,000

Because the total value of Turkey's export trade has shrunk so drastically since 1927, the relative importance of opium exports has not diminished as it would have under more normal conditions. From 1925 until 1928 opium formed an average of 3·8 per cent of the total exports, and since then an average of 2·8 per cent. It ranks eighth in importance among all exports, and fifth among exported products of the soil, i.e. next after tobacco, cotton, cereals, and fruit.

For a country in Turkey's difficult state the prospect of cutting down the production of any commodity which helps to increase exports and which gives employment to the population, is bound to be unwelcome. When the Conference of Drug Manufacturers met in London in 1930 to discuss the allotment of quotas among themselves, Turkey for the first time sent a representative to an international narcotics conference. Hitherto the Turkish Government had refused to adhere to any of the existing drug conventions, and only in 1928 was a law passed making the Ministry of Public Health and Social Welfare responsible for control over raw opium and dangerous drugs, and adopting the import certificate system. By virtue of this law, too, all exports of opium or drugs were to be notified to the consul of the country concerned, but beyond this no provision was made to ensure that opiates would not escape into the illicit traffic. At the Manufacturers' Conference in 1930 the Turkish representative agreed that the question of granting a concession or establishing a Government monopoly would be considered if Turkey were given a place in the quota system. But the quota system was repudiated by the Limitation Conference, and Turkey's plan to set up a monopoly has not yet been carried out.[1]

A new departure in control, however, has been made jointly by the Turkish and the Yugoslav Governments. In 1931 it was agreed between them to create a central bureau for the purpose of controlling production and exports of opium. All exports from either country must be accompanied by a certificate from the bureau, and must be registered by the customs authorities. No opium may be sold or exported except by the definite order of the bureau and, most important function of all, the bureau shall determine in advance how much opium shall be exported in the coming quarter.[2] The method of controlling production has not been explained, nor has any report on the functioning of the bureau yet come to the League. If it is successful its experience may be useful shortly when the limitation

[1] The Turkish representative at the 16th Session of the Advisory Committee said his Government was about to set up a single monopoly factory.

[2] *Advisory Committee's Report to the Council*, 1932, p. 14.

of opium production is undertaken by international agreement. Turkey has already agreed to co-operate in a plan of reduction, if it does not disregard the economic difficulties of the countries affected by it.

The most significant factor in the Turkish opium situation is the manufacture of drugs. The situation has recently improved, since Turkey has ratified the Limitation Convention.[1] Previously her export notification system was not an adequate protection against the illicit traffic, and in spite of the Turkish central criminal police bureau, which is connected with the International Police Organization, a large illicit drug ring was able to operate from Turkey without detection for a number of years. Three large factories were discovered and closed down in 1930. The establishment of the Monopoly which is now under consideration, and the opening of a Government drug factory, will not be a new departure for the Turkish Government, which has already realized the economic value of Government monopoly and Government control of factories. The most significant piece of legislation in 1931 was the creation of a new Ministry of Monopolies and Customs, for the more efficient administration of the enterprises which are under Government control. It should not be difficult to include opium, as well as drug, production in the framework of the Ministry's plans for managing industries, and the experiences of the Turkish Government in this field might do much to assist the drafting and execution of an international agreement for limiting raw opium production.

3. *Persia*

The League Commission of Enquiry into the Production of Opium in Persia has given a complete description of the situation as it existed there in 1926, and there have been few important developments since that time. It is enough, therefore, to indicate

[1] Turkey ratified the Geneva Convention, April 1933.

here the main points of their report to the Council, and to add a brief description of the administrative changes that have been made since on the basis of the Commission's recommendations.

Persia is, of all the countries which produce opium, the most dependent upon it. Like India, Persia grows the opium used in the Far East for smoking, and supplies practically none of the opium used for drug manufacture. But unlike India, Persia has never attempted to control poppy production. Comparison is unfair, however, until one has taken account of the difficult political history of Persia which has rendered peaceful development under a stable government impossible.

The Shanghai Opium Conference of 1909 was attended by a Persian representative, but the resolutions adopted there did not result in an attempt to reduce production. A seven-year law was passed with the object of diminishing opium consumption in Persia, and of abolishing the use of opium dross, but without simultaneous measures for cutting down production these internal restrictions only served to increase the quantity available for export. In 1912 the Persian Government made its attitude clear when, in signing the Hague Opium Convention, it reserved Article 3 (a), which pledged the contracting parties to prevent the export of opium to countries which had prohibited its entry. China, at this time, was probably receiving as much opium from Persia as it previously had from India.

During the British occupation no measures were taken to reduce production. Under the American Financial Administration after 1920 the opium question remained untouched. Indeed, exports rose in one year from 255,000 lb. to 660,000 lb. The Commission of Enquiry reported that at the time of the investigation production was higher than it had ever been known to be before, while the production of food crops was diminishing at a rate that threatened famine.

It is greatly to the credit of the Persian Government that since the Commission's visit it has laid complete plans and passed legislation for the establishment of a system of control and reduction second only to that of India, and much more ambitious than the measures taken in Turkey or in Yugoslavia. How successful those plans will be when they are put into action remains to be seen. Administrative organization is at a lower point here than in the neighbouring country of Turkey; the geographic and climatic factors are infinitely less favourable to agriculture, which is yet the chief industry of the country; the trade balance is adverse, and the country is so poor and under-developed that the destruction of one season's crops can cause a famine taking the lives of one-fifth of the population.[1]

Persia has an area of 628,000 square miles. Only one-third of it is cultivable, and of this area some 110 square miles are sown with poppy. A thousand tons of opium are produced annually, about a million tons of wheat, six hundred thousand tons of barley, and one hundred thousand tons of rice. Thus seen, opium does not seem to be an important crop. A number of circumstances, however, raise it to the level of the chief products of Persia. It grows readily in the dry soil of the central plateau where irrigation is necessary for all crops but less so for opium than for others because being sown in the autumn it requires water at a time when there is a plentiful supply. Again, the necessary labour is available, as the peasants are skilled in the art of collecting the opium juice; the market value is twice that of any other crop for the yield per unit of land; it is the only important crop which is always sure to repay the high cost of transport and to withstand the rude conditions of transportation; it leaves the way clear for planting other crops during the spring and summer, and is commonly supposed to enrich the soil and benefit the succeeding crops.[2]

[1] Estimated toll of the famine of 1918. *Report of the Commission of Enquiry*, Document A. 7, 1927, XI, p. 44.

[2] This may be popular superstition. In China opium is said to impoverish the soil and make crop rotation a necessity.

These factors in the situation indicate the fundamental changes which will have to be made in order to replace poppy with other and more useful crops. Education in the methods of agriculture, the application of dry farming or the building of extensive irrigation systems, seed selection, road building, and rail development, the opening of new markets for Persian products, development of the natural resources, the creation of a favourable balance of trade, carefully planned taxes, subsidies, and bounties for the encouragement of suitable industries and agriculture—in short, the economic regeneration of the country—must be undertaken before the means of eliminating excessive poppy cultivation will be available.

This was the conclusion of the Commission of Enquiry. Ambitious as the programme seems, the Commission was inclined to regard it as both practicable and, indeed, necessary to preserve the economic life of Persia from complete collapse within a few years. Without waiting for the realization of all these measures, the Commission felt that it would be possible, after the attainment of a certain amount of reorganization and control, to begin the substitution of food crops for the poppy. A 15 per cent increase in the production of four of the chief crops, that is, in wheat, barley, rice, and cotton, would mean an increased monetary return to the country of 10,590,000 *tomans* per annum (about £2,250,000 at the present rate of exchange). The return from opium averages 10,500,000 *tomans* annually. As these four crops are cultivated under the same conditions of soil and climate as opium, and as improved agricultural methods are not only possible but are badly needed, the project of substitution is entirely feasible. It is admitted, moreover, in Persia, that if the native consumption of opium ceased, the increased productive capacity of its workers would more than make up for the cost of prohibition.

The struggle of an economically backward people to keep its independence against the superior strength of the industrialized West is always desperate. In the case of Persia there seem to be no odds in her favour. Full of unexploited possibilities of economic development, it still seems almost impossible to make a beginning. There is no money in the country, and foreign loans and concessions entail the danger of foreign intervention, and, moreover, often leave the people as poor as before. The existing railways, and the most important and only really prosperous industry, the extraction and export of oil, have been developed by means of foreign concessions. But both rail and road conditions are so poor that they make the development of industry impossible or too hazardous to be readily undertaken. The oil industry has been enormously prosperous, but nearly all of the wealth it has produced has left the country. The returns to Persia are two: royalties, and the expenditure of the Company in the form of wages and purchase of supplies. These amounted to 148,000,000 *krans* (about £3,000,000) in 1927–28, and to 112,000,000 *krans* (£2,000,000) in 1928–29. The oil exported in the same years, however, was worth £16,000,000 and £18,500,000, whereas the total exports of the country other than oil were worth only £9,000,000 and £10,000,000, in these two years. The benefit to Persia of concessioning her chief natural resource to a foreign country is evidently disputable. Even the inclusion among exports of the returns from oil in the form of royalties and wages and purchases within the country brings the export figure to only 611,000,000 *krans* in 1927–28, while imports in that year totalled 807,000,000 *krans*. In the next year exports, calculated in the same way, were worth 593,000,000 *krans*, and imports 820,000,000 *krans*. But if the exports of the Anglo-Persian Oil Company could be included in the total export figure, the balance of trade would be as favourable as it now is unfavourable, bringing the excess of exports over imports to 453,000,000 *krans* in 1927–28, and to 552,000,000 *krans* in 1928–29.

The importance of this situation to the opium problem is simply that the solution of the latter depends largely upon the wealth of the country, and this in turn upon the development of production and export, and the expenditure of the wealth thus drawn from the country upon the development of further industrial and agricultural enterprises. Secondly, as in the case of Turkey, because the total volume of the export trade is so small, each item in it is precious. In 1927–28, 43,000,000 *krans* worth of opium was exported legally. This was 7 per cent of the total export trade. In the following year 65,000,000 *krans* worth of opium was exported, and as the volume of trade had declined, this figure represented 11 per cent of the total. The immense importance of opium is thus clear.

It may also be indicated by referring to budget reports. In 1927–28 revenue from opium came to 13,390,000 *krans*, which was 3·4 per cent of the total. In the next year opium brought in 16,755,000 *krans*, or 4·2 per cent of the total. On the other hand, the Government spent only 7,000,000 and 9,000,000 *krans* in these two years on agriculture, commerce, and public works. The opium revenue practically covered expenditure on education in each of these two years, and more than covered the cost of posts and telegraphs, of the public debt, of foreign affairs, or of justice and land registration.[1]

The opium revenue until 1927 was made up of a customs export duty, a transport tax, warehouse charges and manipulation fees, and a tax on smoking opium for internal consumption. After the Commission of Enquiry had submitted its report, however, the Persian Government undertook to apply some of its recommendations, and proceeded to create a Government monopoly to control the production of opium. A bill was submitted to the Mejlis by the Government proposing as a finance measure the establishment of an opium monopoly.

[1] Trade and revenue figures are taken from the report of the Department of Overseas Trade on Persia, 1930.

A tax of 10 *krans* per *jarib* (about four shillings per square metre) was to be levied on land sown with poppy. The road tax was abolished, but an export duty of 200 *tomans* per case (£40 per chest of 60 lb.) was to be imposed. Through a five-year exemption from land taxation, and through loans to land-owners from the Government bank, those cultivators who substituted other crops for poppy were to be given State aid. A credit of 2,000,000 *tomans* (£400,000) was to be voted for the purpose of establishing the monopoly and for buying up the first crop of opium. Control was to be followed immediately by measures of reduction of cultivation, of the quantity of exports allowed without import certificates, and of consumption within the country.[1]

The Mejlis accepted the principles outlined in the bill, and in July 1928 passed the law setting up the State Opium Monopoly.[2] Both its aims and its organization are comprehensive and worth close attention. Article 1 announces that: "As from the date of the voting of the present Law, transactions in opium, shireh, and cake opium and bonding, storage, preparation, transport for consumption at home or abroad, and export shall be a State Monopoly, to be known as the STATE OPIUM MONOPOLY." The cultivators are required to submit declarations of their intention to grow opium three months before the season of planting. Surveyors and experts later cover the area under cultivation, determining the exact acreage and estimating the yield. The harvesting is done under the supervision of Monopoly officers, and the opium, which is brought into the district warehouses, is weighed and checked against the estimates of the inspectors. The price paid for the opium is based on a yearly calculation of the current prices and the condition of agriculture. The Monopoly Administration is responsible for making such arrangements with the Ministry of Finance as will permit full

[1] League Document O.C. 661, 1927.
[2] League Document C. 540, M. 194, 1929, XI.

payments to be made to the cultivators within two months of the harvest-time, part-payment being made at the time of delivery.

Although the import certificate system has not yet been adopted, most of the exports are actually made under certificate. The Government has the right to issue permits to merchants for the privilege of exporting opium, and the additional heavy tax already mentioned as levied on every chest leaving the country has been raised by successive stages to 400 *tomans* (1930).

The new law has been in effect since 1928, but very little information has been received at the Secretariat concerning the success of its functioning. The critical period of the last three years may have caused difficulties which need not be anticipated in normal times. But the Monopoly organization is well planned, and given reasonable trade and financial conditions the Persian Government should be able to limit its opium production. The opposition of the merchants is growing stronger, it is true, since the gradual reduction of Indian exports has begun, making a tempting gap for Persian producers to fill. According to the report of the Department of Overseas Trade, British traders are receiving opium in return for their goods in the Persian Gulf, and selling it in the Far East for legitimate consumption in the British possessions.[1] Activities of this sort make the progressive attitude of the Government of India almost useless, at least in so far as it supports the colonial Governments in reducing smoking.

But the possibility of irregular activities will be very much diminished if the proposals of the Monopoly as to its future development are carried out. It has the intention, first, of reducing the cultivation of opium poppy by 10 per cent each year beginning in 1933, and second, to control all exports as well as production. No date has been named, however, for this undertaking. If these plans of the Persian Government prove work-

[1] *Report on the Persian Gulf*, 1929.

able, the world problem of controlling and reducing the cultivation of opium will have entered upon the first stages of its solution. All of the important producers except China will then have organized some machinery for internal control, and all have already agreed to the principle of direct limitation by international agreement and under international supervision.

CONCLUSION

THERE is evidence in the preceding pages that the drug issue is still awaiting ultimate settlement. What is more important, it still awaits a comprehensive plan for such settlement. International control has perhaps proceeded farther in narcotics than in any other industry or enterprise, but precisely because it is a pioneer in the field it has much to suffer from opposition and much to learn from experience.

It must be recognized that what so far has been gained is the acceptance of a principle, the principle that the quantity of narcotic drugs allowed to be manufactured shall not exceed medical requirements. Although machinery has been created to effect that principle, its adequacy, in view of the experience of the last ten years, is open to discussion. For it has become clear that the basic requirement of a competent organization is the investment of a qualified and responsible body with full authority and independence. That principle has received only very limited recognition.

The narcotics problem falls into three parts, the production of opium, the manufacture of drugs, and opium smoking. Each of these has special and distinct features and is, roughly, geographically separate from the other. Each is, moreover, again partitioned on national lines. Control has therefore taken the obvious course and remained divided. The results are clear. The production of drugs in any country has remained unrelated to the needs of the medical world, which is supplied haphazardly and in great excess by free enterprise. Again, the limitation of opium production in one quarter has resulted in increased exports from another rather than in a smaller world production. The complete lack of correlation in the activities of opium producers and drug manufacturers has liberated large quantities of opium for the illicit traffic, and will do so increasingly. The freedom of the opium-smoking colonies from any form of general supervision, and the absence of any connection between monopoly administrations and opium producers, has led to an apparent deadlock in the opium-smoking situation. The whole narcotics problem is thus in a state of anarchy which no amount of control on national lines can possibly cure, and which the existing measure of international supervision is powerless to overcome. The only adequate organization will be one capable of exercising control over widely different sets of conditions, and at the same time of ensuring co-ordination of action and a definite location of responsibility.

It has also become clear that the machinery of control must be adaptable to changing opinion and to new necessity. No problem is static; and this one, like others, is subject to altering conditions. Any body, moreover, which operates on international lines must be capable of adjusting itself to the present rapid progress in administrative method without disrupting organization, for it is essential that the fruits of experience in this field be utilized without delay if administrative organization is to keep abreast of developments in other spheres. This essential quality of adaptability is not found in the existing organization. The Advisory Committee disclaims any power of initiative, and the Central Board, constitutionally less entitled to it, dares use it only with the utmost discretion.

If the narcotics problem is to be finally solved it is on the basis of these principles that control must be organized. That is the problem of the moment, and its solution may lie in one of two directions.

The first has already been touched upon. It is that of the international drug monopoly, run by a competent staff of experts responsible to the League, their salaries budgeted by the League in conjunction with non-member States. The appeal of this proposal lies in its simplicity. It has already been explained that a single drug factory is capable of supplying the world's needs. To staff it would be merely a question of selecting the best men from among the experts of all countries. As a vast public utility the question of private profits would not arise, and salaries could, and should, in view of the responsibility of the positions, be large enough to attract the most efficient men to be had.

An international monopoly would be particularly well adapted to controlling the production of the raw materials. It would be necessary to maintain more than one poppy farm in order to safeguard against the possible failure of crops in any one region, and also for the reason that as long as opium smoking is permitted it is desirable to provide a milder variety for this purpose than for the manufacture of drugs. A farm in Turkey and another in Yugoslavia might supply the factory, and two more, perhaps in the United Provinces and in Afyonkarahisar, the opium smokers. The agents who have successfully run the opium monopoly in India, particularly in recent years, the men who are now gaining experience in Persia, agricultural experts such as those who formulated the plan for crop substitution on the Persian Enquiry Commission, or who staff the agricultural experiment stations in nearly every country—these are some of the sources which might be drawn upon for the formation of a competent staff for running the international opium agency. We are here particularly concerned with opium, but the coca leaf and other narcotic raw materials are capable of similar treatment.

There would, of course, be a board of control. It would have to supervise the operations of the monopoly, and be responsible for the satisfaction of each country's drug requirements. The question of requirements brings us to the Supervisory Body which alone of the existing organization of control would have a part to perform under a system of international monopoly. It would still be necessary to receive and to check the validity of each country's estimate of its requirements, but this accomplished it would no longer be necessary to perform the onerous tasks which now fall on the Permanent Central Board. The quarterly reports on imports and exports, the records of stocks, and the details of manufacture would be automatically eliminated. An international agreement to set up a monopoly of this kind would carry with it the responsibility of every country for preventing a recrudescence of private drug production. To ensure this, and to supervise the retail distribution of the drugs received from the monopoly factory, would be the only duties still devolving upon national administrations. Central police bureaux, which already exist in many countries and whose creation has been urged by the International Police Commission, would be able to perform these duties. It has already been pointed out that nothing more is needed than a little official recognition and encouragement to bring out the latent possibilities of the International Police Organization, which provides exactly the framework wanted for the development of a close network of police control.

In order to locate responsibility for the proper functioning of this international public utility, and to co-ordinate the activity of the various sections, it would be necessary to create an organ partaking of some of the qualities of both the Advisory Committee and the Permanent Central Board. It would receive from the Supervisory Body annually or perhaps every six months, estimates of requirements; from the board of control of the Monopoly factory it would receive reports on the state of production, from the monopoly agencies in control of the poppy plantations reports on the conditions of cultivation, and from the several national administrative units reports regarding medical developments and the control of distribution. This Central Advisory Committee would have to be composed of experts commanding the confidence of the League Assembly, which would provide for their appointment. It might include in its membership, or admit as special assessors, the chief of the International Police Organization, a member of the Supervisory

Body, and a representative of the medical profession. It would be the duty of the Committee to give an account each year to the Assembly of the League of the functioning of the Monopoly, assuring thereby its ultimate control by the representatives of the Governments which created it for their service.

If the Monopoly system is ever adopted it will only be after a struggle, for if it has all the advantages of economy and simplicity, it has also the disadvantages of all innovations. They arouse suspicion and fear. They offer the unknown for the known. They call for all the effort of reorganization in place of the easy continuation of established practice. A more concrete difficulty would be the opposition of the existing drug industry. For the desirability of any measure of reform is rarely apparent to those who are materially interested in maintaining the abuse against which it is directed. But resistance from this source will be weakened if the Limitation Convention is successful. If Government control over manufacture is actually effected, that part of the drug industry which has been supplying the illicit traffic will be entirely suppressed. The rest will probably find the regulations irksome enough to make the prospect of retiring from this branch of the pharmaceutical industry much less unattractive. It is entirely possible, moreover, to arrange for the financial compensation of the firms dispossessed through the establishment of a monopoly. The economy effected in administrative expenditure would more than supply such payments.

There is but one alternative to an international monopoly. Although it lacks the simplicity and economy which commend the monopoly system, it will more readily win support because it can be developed within the framework set up by the Limitation Convention. In fact, it consists simply in a more systematic arrangement of the various functions of supervision and control now incumbent upon the Advisory Committee and the Permanent Central Board, and in the rational reform of these organs. But in no less measure than under an international monopoly must the drug industry be considered as essentially an international public service. It may remain in private hands, but it must be controlled by the instruments which society has known how to construct for its protection.

At present international control in any complete sense does not exist. Even the new Limitation Convention, although it has extended the powers of the Permanent Central Board and created the Supervisory Body, has thereby merely strengthened international supervision, but it has not established international control. There is no organized connection between the Central Board, as an international administrative body, and the national administrative departments for whose success or failure in controlling drug manufacture the Board will be answerable to the Council and the Assembly. It has been seen that the signatories of the Limitation Convention, in accepting the new and important obligation to limit the production of drugs by direct control of manufacture, did not subject themselves, at the same time, to the direct control of the Central Board. Yet it must be obvious that the Board can be an adequate safeguard only if it is given the power to take direct action whenever the necessity arises, and if it is provided at short intervals with the information necessary to keep it constantly in touch with all developments. Under the existing arrangement figures of manufacture, exportation, and stocks are subject to review by the Board only within three months after the end of the year to which they refer. If any country finds itself suddenly a centre of the illicit traffic, supplied with drugs coming from another country, it may notify the Central Board, but the Board is unable to get at the facts and the figures necessary for examining the situation, or to take action on it. Yet it is the organ which should be the effective protection of any country against the danger of addiction.

The Board ought, of course, to receive at once the quarterly reports which each manufacturer, under the terms of the Limitation Convention, must present to his Government. It ought to have the power regularly or at its discretion to send one or more of its members on a visit of inspection. It ought to pass on the validity of every import and every export of drugs, and not alone on those destined for a country not party to the Convention. It ought to be able to make any Government at once answerable to it, and through it to all States members of the League or parties to the Convention, for failure to carry out any of its obligations, and not merely for importing more than its estimate allows.

Of the personnel of the Central Board enough has already been said. It is supremely fitted to act as executor of an international convention. It is impartial and expert, and it has made the best use of its independence. Its success, within the limits of its powers, augurs well for the future of the Supervisory Body which has been created on the same basis and which claims the membership of men who command the highest confidence.

But it is not enough to give the Central Board powers over drug manufacture alone. The correlation necessary between the production of the drugs and of their raw materials requires that supervision of both be the function of one organ. The progress of control over opium cultivation and present preparations for a new limitation conference bring up once more the questions of control which were discussed in 1931. But there is no need to allow the raw opium question to suffer from the timidity which so long delayed the effective control of drug manufacture. Certain fundamental principles are now established which the most wary can accept without hesitation.

First of all, it has been finally established that only quantitative limitation can assure that the production of drugs will not exceed legitimate requirements. Secondly, it is now clear that an independent international organ of supervision is the most effective instrument for control, both because it commands confidence and because it is inherently fitted for the work. These principles therefore must be applied in controlling raw materials.

There is no reason why the application should raise serious difficulties. To determine the quantity of raw opium which may be produced in any year is much easier than to determine the quantities of drugs which ought to be manufactured. It may take the Supervisory Body a number of years, after studying the successive estimates submitted by each country, to establish a really satisfactory figure of legitimate consumption. Nor will it be a simple matter for Governments to ascertain what quantity represents a reasonable medical consumption. But whatever the accepted total estimate may be, the quantity of raw materials necessary will be determined automatically on that basis. The quantities used by the opium-smoking monopolies have been known for a number of years. To establish the figure of each year's legitimate production can therefore scarcely be called a problem.

There remains the question of the constitution of the organ which will exercise international supervision over the production of opium. Two alternatives are possible. Either a new organ must be created or the Permanent Central Board and the Supervisory Body must perform this function, adding each to its membership one or two experts on raw opium production. The only argument in favour of the first course is its strict formality. As the Central Board and the Supervisory Body are creatures respectively of the Geneva and the Limitation Conventions, the question could be raised whether a third convention, with possibly a different set of adherents, could be allowed to widen the established scope of their functions. But to establish a new organ to supervise the production of raw materials separately from drug manufacture seems both an unnecessary complication of machinery and a contradiction of the essential unity of the narcotics problem. A single organ of supervision ought to be responsible for its entire control. It is not likely that the volume of work would prove too great for the Central Board, but if a separate organ had to be created for this reason it should act as a committee of the Board, standing in the same relationship to it as the Supervisory Body. The Central Board, however, would probably be able to take care of the additional work of supervising opium production. The chief burden of duties would in any case fall upon the several national departments of opium control.

The Government monopolies which have been set up in the important producing countries will prove valuable in assuring control at the centre. Few of the manufacturing countries have the production of drugs as well in hand as some of the opium-growing countries have the cultivation of poppy. Whereas the Limitation Convention had to provide for national administrative machinery suitable for taking part in the larger scheme of international supervision, the coming raw-opium convention will not have to do this. It can base its provisions upon existing systems of control, at most providing for their perpetuation. But in becoming parts of an international system these departments, whether regulating private enterprise as in Yugoslavia and Turkey, or administering a Government monopoly as in India and Persia, will have to accept one fundamental change. They may now, in determining the area to be sown in poppy, use their own discretion, based as it is on such considerations as the state of demand and of prices, on the national economic situation, or on such local arrangements for reduction as they may have decided upon. But in the future, if they admit the implications of the principle of international supervision, to which they have already agreed, they will limit the areas of poppy cultivation to the figure prescribed by the Central Board or the Supervisory Body.

It is along some such lines as these that the control of narcotic drugs must be organized if the world is to have reasonable assurance of protection from the menace of addiction. But it is not enough that there should be safeguards against the dangers that are now known to exist, nor that the methods of organizing these safeguards should embody the highest attainments of administrative science. For the conditions of this problem, it has already been said, are not static. Science will advance and invent new narcotic poisons. The medical profession will need new drugs and discard the use of old ones. The devices of the illicit traffic are without end. On the other hand, there will also be developments in administrative methods. Changing economic and political conditions will have a direct bearing upon some of the narcotic problems. Some provision will have to be made to maintain in the future, among constantly changing conditions, the effective control of the drug traffic which these projects make possible under present circumstances.

It is at this point that the Advisory Committee must be reconsidered, chiefly because this is the type of function which it ought to have fulfilled, and also because it is possible by correcting the fundamental errors in its constitution to fit it for this essential task.

A detailed discussion of the Committee's history has already been given, but it may be well to recall two things. One is that the Committee (until 1931) was composed of representatives of the principal manufacturing and producing countries, some of them diplomats, some administrative experts, some ex-colonial officials. The other is that, in all the course of its existence, every comprehensive plan of control, every project of reform ever considered by the Committee was presented to it by some outside agency, by the League Assessors, or by a minority in the Committee itself, too small to be effective. Nearly always such projects were rejected. Only the determination of certain consuming countries acting through the medium of the League Assembly finally made possible the Limitation Convention. The very principle underlying it was rejected time after time by the Committee. The Geneva Conference was due to the efforts of a semi-official American delegation which asked to bring a plan for limiting drug production before the Committee. A French

agricultural expert formulated the ingenious plan of crop substitution for the solution of the opium problem in Persia. Mr.
Sirks, as assessor, formulated the scheme of international police
control. And, not least, the representatives of consuming
countries, at first M. Cavazzoni alone, and since 1931 seven
others, must be credited with bringing before the Committee
such drastic suggestions for reform as that of the uniform
organization of national administrations, and the adoption of
national monopoly control. An unnamed Chinese physician
originated the idea of an international monopoly, and Mr. Blanco,
an expert who, in a private capacity, makes it his business to
supply the public with information on narcotics control, produced the Scheme of Stipulated Supply which reopened the
whole question of direct limitation. It was he, also, who supported the opposition which finally destroyed the quota system.

It is clear that such elements must be officially recognized and
united in a policy-forming body. Individuals who know the
drug question thoroughly, who have an informed interest in
international control, are surely best qualified to represent the
general public whose concern is only that it be assured an
adequate medical drug supply, and that it be protected from the
illicit traffic. But it is also essential to give a place to individuals
who, while approaching the problem from the standpoint of the
consumer, are especially qualified to deal with certain aspects of
it. There should be at least two members of the medical profession, familiar with the pathological problems involved, with the
care of addicts, and with new uses and substitutes for the various
drugs. There should be a representative of the International
Police Organization. There should be a representative of the
Permanent Central Board, of the International Health Organization, and possibly of an institute of agriculture. There
should be representatives of one or two of the large associations
in the Far East which are concerned with the elimination of
smoking. The new Advisory Committee should in brief be

composed of individuals whose interest and experience qualify them to formulate progressively the policy of narcotics control in the interest of the consuming public. It should reflect broadly every important aspect of the narcotics problem, and yet retain the flexibility and impartiality necessary to grasp the widest view of its subject. This is not the organ for technicians, Government representatives, or administrative officials. Their function is to act. The function of this body would be to instruct them in their actions, in other words, to direct control in accordance with changing opinion and new developments. These principles are not new. In varying degrees they have already been applied in the organization of the League and of the International Labour Conference. If they are complex it must be remembered that complexity will be an inescapable condition of organization as long as the simple aim of rendering public service remains hedged about with the antique claims of nationalisms, vested interests, and unbridled economic enterprise.

BIBLIOGRAPHY

General Works

ALEXANDER, H. G., JOSEPH GUNDRY ALEXANDER, Swarthmore, 1921. Narcotics in India and South Asia. London, 1930.

ANSTEY, VERA, The Economic Development of India. London, 1929.

ASHLEY, the Hon. EVELYN, M.P., The Life and Correspondence of Henry John Temple Viscount Palmerston. London, 1879. In two volumes.

BANERJEE, PRAMATHANATH, A History of Indian Taxation. London, 1930.
  Provincial Finance in India. London, 1929.

CAPUS, G., et BOIS, D., Les Produits Coloniaux: origine, production, commerce. Paris, 1912.

CHANUT, Le Régime de l'Opium en Droit international. Paris, 1933.

COYAJEE, Sir J. C., India and the League of Nations. Waltair, 1932.

CRANE, C. K., The Essential International Narcotic Problem in 1928 and a Solution. Los Angeles, 1929.

FOSDICK, RAYMOND B., European Police Organization. New York, 1915.

GAVIT, Opium. London, 1925.

GODWIN, GEORGE, Cain, or the Future of Crime. London, 1928.

GREAVES, H. R. G., The League Committees and World Order. London, 1931.

HOIJER, OLAF, Le Trafic de l'Opium et d'autres Stupéfiants: étude de droit international et d'histoire diplomatique. Paris, 1925.

LIAIS, MICHEL, La Question des Stupéfiants. Paris, 1928.

MACCALLUM, ELIZABETH, Twenty Years of Persian Opium (1908–1929), for the Foreign Policy Association. New York, 1928.

MAY, Herbert L., Survey of Smoking Opium Conditions in the Far East, a report to the Executive Board of the Foreign Policy Association. New York, 1927.

MILLER, DAVID HUNTER, The Drafting of the Covenant. New York, 1928.

MORLEY, JOHN, The Life of William Ewart Gladstone. London, 1903. In three volumes.

NELIGAN, A. R., The Opium Question with Special Reference to Persia. London, 1927.

ROWNTREE, JOSHUA, The Imperial Drug Trade. London, 1905.

SINHA, J. C., Economic Annals of Bengal. London, 1927.

TOYNBEE, ARNOLD J., and KIRKWOOD, KENNETH P., Turkey. The Modern World Series. London, 1926.

TURNER, F. S., British Opium Policy and its Results to India and China. London, 1876.

WILLOUGHBY, W. W., Opium as an International Problem: the Geneva Conferences. Baltimore, 1925.

WISSLER, ALBERT, Die Opiumfrage. Jena, 1931.

WOODS, ARTHUR, Dangerous Drugs. New Haven, 1931.

Official Records, Documents, and Statistics

Report of the International Opium Conference. Shanghai, 1909.

Conference internationale de l'Opium, 1912. Actes et Documents. La Haye, 1912.

LEAGUE OF NATIONS.

Minutes of the First (etc.) Session of the Council. Geneva, 1920–33.

Records of the First (etc.) Assembly. Plenary meetings. Meetings of the Committees. Geneva, 1920–33.

Report of the Advisory Committee on the Traffic in Opium and Other Dangerous Drugs. First (etc.) Session, Geneva, 1921–33.

Permanent Central Opium Board. Reports to the Council on the Work of the First (etc.) Session. Geneva, 1930–33.

International Opium Convention signed at The Hague, January 23, 1912. Geneva, 1923.

First Opium Conference, November 3, 1924–February 11, 1925. Minutes and Annexes. Geneva, 1925.

First Opium Conference. Agreement, Protocol, Final Act. Geneva, 1925.

Second Geneva Opium Conference, November 24–December 3, 1924. Plenary Meetings. Meetings of the Committees and Sub-Committees. In two volumes. Geneva, 1925.

Second Opium Conference. Convention, Protocol, Final Act. Geneva, 1925.

Records of the Conference for the Limitation of the Manufacture of Narcotic Drugs, Geneva, May 22 to July 13, 1931. Geneva, 1931.

Convention for Limiting the Manufacture and Regulating the Distribution of Narcotic Drugs. Geneva, 1931.

BIBLIOGRAPHY

LEAGUE OF NATIONS—*continued.*
Conference on the Suppression of Opium Smoking, Bangkok, November 9 to 27, 1931. Minutes of the meetings and documents submitted to the Conference. Geneva, 1932.
Conference on the Suppression of Opium Smoking. Agreement and Final Act. Geneva, 1932.
Commission of Enquiry into the Production of Opium in Persia. Report to the Council. Geneva, 1926.
Commission of Enquiry into the Control of Opium-Smoking in the Far East. Report to the Council. Geneva, 1930.
Analysis of the International Trade in Morphine, Diacetylmorphine, and Cocaine for the years 1925–29. Official No.: C. 718, M. 306, 1930, XI.
La Consommation Mondiale en Opiacés et en Cocaine. No. officiel: O.C. 1112. Genève, 1929.
Raw Opium Statistics (provisional). Conf. L. F. S./60. Geneva, June 11, 1931.

Publications of the International Criminal Police Commission.
La Co-opération internationale dans la domaine de la Police judiciaire. Mémoire édité par la Commission internationale de Police criminelle. Vienne, 1928.
Résolutions de la Commission internationale de Police criminelle à Vienne, 10–12 septembre, 1928; 20–22 janvier, 1930.
Résolutions du IIIième Congrés international de Police à Anvers, 25–30 septembre, 1930.
Rapport de la Direction sur la représentation de la Commission internationale de Police criminelle dans les Comités de la Société des Nations. Vienne, 24 janvier, 1930. (Société des Nations, Document O.C. 1151, 1931.)

BELL, H. T. MONTAGUE, Near East Year Book and Who's Who, 1927. London 1927. . . .

ROYAL INSTITUTE OF STATISTICS: International Yearbook of Agricultural Statistics, 1930–31.

Japanese Imperial Decree, No. 38. Tokyo, 1930.

UNITED KINGDOM.
Dangerous Drugs Act, 1920. 10 and 11 Geo. V, ch. 46.
Dangerous Drugs Act, 1925. 15 and 16 Geo. V, ch. 74.
Hansard, 1891–95.

INTERNATIONAL NARCOTICS CONTROL

U.S.A.
  Opium and Narcotic Laws. U.S.A. 60th Congress, No. 221
    H.R. 27427.
  Conference on Narcotic Education. U.S.A. Hearings before the
    Committee on Education, House of Representatives. H.J.
    Res. 65, 1926.

INDIA.
  Proposals for Indian Constitutional Reforms. Command Paper
    4268. London, 1933.
  India in 1922–23 . . . '30. A statement prepared for presentation
    to Parliament in accordance with the requirements of the
    Government of India Act. Calcutta, 1923–32.
  Legislative Assembly Debates, 1921. Delhi, 1921.
  Reports on the Operations of the Opium Department, 1910–11
    to 1930–31. Ghazipur, 1911–31.
  Finance and Revenue Accounts of the Government of India,
    1900–01 to 1911–12, Calcutta 1902 to 1913; 1912–13 to
    1922–23, Delhi 1914 to 1924; 1923–24 to 1930–31, Calcutta
    1925 to 1932.
  Statistical Abstract relating to British India, 1918–19 to 1923–24.
    London 1921–26.
  Agricultural Statistics of India, 1900–01 to 1930–31. Calcutta,
    1901–32.
  Bombay Opium Manual, 1924. Bombay, 1925.
  Bombay Legislative Council Debates, 1933, February. Bombay,
    1933.
  Reports on the Administration of the Excise Department in the
    Bombay Presidency, Sind, and Aden, 1922–23 to 1929–30.
    Bombay, 1923–31.
  Report on the Administration of the Excise Department in the
    Province of Assam, 1917–18 to 1930–31. Shillong, 1918–31.
  Report on the Administration of the Excise Department in the
    Presidency of Bengal, 1917–18 to 1930–31. Calcutta, 1918–31.
  Report on the Administration of the Excise Department in the·
    Province of Bihar and Orissa, 1917–18 to 1930–31. Patna,
    1918–31.
  Report on the Administration of the Excise Department in Burma,
    during the year ended March 31, 1917, to the year ended
    March 31, 1931. Rangoon, 1918–32.

BIBLIOGRAPHY

INDIA—*continued.*

Report on the Excise Revenue of the Central Provinces and Berar, 1917–18 to 1921–22; 1923 to 1931. Nagpur, 1918–32.

Report on the Administration of the Abkari Revenue, Presidency of Fort St. George, 1917–18 to 1922–23. Madras, 1918–24.

Report on the Administration of the Excise Revenue, Presidency of Fort St. George, 1923–24 to 1930–31. Madras, 1924–31.

Report on the Excise Administration of the Punjab, 1917–18 to 1929–30. Lahore, 1919–31.

Report on the Excise Administration of the United Provinces for the year ending March 31, 1918, to the year ending March 31, 1931. Allahabad, 1918–32.

PERSIA.

U.K. Department of Overseas Trade. Economic Conditions in the Persian Gulf, April 1929. Report by Lieut.-Commander Forester, acting British Vice-Consul at Bushire. London, 1929.

U.K. Department of Overseas Trade. Economic Conditions in Persia, dated March 1930. Report by E. R. Lingeman, Officer in Charge of Commercial Affairs, British Legation, Teheran. London, 1930.

Correspondence Respecting the Affairs of Persia. Parliamentary Command Paper. Persia, No. 1, 1914.

Statistique Commerciale de la Perse. Tableau Général du Commerce avec les pays étrangers, 1922–23 to 1928–29. Téhéran, 1923–29.

TURKEY.

U.K. Department of Overseas Trade. Economic Conditions in Turkey. Report by Colonel H. Woods, O.B.E., Commercial Secretary to His Majesty's Embassy, Istanbul. London, 1932.

République Turque, Office Centrale de Statistique:

Annuaire Statistique, 1928, 1929, 1930–31, 1931–32. Ankara.

Compte Rendu du Recensement Agricole de 1927. Angora, 1929.

Recensement Générale de la Population, 1927. Angora, 1928.

Statistique Mensuelle de Commerce, 1925–30. Angora, 1925–30.

YUGOSLAVIA.

Economic Yugoslavia. Ed. by Office for Foreign Trade, Ministry of Commerce and Industry. Belgrade, 1930.

281

YUGOSLAVIA—*continued.*

Kingdom of Yugoslavia, 1919–29, publ. by Press Bureau of the Presidency of the Ministerial Council. Belgrade, 1930.

Ministère de l'Agriculture et des Eaux: Supérficie productive et Rendement des Plantes Cultivées, 1923–24. Belgrade, 1924.

Direction Générale des Douanes: Statistique du Commerce Extérieure du Royaume des Serbes, Croates, Slovènes, 1928–1932. Belgrade, 1929–33.

INDEX

283

INDEX

INDEX

INDEX